Rough Justice

Citizens' Experiences of Mistreatment and Injustice in the Early Stages of Law Enforcement

Roger Williams

With a Foreword by David Wilson

 WATERSIDE PRESS

Rough Justice
Citizens' Experiences of Mistreatment and Injustice in the Early Stages of Law Enforcement
by Roger Williams

ISBN 978-1-909976-18-4 (Paperback)
ISBN 978-1-908162-92-2 (Epub ebook)
ISBN 978-1-908162-93-9 (Adobe ebook)

Main UK distributor Gardners Books, 1 Whittle Drive, Eastbourne, East Sussex, BN23 6QH. Tel: +44 (0)1323 521777; sales@gardners.com; www.gardners.com

North American distribution Ingram Book Company, One Ingram Blvd, La Vergne, TN 37086, USA. Tel: (+1) 615 793 5000; inquiry@ingramcontent.com

Cataloguing-In-Publication Data A catalogue record for this book can be obtained from the British Library.

Printed by CPI Group, Chippenham, UK.

e-book *Rough Justice* is available as an ebook and also to subscribers of Myilibrary, Dawsonera, ebrary, and Ebscohost.

Published 2015 by
Waterside Press
Sherfield Gables
Sherfield-on-Loddon
Hook, Hampshire
United Kingdom RG27 0JG

Telephone +44(0)1256 882250
E-mail enquiries@watersidepress.co.uk
Online catalogue WatersidePress.co.uk

Table of Contents

Preface and Acknowledgements

I have compiled this book as an ordinary citizen. A layman who found himself unwittingly caught up in a highly professionalised criminal process. I then found that there were others with similar experiences — 'little people' up against the might of the state, usually with no prior involvement with law enforcement. Their feelings ranged across a wide spectrum: admittedly sometimes satisfaction but frequently discontent due, e.g. to frustration, confusion or helplessness in the face of the exercise of police or other powers.

I also began to learn of techniques to keep the citizen in place sometimes bordering on malpractice or even corruption, leading to anger and mistrust. The more I discovered the more I became concerned as I met and talked with other people who had poor experiences of our so-called unrivalled British justice — and those experiences kept on coming my way. The book contains some of these stories. It could of course happen to you.

I hope what follows will not just highlight problems but fuel a robust debate about our system of law enforcement, especially as it concerns police forces, their tactics, integrity and service on offer, that it might:

- become a beacon that attracts further victims of injustice to step forward, the silent majority, and to press their local MPs for improvements;
- prompt those in the administration, scrutiny of and policing of criminal justice to take a critical look at what goes on around them and seek to influence better practices, integrity, decency and other things that, if missing, cause citizens to lose confidence;
- bring the Government to stop 'tinkering around the edges' and put forward bold, far-reaching organizational and legislative proposals to resolve the kind of shortcomings described; and
- increase the investigation into and prosecution of corrupt police and other criminal justice personnel who, all too often it seems, can avoid the consequences of their actions or inactions.

Wider revisions may be required but at the heart of current policing problems and public disquiet is the cosy relationships each local Professional Standards Department (PSD)[1] enjoys with its respective police force; the currently toothless Independent Police Complaints Commission (IPCC); and the rest of the police complaints system. The Parliamentary Home Affairs Committee (HAC) (and thus Government) is well aware of many of the IPCC's shortcomings, but does not appear to have focused sufficiently on the inadequate service provided to both the IPCC and the public by local PSDs.

The Crown Prosecution Service (CPS) does much good work but its pursuit of erring police officers and other public servants appears to be less impressive, although often inadequately served by police evidence and a system of split responsibilities.

Consequently, the need for corrective changes is wide-reaching. Even the modern-day police and crime commissioners (PCCs) fall short of public expectations. However, in my view HM Inspectorate of Constabulary (HMIC) has much to offer, but a different approach and additional powers would release greater potential. I'm not convinced that the Government knows what corrective action to take, but only it can bring about the necessary legislative changes. An updating of the Police Reform Act 2002 is unquestionably necessary. The question is: 'Which Government will have the political courage and will to take on the challenge of systemic reform?'

Re-branding or re-naming exercises are not sufficient. Several departments have been dealt with in this way over the last decade but all, not to put too fine a point on it, have failed to meet expectations.

To paraphrase John Emerich Edward Dalberg Acton, first Baron Acton,[2] 'Power corrupts; absolute power corrupts absolutely'. I think most people would agree and I suggest that, as citizens and as a society, we allow politicians too much leeway. And as Edward Burke, to whom this book is dedicated in a page or so, wisely stated, 'The only thing necessary for the triumph of evil is for good men to do nothing.'[3]

Recognising the tendency of power to corrupt and rather than do nothing

---

1.   Or in London the Met's Department of Professional Standards (DPS). To avoid continual repetition when describing PSDs in general I use that term to encompass the Met's DPS unless stated otherwise.
2.   1834-1902. In a letter to Bishop Mandell Creighton in 1887.
3.   1729-1797. (Although there is some debate re the true origins of the sentiment).

I have written this book. Motivated by my own experiences of untruths and injustice at the hands of the police, I began years of private research, delving into public records, newspapers, the archives, statistics, the stories of those who contacted me when they heard what I was doing and whatever other relevant information I could unearth (including by making frequent requests under freedom of information (FOI) laws).

As already indicated, I am no expert but I have learned a great deal and received much help, encouragement and data as I went along. Further, I hope that not being part of the system actually gives me some advantage—untainted as I am by handed-on wisdom, working cultures or the entrenched ideas of many criminal justice practitioners. I apologise for anything which, as a layman and non-expert, I may have misunderstood or failed to grasp. However, if a keen citizen observer cannot understand the way powers are exercised when the law is being enforced that is surely a defect in itself. It is essential to my mind that we should employ simple processes and that those who enjoy powers over citizens should not be able to hide behind obscurities, whether created by legislation or invented by themselves.

At the end of the book in *Chapter 24*, I ask 'What's to Be Done (and by Whom)?' with some suggestions but mainly with the intention that other people will debate these issues and find answers.

Much of the book focuses on the police. Few readers I guess are likely to disagree that they and other law enforcement agents have a difficult but essential job to do (and I believe that many do commendable work). An independent police force, like an independent press, is essential, yet there are too many examples of situations in which police officers adopt a 'because we can-approach', emboldened by the fact that there is no *effective* body to check or brake or warn or restrain them. Or, criminal proceedings and the ordinary courts apart, which is the exception, to effectively punish them. Even some MPs have experienced this approach which, surely, confirms that it is in the interests of the whole country to seek change: an unfettered police force but with essential deterrents to 'freestyle' policing.

Names, Places, Locations, Outcomes: An Important Note

Some of the names, places and other identifying features in this book have been altered. My contributors' experiences were communicated largely in confidence. Nowhere is the purpose to 'point a finger' at individuals or organizations but to outline the scale of a problem that I genuinely believe needs correcting. Where something is in the public domain I have tried to include references to existing published materials, official or otherwise. Every effort has been made to ensure accuracy, but the nature of some proceedings is that they 'linger on' and—another criticism—occasionally disappear from public view altogether. Day-to-day developments and sometimes final outcomes cannot always be easily traced. Readers should treat claims and allegations as precisely this pending news of any final ruling, decision, appeal or similar. The opinions are mine alone and not of the publishers others.

Acknowledgements

I would like to thank all those who have helped with this discourse. Publication of it would have remained stillborn without my wife's support, the contributions it contains, proof readers and superb (and invaluable) technical support. Thank you all.

I'd also like to thank and commend the editors of *The Independent* and *The Guardian* newspapers who, to my mind, have proved via their numerous articles that they in particular understand that there *is* a problem and have done all that they can to publicise issues of the kind raised in the book.

Thanks to Bryan Gibson and the staff at Waterside Press who have worked wonders with my draft and produced what I hope you will find is a powerful argument for change. Also to David Wilson for his kind Foreword.

Last but not least, thank you dear reader for your time and attention. I have done my best to focus minds on the need for change—please do *your* best to create the pressure that makes it happen.

For those with a contribution to make to any later edition of this book, please send your experiences to me in confidence by email via my publishers whose contact details appear on page ii.

Roger W Williams, Limousin, France, Winter 2013/14

Foreword

No one actually sings a 'social contract' — that supposed deal which is done between the individual and the State and which is enshrined in our political philosophy. We simply take it for granted that as citizens we give up a little of our personal freedoms in return for the protection that the State affords to us all. To do otherwise would lead to the nightmare that Hobbes so vividly described as 'the life of man, solitary, poor, nasty, brutish and short'.

But there are problems too as well as advantages of having the State's protection. What should we do if we want to opt out of the State, or re-negotiate our relationship with it? What if the State requires us to do something with which we fundamentally disagree on either a moral, or practical level?

Of course most of us never really encounter the 'State', beyond paying our taxes and using public roads, hospitals or schools. And, perhaps the most visible agents of the State — the Police — are characterised as being 'the best in the World'. They are accountable, professional and beyond reproach. We should be grateful, we are told, for their protection and marvel at their professionalism.

Now enter the World that Roger Williams describes in his extraordinary book. A World where these agents of the State are anything but accountable, professional and beyond reproach. This book should remind us all that our 'social contract' comes with some frightening downsides.

Professor David Wilson, Birmingham City University, January 2015

About the author

Roger Williams is an Engineer (C Eng. FI Mech E, FI E&T) who initially trained in Hatfield, Hertfordshire. After experiencing injustice at the hands of police and prosecutors he eventually complained to the Independent Police Complaints Commission (IPCC) expecting that it would 'sort this out'. Considering himself totally let-down and, with previous writing and research experience, he set out to learn more about the early stages of the criminal justice system and, finding others with similar experiences, to do what he could to try and constructively improve such arrangements.

Aside from many magazine pieces, he has published 20 books on motoring (Veloce Publishing).

The author of the Foreword

David Wilson is one of the UK's leading criminologists and presenter of a number of crime-related TV programmes. Based at Birmingham City University where he is Director of the Centre for Applied Criminology, his books for Waterside Press include *Serial Killers* (2007) and *Mary Ann Cotton* (2013). He is co-author of *What Everyone in Britain Should Know About the Police* (2nd ed. Blackstone Press, 2001) (with John Ashton and Douglas Sharp).

Introduction

Could it happen to you? Much has and will no doubt be written about the bigger well-publicised police errors and miscarriages of justice. Over the years there has been a worrying number of high profile police actions or inactions, some of which are currently under investigation or re-investigation, which all (to quote the Parliamentary Home Affairs Select Committee) 'cast doubt on police integrity and competence'. They undermine public confidence too. However, I do not propose to focus on any of these, but on the 'smaller' and often less visible injustices that take place, it would appear daily, and which could indeed happen to anyone.

Often, lesser issues are not brought to the public's attention, at least not on a joined-up basis, although numerous newspaper pieces wave 'warning-flags', which I draw attention to shortly. However the media needs to switch to the latest attention-grabbing headline so the smaller injustices do not receive constant or any publicity and the consequential focus of those in a place to make a difference. This book recounts just some police-related alleged injustices that, although not always headline grabbing, are just as individually distressing to those involved as some of the more widely publicised stories.

In fact the police have a great deal going for them. First in line are the many hard-working honest officers. And a host of crime fiction writers devote hours into weaving ingenious plots in which our devoted, virtuous fictional heroes eventually crack crimes and mysteries after dogged persistence. Although often with slightly flawed idiosyncrasies, nevertheless the collective image generated is one of thoughtful, scrupulously fair, resourceful, honest, dedication. Furthermore, in real life, the police put a great deal of effort and resources into creating a positive image by using TV programmes like *Crimewatch* and *Traffic Cops*. The programme-makers like such programmes because they provide low-cost TV and the police see the programmes as a way of enhancing their image. However, police time and effort might possibly be better spent policing more equitably, fairly and effectively. If that were to become a reality, their need for image-creation might be less essential.

In spite of their work, the image most people seem to carry of the police is that they are never there when you want them and when you are unlucky enough to get their attention the outcome is all too often one of shortcomings or in some cases injustice or lack of integrity. This book opens with a series of individual experiences and I thank all who were angry yet brave enough to contribute to this project by providing me with the details of their rough justice experiences. My objective is to air what I've come to realise is a significant problem in the hope that the powers-that-be will start to consider alternatives to the 'we're-untouchable'-style of policing in the UK.

If interested at all, the police will likely plead limited resources, too much paperwork and/or financial cutbacks. However, in many of the examples outlined here they have actually squandered resources, time and thus money, while other instances suggest poor judgement or mistakes that should have been avoided. In several cases, an early abject apology might have concluded the matter but that solution is rarely on the police agenda. Sadly there are also worrying high profile cases, if not quite on the scale of Hillsborough still involving what seem to be systemic failings.

Some officers *are* disciplined and some convicted of offences in the courts. Misconduct, perverting the course of justice, assault, violence, threatening behaviour and/or battery are recorded and these cases bring one to wonder about the culture of the police, about how much supervision was exercised or whether the police are secure in the belief that whatever they say or do is usually accepted by the courts and the IPCC. The latter too rarely takes the police seriously to task. As a result, more and more disillusioned members of the public, not to mention of the media, are rightly challenging both the police and the IPCC with increasing frequency. However, even when the IPCC does recognise police corruption or ineptitude and makes, often albeit weak, penalty recommendations, the police dilute or simply ignore the IPCC's 'recommendations'. This cannot be allowed to continue.

With an organization as large as the combined police forces of the country there have and will always be a few 'bad-apples'. But it seems that these bad-apples are becoming more numerous, that their exploits are getting more publicity and that they seem to be progressing to greater degrees of illegality. This is of concern for many UK citizens, particularly those who have direct experience of being dealt with by the system. So, unfortunately, it is the negative side of policing that, with no apologies, this book focuses upon. But it also includes countless constructive and remedial suggestions.

Part 1, 'Individual Experiences and Accounts', focuses on real-life individuals' true stories of mistreatment or injustice. Mostly I have used fictitious names of people or places unrelated to anyone living or dead and have in some cases masked the location or police force concerned. That part also includes some undisguised information where it is already well in the public domain or facts are documented in official sources such as reports, transcripts of Parliamentary or other proceedings, or reliable media coverage. I have tried to present this information in as balanced a way as possible and to make sure that it is accurate and fully up-to-date and apologise now if any significant developments have escaped me. *Part 1* can be read in conjunction with *Appendix 2*, 'Some further Examples of Cause for Concern: No Smoke Without Fire', which includes references to some of the injustices I came across during my research.

While it is impossible to do more than speculate, if one considers the entire spectrum of malpractice from procedural short cuts right through to outright corruption, I believe certain police officers in the UK must adopt a less than scrupulous way of exercising their considerable power. From my research, I think failings in levels of integrity and decency are perhaps more widespread than people might think.

To allow the reader to appreciate the separation between the departments involved and to emphasise that the common responsibility lies solely with Government, I have included, in *Appendix 1*, a summary of criminal justice organizations at the 'front end' of the criminal justice process.

My analysis of the major elements of pre-court 'checks and balances' are detailed in *Part 2* whilst *Part 3*, 'Summing-up', contains a number of what I hope are constructive suggestions. The list is a substantial one and some may think that it makes for uncomfortable reading. But I believe that many of these proposals need to be addressed if confidence in the police and criminal justice system are to be maintained or re-established.

I cannot conclude without thanking all the contributors to this book, some extremely scarred by their experiences, without whose help, support and information this book would not have been possible. As can be seen from their stories there is considerable bad-feeling out there towards the police, justice system and authorities which, frankly, I had absolutely no awareness of until I began to receive information.

Readers without contact with the police are likely to be unaware of the dramatic change in mind-set that many citizens experience after contact with our modern police forces—or that the negative feeling often only gets more intense as they experience the supposed appeal procedures. And as one correspondent explains in *Chapter 7*, one bad experience can last a lifetime leading to mistrust in the police and other public authorities.

Once Pandora's Box is opened-up there is revealed not just a catalogue of bad experiences but inadequate legislation, dubious procedures such as the police investigating themselves, an inability to admit mistakes and poor regulation. We need to close that box using public pressure, our political representatives and the democratic process.

Acronyms

The following are some of the main acronyms used in this book:

ABE — Achieving best evidence
ABH — Actual bodily harm
ACPO — Association of Chief Police Officers
CAB — Citizens Advice Bureau
CPS — Crown Prosecution Service
CSEW — *Crime Survey for England and Wales*
DBS — Disclosure and Barring Service
DI — detective inspector
DPG — Diplomatic Protection Group
DPP — Director of Public Prosecutions
DPS — Department of Professional Standards (or PSD below in the case of the
    Metropolitan Police)
FASO — False Allegations Support Organization
FGM — Female genital mutilation
FOI — Freedom of information
GHOSH test — to see whether dishonesty exists for theft (see *Chapter 2*)
HAC — Home Affairs Committee (Parliamentary Home Affairs Select Committee)
HMRC — HM Revenue & Customs
HMIC — Her Majesty's Inspectorate of Constabulary
HOCR — Home Office Counting Rules
IO — Investigating officer.
IPCC — Independent Police Complaints Commission
Met — Metropolitan Police Service
NCA — National Crime Agency (previously called National Crime Squad (NCS))
NCIS — National Criminal Intelligence Service
NCRS — National Crime Recording Standard
NSPCC — National Society for the Prevention of Cruelty to Children
PASC — Public Administration Select Committee
PCA — Police Complaints Authority
PCC — Police and Crime Commissioner

PCP—Police and Crime Panel

PIDA—Public Interest Disclosure Act 1998

PIN—Police Information Notice

PNC—Police National Computer

PSD—Professional Standards Department (of the Metropolitan Police Service)

PTSD—Post-traumatic stress disorder

RMG—Rape Monitoring Group

RSA—Royal Society for the Encouragement of Arts, Manufactures and Commerce

SOCA—Serious Organized Crime Agency[4]

URL—Uniform Resource Locator (frequently called a web address)

WAR—Women Against Rape

ZT—Zero-tolerance

---

4. SOCA was superseded on 7th October 2013 as explained at http://www.ipcc.gov.uk/page/
serious-organised-crime-agency-soca-replaced-national-crime-agency-nca The NCA says it
has a wide remit, tackling serious and organized crime, strengthening our borders, fighting
fraud and cyber crime and protecting children and young people from sexual abuse and
exploitation. See http://www.nationalcrimeagency.gov.uk/about-us/what-we-do

PART 1

Contributions, Media and Experiences

CHAPTER 1

Conspiracy, Cover-up or Both?

The problems for this married couple, we'll call the husband Chris, started a couple of years ago when they were out of the country on holiday. Up until going away Chris had been working to publicise his local community's attention to some issues involving a county councillor who Chris, along with some local residents, were unhappy about. During Chris's absence someone vandalised the councillor's wife's car and not unreasonably the councillor complained to the police. The police visited the councillor who took the opportunity to change the focus of the discussion to several screenshots of an anonymous blogger's entries on his internet blog and in particular to a couple of innocuous emails that had passed between Chris and the councillor. The latter claimed that he was being harassed.

The police subsequently informed the local press that the anonymous blogs had been traced back to Chris via his internet provider. The police arrested Chris's wife at her place of work and Chris, using handcuffs, from his home by entering his property. No charges were brought. However, even were the claims of harassment true, the police had no right of entry to their home so Chris sued them for trespass, false imprisonment and assault.

For the subsequent years the police maintained they had acted properly in spite of solicitors' letters pointing out police errors. The first weaknesses in the police case surfaced a short time before trial when they said they would accept liability provided Chris and his wife signed a confidentiality clause. The condition was rejected. More discussions took place up until a couple of days before trial when the police capitulated and accepted full liability for damages and costs without a confidentiality clause. The cost of legal wrangling accrued over three years amounted to a very large sum indeed, but clearly the police tactic had been to wear Chris down, deplete the couple's financial reserves and presumably they were expected to just 'slip away' (as many would do). However Chris stuck it out whilst pointing out that the police would have saved over £100,000 had they apologised for their errors soon after the event instead of squandering supposedly scarce resources on what he felt was mismanagement and cover-ups.

About half-way through this legal wrangle a further complication/case arose when Chris received an email. The message appeared to come from another councillor, this time a local councillor who Chris and his wife felt was doing a good job and with whom they had a good relationship. The message requested any information they had on the county councillor who was standing for re-election. Chris had been assembling information on various potential candidates, intending to disseminate this as appropriate at re-election time so, using the 'Return' button on his email software, Chris despatched, he thought to his local councillor, a number of papers relating to the county councillor in question. A short time later a solicitor acting for the county councillor sent Chris a letter threatening legal action if the information on the councillor was distributed. Chris ignored the threats and prepared a leaflet for distribution that included some of the contested information.

Puzzled as to how the county councillor's solicitor got hold of the information, Chris, his wife and the local councillor jointly complained to the police. They had found that the original incoming email requesting information and several subsequent incoming emails had used a minutely altered email address that at first glance looked like the local councillor's address. They all felt the emails were evidence of data theft obtained by identity fraud and by guile ('blagging' in modern parlance) and made written statements to the police questioning how the county councillor had been in possession of the illegally obtained information. The police assigned an officer to the case but, to Chris's knowledge, the officer never sought an explanation from or visited the county councillor to ascertain how he and his solicitor had come by the data. But they did insist that no offence had been committed.

Consequently, Chris lodged his first complaint alleging that the police—and this officer in particular—had not exercised a proper duty of care by investigating the complaint appropriately. As with all complaints, the matter was passed to the force's Professional Standards Department where a different officer declared it was an internal issue and that there were no grounds to launch an investigation. Chris appealed to the Independent Police Complaints Commission (his first of what subsequently turned out to be four appeals) against the PSD decision and inaction. This appeal was upheld and the IPCC ordered the PSD to investigate the complaint. This task was passed to a detective inspector to explore the case and the first PSD officer's alleged inadequate duty of care by visiting the county councillor to ascertain how he came by these blagged documents. The IPCC also agreed the complaint was not an 'internal issue'.

A PSD detective inspector met the complainants and proposed they withdraw their complaint against the first PSD officer in which case the DI proposed that that officer would write a letter to the county councillor seeking an explanation as to how he came by the blagged/confidential documents. The DI went on to explain that she did not have a 'complaint withdrawal' form with her but would emailed one to Chris. She asked what else the complainants wanted added to any such letter. Chris said he'd type out his suggestions, which were duly sent to the PSD's DI. The DI replied with a copy of the complaint withdrawal form that she had completed and asked Chris and his wife to sign it. At the same time the DI told Chris that their draft wording wasn't satisfactory and suggested alternative wording while making it clear that no letter would be sent to the county councillor if the signed withdrawal form was not returned. Chris and his wife signed the form withdrawing their complaint against the PSD officer, but in spite of several phone calls to the DI asking what response they had received from the county councillor, neither PSD officer was prepared to divulge that or any other information about a subsequent investigation or even whether an investigation had taken place. Chris wrote to the chief constable but his letter was not answered nor even acknowledged.

Three subsequent letters to the chief constable all failed to illicit a response so Chris wrote a further complaint to the police alleging the DI's misconduct, bribery or blackmail. In due course the PSD replied telling Chris that they had forwarded his complaint to the IPCC but simultaneously they had requested dispensation not to investigate the complaint because they felt it vexatious, without foundation and that it was intended to worry, annoy or embarrass. Consequently Chris lodged his second appeal to the IPCC which upheld the appeal and required the PSD to investigate the DI's actions. At this point the DI resigned from the police force. As with all other police officers, resignation mostly avoids further involvement or consequences of their alleged actions.

Nevertheless an investigation was initiated and allocated to another DI within the same PSD — thus both DIs worked for the same PSD and consequently were one-time colleagues. In due course the second DI reported that the first, now resigned, DI had committed no offence and no action was to be taken. Chris submitted his third appeal to the IPCC. The IPCC subsequently found there had been a clear breach of standards and that the force needed to:

- learn from the situation;
- apologise for failures in dealing with the case; and
- place a misconduct verdict in the first DI's records.

Indeed, shortly thereafter, a detective superintendent from the PSD wrote to the effect that they recognised that Chris and his wife had not received the standard of service that they should have expected. He said that, having received the IPCC appeal findings, they were considering their recommendations in full and would take any necessary action to ensure that they learned from this case. Chris in turn welcomed the statement but replied pointing out that the police had apparently still not made any effort to investigate the initial complaints of stolen identity, concerning the IP address, theft of confidential documents and blagging.

Consequently, Chris lodged a civil action. Usually three-year process, while his suit was in progress two different police officers arrived at Chris's house, demanded entry, arrested him and not only harassed him but refused to give further details of who had directed their visit and why he was being arrested. The officers also told him that it was necessary to handcuff him within house. Fortunately, Chris took a covert video of events showing him to be polite, co-operative and courteous and that he was indeed handcuffed. Chris was taken to and detained at the police station for most of that day and later interviewed by a third police officer in the presence of his solicitor in the twin-taped interview-room there.

However 18-months later the arresting constables wrote post-arrest statements that alleged he was shouting, screaming and abusive and that, outside the property, he had tried to walk towards his car. The officers' statements recorded that they asked him where he was going and that they needed to apply handcuffs. The video shows all these statements were fabrications. However the interviewing officer also fabricated much of his subsequent written statement of the post-arrest police station interview. In spite of Chris's solicitor's presence and official police interview recordings (a copy of the interview tape was provided to Chris's solicitor) the interviewing police officer fabricated what Chris felt was a derogatory but probably untrue written statement.

A fourth appeal to the IPCC followed. Chris complained that all three officers had not only inaccurately recorded the events that had taken place 18-months earlier, both at his home and later that day at the police station, but the statements had been prepared with the coordination of the force's Legal Services Department once Chris's legal challenge had became known. It transpired that the legal representative for the police had interviewed the PCs 18-months after the arrest and station interview, taken notes and drafted the second statements that partly contradicted the officers' first statements. There were consequently a total of 12 emails exchanged between the officers and the force's legal expert culminating in the new signed statements. However it was these latter statements that were shown to be erroneous by the video/audio evidence supplied by Chris to the IPCC as part of this fourth appeal. He estimates there were in the order of 50 deviations from the truth across the three officers' final statements and is convinced he provided the evidence to the IPCC proving his allegation that the officers collectively were perverting the course of justice.

Chris was prevented from calling the Legal Services Department's representative as a witness—apparently she was no longer employed by that police force. His fourth appeal to the IPCC also included a copy of a letter from the investigating officer as follows:

[D]ue to an error on the part of Xxxx police, data relating to you has been viewed by a third party. The third party who had access to your personal data works for Xxxx police and, to my knowledge, the data has not been divulged to any person outside the organization....The matter is currently being investigated by the Xxxx PSD team and has been referred to the office of the Information Commissioner...Please accept my apologies on behalf of Xxxx police for this lack of professional care.

However, the letter did not refer to the fact that the PSD investigating officer had also attempted to retrieve the emails from the database but found that they had been deleted.

The IPCC told Chris that, in spite of the associated database insecurities, they were only going to look at the main issue of his appeal (concerning allegations of perverting the course of justice), apparently taking the view that third-party access to and deletions from police computer records was not something worthy of their consideration. Indeed there was no reference to either computer-related aspect in the IPCC response. The following are extracts from it (with certain words deleted for reasons of confidentiality):

When determining whether your complaints are upheld, I have applied the civil standard of proof. This means I have considered whether it is more likely than not that the conduct took place as you allege. Having examined all the evidence I am not satisfied that your allegation that officers intended to pervert the course of justice has reached the standard required to be upheld, though it is clear that individual allegations about inaccuracies in their statements are correct and the overall complaint is partially upheld on these grounds. I have reached this conclusion for the following reasons:

Your overarching complaint is that the officers have attempted to pervert the course of justice, possibly in conspiracy with others and have thus committed misconduct in a public office. You have cited inaccuracies in three officers' statements as evidence for your view that this is the case. The investigating officer has agreed with your view in some instances and not in others. CPS guidance relating to the offence of perverting the course of justice states that:

The offence is committed where a person:
- does an act (a positive act or series of acts is required; mere inaction is insufficient);
- which has a tendency to pervert; and
- which is intended to pervert the course of public justice.'

While I accept that there were numerous small inaccuracies in the officers' statements [which ultimately led to the civil action being settled in Mr A's favour] I do not consider that the officers were attempting to pervert the course of justice or wilfully neglecting to perform their duties. This is because there is no evidence that they intended to do so.

The alternative explanation is that PC Y and PC Z were not sufficiently mindful of the need to ensure that their statements (both about the arrest and for the civil claim) were accurate reflections of events and were not influenced by the conflict which they and Mr A had when they tried to arrest him. I find this explanation to be more credible because they were aware at the time that they made their statements that the arrest had been recorded. It would therefore have been both foolish and counterproductive to produce statements which they knew and intended to be inaccurate, given that there was objective independent evidence to disprove them. The same argument applies to PC Z's account of Mr A's interview.

Later in the letter, the IPCC case officer concluded (the IPCC using bold type where shown below):

After considering all the information available I have now made a decision about your appeal. I have upheld your appeal. Xxxx Police are therefore recommended to implement steps to ensure that DC X and PCs Y and Z focus on the importance of making accurate statements as part of their continuing professional development and that this is monitored by their line managers for an appropriate period.

You are not able to appeal against the assessment of your appeal. If you have any questions or need more information about the appeal decision please contact me using the details shown at the end of this letter.

Chris still hopes that the Office of the Information Commissioner will address the question of police computer security and that in the interests of justice the Xxxx police will explore their database back-up records. Chris seeks a meeting with the PSD officers to clarify these details and understand the ongoing investigations in more detail. That meeting is currently proving more difficult to arrange than should be the case given this case's history.

Meanwhile whilst there have already been huge costs involved in fighting what Chris believes to be conspiracy and/or corruption, it seems unlikely that the financial outlay is concluded in the light of the latest turn of events. Furthermore, even though Chris received some damages the stress, time, pressures, humiliation, police determination and consequent tasks imposed on Chris and his wife continued over a long period.

Comment

It would seem that the IPCC considered the proved inaccuracies in the three police officers' written statements to be slightly undesirable but nothing more than a blip in their professional development. I find that worrying, particularly when you consider police officers' statements are frequently instrumental in a CPS decision to prosecute suspects and subsequently as evidence in a court of law. Consequently, the accuracy of police information generally—and statements in particular—seems of paramount importance to the administration of justice. Small wonder that the public is uncomfortable about aspects of the justice system and many wonder when do inaccuracies turn to lies and lies to corruption and why are so many IPCC outcomes so police-orientated?

Then we have the computer security questions, not to mention wondering why the IPCC is so unconcerned about 12 evidential emails that have been deleted from a police database that it elects not to consider this while protecting itself by declaring that there is no appeal from its decision. How can the IPCC be respected as the police 'watchdog' if it ignores fundamentals such as police data integrity and security?

A police IT system will have a data back-up policy in place. Consequently, even if the deleted emails are not in the current file, they ought to be in a back-up file... if the police wish to find them that is. If unable to recover them, specialists (e.g. Kroll Ontrack UK[1]) will likely be able to do so. Alternatively, other companies (such as Kroll's sister company Kroll Ontrack Digital Forensics Investigations[2]) handle IP theft, fraud, corporate computer misuse, criminal defence and, perhaps particularly relevant, internal and external computer hacking, if the police really want to resolve several computer-related issues in this case and bring the perpetrator(s) to justice.

---

1.   See http://www.krollontrack.co.uk
2.   See http://www.ediscovery.com/eu/solutions/digital-forensic-investigations/

CHAPTER 2

Police Non-attendance

The pseudonym for this contributor is Douglas, who had rented a couple of unfurnished rooms at a private house for about 12 years. He used one for his bed-sit and for storing his personal items and one as an office, but hadn't actually slept in the bed-sit for a number of years as he was living with his girlfriend. As usual, he called on the landlord to pay his rent on the first of the month. Nothing out of the ordinary was said but a few days later he received a telephone call from the landlord saying he needed the rooms for a friend who was homeless so, as this friend's need was greater than Douglas's, would Douglas empty his belongings soon. The conversation took place on a Friday but after a short discussion Douglas agreed to move his belongings on the Monday, i.e. after the weekend.

When Douglas arrived at the property on the Monday both doors to his rooms were hanging off their hinges. They looked as if they had been kicked-in, indeed when Douglas asked the landlord what had happened he was told that the landlord's brother had broken into Douglas's rooms. Furthermore most of Douglas's belongings were missing including £4,000 worth of tools, personal items and, from the office, all the business's records such as copy-invoices, tax and VAT records.

Douglas telephoned the police to inform them of the theft/break-in and was told officers would attend at some point but not that day, the Monday, as they were short-staffed. However, in spite of Douglas making numerous telephone calls in the days that followed, the police failed to attend. Eventually the police told him that his request was not urgent and they would get there at some point. Douglas then made a point of calling the police daily until, three weeks after he reported the theft, the police finally visited the property although Douglas was not aware that they were coming so wasn't present.

A short while later the police telephoned Douglas to tell him that:
    (a) as the landlord lived at the property the landlord was within his rights to break into the rooms;

(b) the landlord stated that Douglas was in arrears with his rent;

(c) Douglas may not return to the property to remove any further belongings himself (and was advised to arrange collection by a third party or risk arrest for trespass); and finally that

(d) this complaint was *civil* and not *criminal* and not therefore a matter for the police.

There is no doubt that any underlying property issues are civil matters but that should never be used to mask the fact of criminality and the need for an investigation. It is too easy an opt out for the police. It is reminiscent of the now long discredited approach to family violence and 'neighbour quarrels', both for many years wrongly categorised as 'domestics' and thus nor warranting police intervention except in the most serious of cases.

Douglas insisted on providing the police with a written voluntary statement/complaint and photographs and asked if, when attending the property, they had carried out a GHOSH test to ascertain if a crime had been committed or not. The police asked Douglas what a GHOSH test was! Douglas explained that it was a court test for dishonesty in theft as follows:

Following the decision in *R v Ghosh* [1982] 2 All ER 689 the jury should if necessary be directed to apply a two part test. First, was what the defendant did dishonest by the ordinary standards of reasonable honest people; and, if so, did the defendant realise that what he did was dishonest by those (rather than his own) standards.

No response was forthcoming.

Douglas took advice regarding his and a landlord's rights in law and established that a landlord is required by common law to allow his tenants 'exclusive possession' and 'quiet enjoyment' of the premises during the tenancy. Further, landlords are obligated to protect a tenant from disturbance by all and sundry including the landlord unless they give reasonable notice, get the tenant's consent, obtain a court order or if there is good reason (e.g. to carry out any repairs for which they are responsible). Even in the last event, a landlord must nevertheless ask the tenant's permission and provide a minimum of 24-hours' notice. In fact a landlord risks prosecution for harassment under the Protection From Eviction Act 1977 if he or she enters a let property without the tenant's explicit permission—all basic common matters every police officer will, or certainly should, be aware of.

Having established his rights in law, Douglas returned to the police station and reiterated his complaint, provided the police with evidence regarding the rent not being in arrears, text messages from the landlord clearly indicating that his brother had broken into the rooms and insisted that the landlord and his brother were totally 'out of order'. The police still took no interest saying the matter was civil and beyond their control, leaving Douglas to conclude that the police were seeking to avoid one or more entries in the crime figures for their area, which is one way to improve their crime statistics, save themselves some work and possibly embarrassment in court when having to explain that they failed to attend the crime scene for three weeks. Sadly, Douglas was too disgusted to take his complaint further.

It is impossible to be sure but it seems likely that the initial slow response was the consequence of the police call-centre's prioritisation of the burglary. The subsequent visit by the police and their categorising the matter as civil looks to be a further example of 'screening-out' as described in *Chapter 13*. This categorisation saves a great deal of work if the police can walk away from an investigation and as explained in that chapter is a contributing factor to the reliability of the nationwide annual *Crime Statistics*.

CHAPTER 3

Conspiracy, Cover-up or Both? (2)

Paul is the name we'll use to identify this extraordinary victim who alleges persistent police corruption, conspiracy and cover-ups over many years following an initial civil financial dispute with his ex-partner regarding the division of the equity in their home. The partner was refusing to return Paul the money he had put into their house. They both continued living in the house but there was an uncomfortable atmosphere and Paul's ex-partner made no secret of the fact that she wanted sole possession. Possession was not in dispute but Paul's solicitor had nevertheless told him to stay in the house until a financial settlement was agreed. Paul stresses he was not asking for a share of the house, just the return of money he had invested in it. The partner seemed convinced, in spite of explanations to the contrary, that Paul wanted 50 per cent of the value of the house.

Ultimately, the ex-partner and her brother, who had some experience of the law, went to a police station requesting the police remove Paul from the home and they predicted that there was going to be a breach of the peace. About a week later at about 1.30 am Paul was woken by two uniformed police officers who threatened to arrest him if he did not leave the house immediately. Paul explained that there was an ongoing civil dispute between himself and his ex-partner, but the police refused to listen claiming that they knew the lady and that she wanted Paul out. On the advice of his solicitor Paul left peacefully, witnessed by the next door neighbour who saw the police officers arrive and leave and gave a statement confirming that there was no shouting, swearing or any breach of the peace (relevant later in the account).

Paul's son was in the house and also saw what was going on and accompanied Paul to the police station the next day to complain about the earlier actions of the two officers. Paul's son also witnessed the police refusing to record his father's complaint — in fact the duty-sergeant not only refused to do so but also threatened to arrest Paul if he returned home.

The police kept changing the reason why Paul had been evicted. The one reason the police favoured was a 'possible breach of the peace' but they refused to show Paul his ex-partner's statement for three years so, initially, Paul never really knew what he was being accused of.

When Paul did finally receive copies of the statements provided by the ex-partner and her brother, they gave no real reason for their complaint other than they predicted a breach of the peace. But that had never happened and this is one of several particularly obtuse aspects of this case. Paul was not being accused of anything other that a *possible* breach of the peace but it took the police eight years to admit nothing had happened, that there was no breach of the peace, although one of the officers, a PC 1, together with Paul's ex-partner had recorded signed statements that Paul was shouting and swearing when evicted.

Even though the police had intervened in a civil matter, Paul wasn't sure if it was an unusual collection of circumstances or that the officers were deliberately flouting the law. For six-months he complained to the police in numerous letters about his unlawful eviction but the police said they had made a thorough investigation and the matter was now closed. One of the contacts Paul made was with the False Allegations Support Organization (FASO)[1] — a voluntary body dedicated to providing support to anyone affected by a false allegation. They advised Paul contact the Independent Police Complaints Commission (IPCC) which responded that the police had not recorded his complaint and advised him to formally complain to IPCC about this. The IPCC took about a month and then upheld the matter telling the police force involved that they should record the complaint and investigate the matter.

The police started their investigation whereupon PC 1, one of the evicting officers, resigned while under investigation. Consequently the Professional Standards Department refused to question him. The other officer, PC 2, couldn't remember what had happened. The PSD investigators declined to interview Paul's two witnesses, his son and his neighbour, but nevertheless cleared both officers. They did produce a crime report claiming Paul was shouting and swearing at the officers so Paul complained to the IPCC about the police's biased investigation and the falsified crime report. The IPCC

---

1.   FASO is a (voluntary) organization 'dedicated to supporting anyone affected by a false
      allegation of abuse' and operates a national helpline: See http://www.false-allegations.org.uk

sided with the police and concluded that the officers had acted appropriately.

Paul then spent nearly two years writing letters, phoning and complaining to anyone he thought might be able to help him establish the truth. The Citizens Advice Bureau (CAB) proved helpful, but told Paul that he would have to take the IPCC to court or give up. With the help of one of the duty solicitors at the CAB he indeed took the IPCC to the High Court, represented himself, requested and received a fee exception, but admits to struggling with paperwork he rarely understood. In fact, his understanding and preparation for his case was further confused by the court giving him the wrong date for the disclosure of papers. Consequently the IPCC tried to cancel the hearing. Paul was lucky to get a letter from the manager of the court submissions office confirming Paul had been given an incorrect date. Nevertheless the court papers and letters were so hard to understand that Paul tells me he was constantly going to the Royal Courts of Justice asking anyone and everyone for guidance as to what he needed to do.

Eventually, he received a letter with a date for, he thought, a hearing allowing an extension of time. The judge did give him permission for such an extension but Paul sat down wondering why the IPCC/police's barrister was starting to explain what the police had accused him of. He couldn't grasp why the full case was being discussed but, although completely out of his depth, he continued trying to defend his complaint. Paul's neighbour was not called to the hearing, probably as the police admitted years later, because they knew that there had been no shouting, swearing or breach of the peace. Paul's son did appear at the hearing and gave evidence but, to his disappointment, was not cross-examined by the police barrister. Paul's son was convinced that the police barrister would dispute his evidence but, presumably by this time the police knew they had no case. Nevertheless the judge seemed disinterested in Paul or his evidence so Paul lost that hearing.

The police barrister asked for costs but the judge said no and the IPCC did not apply for costs. That subsequently proved a dilemma when Paul next met the CAB solicitors—should the police be included or not included on the next summons. Some advisors said yes, some said no, but Paul just went along with their final decision and the police were included on the next application even though it was really the IPCC Paul was taking to court. With more help from the CAB Paul applied for and was granted *pro bono* representation by a barrister, who proved to be impressive. The barrister applied for an appeal. There is a time limit for appeals that added to Paul's pressures, particularly since his barrister wasn't sure if he would succeed with the appeal but he wrote a great argument and an application for judicial review was granted.

During the judicial review the judge stated (author's note, two names have been blanked for reasons of security):

> Given the information available beforehand to the police officers concerned, their conduct in awakening and removing Mr X from his home in the middle of the night in the claimed belief of an apprehended breach of the peace, the matter deserved, in my view, a more vigorous and thorough investigation by Z Constabulary of the available and potentially available evidence. It also called for close scrutiny of the officers' accounts. In my view, for reasons advanced, there is a strong arguable case that the Independent Police Complaints Commission should have directed a reinvestigation of the matter, rather than merely review the Constabulary's investigation.

Paul applied for compensation from the IPCC but they refused. Again the CAB came to his aid by telling him to get a law costs draftsman to work out a bill of costs, whereupon the IPCC paid up without the need to go back to the High Court. The IPCC admitted the police officers had in fact acted unlawfully and offered a meeting at their head office in Holborn where Paul received an apology and was awarded by the IPCC, after intense negotiation, £3,000 compensation. Nick Hardwick (then chair of the IPCC) said (one name and one date have been blanked for reasons of security):

> [I]f the force had said to Mr X in Christmas 2xxx that the officers had made a mistake and got the law wrong, this would never have come so far. The system itself is worse than what happened to him in the first place.

Nevertheless the police continued to defend their officers' actions and declined a reinvestigation, an apology and compensation. However having been granted a judicial review Paul was able to apply for legal aid to continue his case against the police and in due course they blamed the officer who had resigned and said they would give the other officer 'management words of advice'.

After a long search, Paul found ex-PC 1's home address and filmed an interview with him. He confirmed that Paul had stayed calm on the night of the incident and did not shout or swear but also claimed that he was not the officer who wrote the 'shouting and swearing' crime report. Some years later this claim proved untrue. Ex-PC 1 refused to provide Paul with a written statement to help clear his name. Nevertheless when this new video evidence was offered to the police solicitor disproving their claims of the evidence they had, the solicitor threatened to sue Paul for defamation. The police took that solicitor off the case one month later.

Bringing the case to court was a long drawn out struggle but eventually a three-day hearing in the county court was fixed. The judge agreed that there had been no shouting and swearing and that the two officers were guilty of assault, intimidation, breach of human rights and unlawful eviction. Paul's ex-partner and ex-PC 1 refused to attend the court but Paul was awarded a small amount of damages plus 80 per cent of his costs. The police continued to claim that the officers were attending a difficult situation and had taken a pragmatic approach. Twelve-months after the award Paul was yet to receive his damages and costs but holding out for the full sum allotted by the court.

Paul's MP proved most helpful and tried to arrange a meeting with a chief superintendent to ask why someone had made false allegations and to enquire how it was possible to arrange an unlawful, premeditated eviction. It took six months before a meeting was arranged: not however with the chief superintendent, who declined to attend, but with an inspector. Paul asked why no-one had been prosecuted now that it was established the officers had acted unlawfully. The inspector continued to claim that someone had made a mistake but Paul told him, 'Eight years is not a mistake, it's a cover-up.' Paul was given an apology and a copy of the updated crime report stating, '[I]t was proven in court that the incident did not happen'. The inspector admitted PC 1 had fabricated the shouting and swearing crime report. Even though Paul's ex and PC 2 both knew that no shouting or swearing had taken-place on the evening of the incident, they were not prosecuted and PC 2 was given 'words of management advice'.

The police are still in denial bearing in mind the evidence and court findings and will still not admit their officers did wrong. With further help from Paul's MP another meeting took place with the police where they admitted PC 1 had fabricated the crime report but no charges, prosecutions, dismissals and no blame was attached for the subsequent cover-up. They said it was just a mistake.

Paul has written to the police and crime commissioner (PCC) who did not even reply to his first two letters. An assistant replied to his third letter but used facts that have been shown in court to be false, thus it seems the PCC is regurgitating the same police script. Paul pointed out these mistakes to the PCC in another letter but was not afforded the courtesy of a reply. He is still in touch with his MP who is trying to get anyone, including the Parliamentary Home Affairs Select Committee (HAC), to look at the corruption within the police.

Paul is also persistent in his efforts to get the police to bring to account the officers who lied. He's written to the Prime Minister but is still waiting for a reply and the chief constable is refusing to meet him. However, Paul's correspondence with Keith Vaz MP, chairman of the HAC has resulted in the assistant chief constable offering a meeting with 'a senior officer' (but not the chief constable).

Comment

Paul spent two years trying to meet the most senior police officer but eventually the deputy chief constable and chief superintendent met with him. The meeting lasted six hours. The two claimed that their officers did not accuse him of 'shouting and swearing' even though the arresting officers' crime report clearly stated he was. Ultimately the deputy chief agreed to have Paul's ex-partner questioned again but, unsurprisingly, she stuck by her original story in spite of three people's evidence to the contrary. Also unsurprisingly perhaps, the interviewing officers accepted Paul's ex-partner's version of events so Paul is now attempting a further *judicial review* of the police investigation report and still hopes to see the original arresting officers prosecuted ... one day.

CHAPTER 4

Sexual Abuse: Fact and Fiction

Compare and contrast the experiences of just some of those living in the metropolitan area, their sexual abuse experiences with the spin issued by the Metropolitan Police Service and the Rape Monitoring Group of Her Majesty's Inspector of Constabulary. My interest in the diligence and compassion provided to rape victims by the Met was initiated by the harrowing contribution that follows. I have made some minor alterations for clarification or to ensure anonymity but first I need to set the scene by explaining that, to quote the Met's own publicity,

> Sapphire is a unit of specialist officers whose role is to investigate rapes and other serious sexual violence. This includes providing care and support to the victims, as well as investigating the offence to the satisfaction of the victim and bringing the offender to justice..

That 'spin' contrasts with this contributor's actual experiences:

> In [date deleted] I reported rape by my (now) ex-partner to Sapphire (who deal with sexual offences in London). The 'investigation' was poor. I had a medical examination but the police didn't send it off for analysis. They left it a week to take a witness statement from the first person I told (by the time they bothered she had forgotten some of what I had told her). I was being intimidated by his colleagues when he was on bail, the police refused to deal with it as witness intimidation—instead she was arrested for harassment (she was an ex-girlfriend of his who had been harassing me for months before the rape). When the police bothered to contact three independent witnesses they tried talking one of them out of giving a statement and indeed never bothered to take one! When my ex-partner broke bail directly to harass me the Sapphire officer refused to arrest him as she said 'I don't think you're in any danger of him'. I begged her to keep

him away as he had been in touch many times, crying and begging forgiveness. The Sapphire officer didn't, and I ended-up back with him.

Initially my ex was remorseful and apologetic, but the abuse started again. In [date deleted] more of his colleagues started again, physically attacking me in the street and at my front door (in front of my son), bringing acid to throw in my face and telling me I'd be stabbed through the heart. I emailed a previous officer to report it but he never even bothered to reply to the email.

The second time my ex raped me was [date deleted but about a year later]. I told my GP (always very supportive, saved my sanity) but I didn't tell the police straightaway because of how they'd let me down the previous year. In [date deleted] my ex tried to kill me in his car. I got a restraining order out against him but it didn't stop. In [date deleted but one month later], three officers arrived at my (place of work) to arrest ME for 'harassment' of him. As the restraining order hadn't stopped his associates' abuse I told his employers (because of his job) I'd got the restraining order and that he'd got his job using fraudulent documents (proved at my trial). I thought if I spoke out about him I'd be safe, how wrong I was. He had planted evidence and the lies from his witnesses in their statements were unbelievable but [this was] provable if the police had investigated them. Phone records, CCTV would have proved I wasn't where they said I was when I was meant to have harassed them. My Oyster records could show I was some-where else. One of them told the police I'd been spoken to by the police before about harassment, which was the first I'd heard of it and the police had never spoken to me because I hadn't done anything, which again was provable. The officer investigating lied in her statement to the CPS. I have the proof—I got a copy of my taped interview and her sworn statement to the CPS where she says things that never happened in interview. She also told them the planted evidence was found on my laptop when it wasn't, their own technical report showed that.

I complained to the IPCC. They refused to investigate the incidents before my arrest because their guidelines say it wouldn't be fair for officers to have to account for their actions over 12 months and most of them were over 12 months old! After my IPCC complaint I met with officers at [location deleted] and told them I wanted to report the second rape and the attempt to kill me but they never got back to me to arrange for me to give an ABE (achieving best evidence format). I did go back to a different station in [date deleted] and saw a lovely police officer who did take me seriously and different Sapphire officers who arranged an ABE. They arrested my ex, but when I was found guilty of harassment they dropped it. They dropped it before they had got my medical evidence (my GP reports that showed I reported the second rape to her), before they contacted another of his ex's who had also got a restraining order out against him after he abused her, and most importantly—back in 2009 the police advised me to record him so I could prove harassment—and I had him on tape saying he was going to 'rape my friend *as well*', as well as other disgusting threats like he would hunt me down, drive his car into my flat when my son and I were there, that he would be in my life forever.

In [date deleted but 12 months later] I was put on trial. It was like Monty Python: I was convicted on planted evidence.

So I find an organization called Women Against Rape (WAR) who help people like me. And we had meetings with the CPS, with Sapphire etc. and they all pass the buck. I complain again to the IPCC, about the copper who lied to the CPS to get me charged—the IPCC said it 'Wasn't in the public interest' to investigate her. They upheld a few of my complaints, but when the DPS have investigated their colleagues in my case, they lied and the DPS take their word for it. Finally, the IPCC had to (on a technicality) order a re-investigation into the two rapes so they gave it to an 'independent' Sapphire to investigate but, out of all the Sapphire units in London, they gave it to the one who I believe my ex has ties to the police (a co-incidence?). This Sapphire investigates and says that although there were flaws in both investigations none of the officers are guilty of misconduct. The report by the officer in the first [date deleted] rape who had refused to arrest him for breaking bail had mysteriously vanished. Another officer 'retired' so can't be held accountable.

But this investigation has shown that the officer in charge of the 2nd rape investigation falsified documents—he has written in black and white that on a date in [date deleted] he collected the recordings of my ex threatening to rape again, transcribed them and then made the decision to close the case. I can prove he never did. So I have appealed this decision to the IPCC. I should have heard from them eight weeks ago as to whether this appeal has been successful, but surprise, surprise, it's only just been allocated to an IPCC caseworker and they aren't returning my emails—I'm guessing they're sitting up in Xxxx biding time, trying to work out how to cover this up. I don't know quite how they're going to, but I'm sure they'll give it their best shot!

So I am waiting for the final whitewash by the IPCC. I know I might sound light hearted about this, but I can't put into words the devastation this has caused me and gallows humour is the only way I avoid ending in a psych ward. That and now working for [deleted] has taught me that mine isn't a one off case, like the police would have us believe. So many women who report to Sapphire go through the same, and the IPCC just cover it all up. I'm lucky I've had two of my complaints upheld, I know hardly any are. But what's the point in upheld complaints when the officers don't get punished? At most they get 'words of advice'. It's an outrage.

And of course the worst thing about all this isn't even my conviction, it's the fact that the man who raped and abused me for years is seen as the victim and is free to carry on raping and abusing other women. The police knew he was engaged in other (some provable) crimes, but refused to investigate them. Instead the police charged me on planted evidence—I think to shut me up, so I wouldn't be a credible witness, I think he's being protected by a lot of people.

When I was arrested, I was entitled to see the police report into the first rape as we asked for a bad character reference—and my god, it's a sight for sore eyes. If members of the public saw how the police really 'investigate' rape they'd be shocked, and even more shocked at the way the IPCC close down complaints so the officers involved aren't held accountable.

So not a great deal of 'care and support' here—in fact the Met managed to ignore then prosecute the victim for harassment! While I explore the spin aspects of Met/HMIC reports later, I want to contrast the above reality with the Met's publicity already outlined at the start of this chapter.

Our contributor's story assumes even greater significance when we consider what other known sexual abuse cases were simultaneously occurring in Met's area. Indeed, two serial-rapists were going free:

(1) taxi driver John Worboys, where the nature of the investigation and more recent court rulings in favour of two victims of rape and sexual abuse lays the police open to claims for damages and compensation from an estimated 105 additional victims; and

(2) Kirk Reid, a women's football referee.

The Met's incompetence over the Worboys rape investigations took many years to surface but started with them ignoring not only the first complaint in 2002 but many others thereafter. Taxi driver Worboys drove a black cab and adopted a technique of drugging then raping his victims on its back seat. By the time of his arrest in February 2008, he had drug-raped at least 14 women complainants—but subsequently had attacked 29 victims with more women, on hearing of his arrest, reporting similar attacks. Of course there may still be others who cannot bring themselves to report their abuse.

As serious and unsettling as this is, the case takes on a whole new dimension when it is noted that the Met had Worboys down as a suspect of numerous sex attacks since as early as 2004, but failed to connect-up the dots and so did nothing about it until 2007 when they *did* arrest him. But they released him without charge. However it transpired that, simultaneously, the Met's rape-investigating shortcomings were being replicated by their failure to apprehend a second serial rapist—Kirk Reid.

Worboys was found guilty of 19 charges of drugging and sexually assaulting women and given an indeterminate jail sentence in March 2009. After his arrest in 2008 (and no doubt with the Reid case hanging over them), the Met's flawed responses to numerous allegations of rape reached such a level that the IPCC was invited to carry out an inquiry into why the police had released Worboys the previous year. In fact, that IPCC investigation was extended to a second one into the Reid case. Sandra Laville, writing in the *Guardian* on 27th March 2009 the under the headline 'Missed clues left London chef free to attack women' noted that the judge had described the police investigation as 'inadequate'. She went on to describe how:

The Metropolitan police force is facing a crisis in public confidence following fresh revelations of serious mistakes that left a serial rapist free to attack scores

of women ... Only weeks after acknowledging failures in the investigation of the
black-cab rapist John Worboys, Scotland Yard is under a barrage of criticism
for not catching and stopping Kirk Reid, a south London chef who raped and
sexually assaulted more than 71 women over eight years.

Laville explained how Reid had been suspected of a series of sex attacks in
2004 and crossed the police radar at least 12 times, but no-one had pursued
inquiries into him. He went on to attack at least 20 women, leaving the Met
facing another 'Macpherson moment' over its rape and sex crime investigations.[1] Reid attacked in south London in the early hours of the morning,
targeting women walking home alone.

He was finally identified after the investigation was passed to an experienced detective who took just hours to identify him as a prime suspect and
match his DNA to that from assaults in 2001 and 2002. Detective Inspector
Justin Davies was in fact praised by the judge for his excellent work.

John Yates, the Met assistant commissioner and national police spokesperson on rape and sexual assault, was reported as acknowledging both that
there had been errors: and comparisons with the aftermath of the Lawrence
case: 'Nothing can adequately excuse the failure to follow up straightforward lines of inquiry that should have seen Reid arrested at that time [i.e. in
2004].' Yates stressed examples of good police work across the country into
rape allegations, but 'too many and significant inconsistencies in the investigative response at every level', not only in London but across England and
Wales such that 'Rape cases simply do not get the attention they deserve.'

The IPCC also declared that the Reid case gave 'real cause for concern.'
IPCC commissioner Deborah Glass was quoted as saying that: there had
been a number of cases in which the response by police to victims of sexual
offences had been called into question such that there was 'a real need for
independent scrutiny.'

The Metropolitan Police Commissioner Sir Paul Stephenson expressed his
very real concerns about public confidence in his force ebbing away after its
repeated failures in such inquiries. An internal review had identified various
concerns in the standard of investigations and efforts were being made to

---

1.   A reference to criticism that engulfed Scotland Yard following the racist murder of Stephen
     Lawrence.

'learn lessons'

An IPCC investigation into failings in both the Worboys and Reid cases identified a series of failings in a rape inquiry in 2005. Four officers were to be disciplined as a result by the Met's DPS. The report on that case contained testimony from senior members of the specialised sex crime investigative Sapphire which described a department 'in crisis' because management—who were concerned with hitting national targets—considered car crime a higher priority than rape and sex offences.

There were further ramifications following the Worboys case later but, chronologically, we need to explore the IPCC Worboys investigation. The Met voluntarily referred their management and investigation of that case to the IPCC in January 2009. In January 2010, it concluded that:

> Five police officers have been disciplined and the Independent Police Complaints Commission (IPCC) has called for changes to the way police deal with victims of sexual offences following its investigation into the Metropolitan Police Service's enquiry into John Worboys.

> The investigation discovered missed opportunities due to individual errors of judgement as well as more systemic issues. It found that there was a case to answer by five police officers, two Detective Constables, a Detective Sergeant and two Detective Inspectors and all have been disciplined as a result.

> On 26 July 2007, a woman called the Met and reported that she had been sexually assaulted by the driver of a London taxi. An investigation began and John Worboys was arrested the next day. He was bailed pending further inquiries but the investigation was closed in October 2007, as it was decided that there was insufficient evidence to take to the Crown Prosecution Service.

> He went on to attack a further seven women before he was arrested for a second time and subsequently charged in February 2008. In March 2009, he was convicted of 19 charges, including one count of rape and four sexual assaults from October 2006 to February 2008. He was sentenced to an indeterminate sentence on 21 April 2009 at Croydon Crown Court.

The Met conducted an internal review of their overall handling of the Worboys investigation which concluded in October 2008, which led to a number of recommendations as to the way victims of sexual assaults are dealt with and organizational changes. They then voluntarily referred their handling of the case to the IPCC in January 2009. Following this referral, the IPCC received two complaints, one from the woman who was assaulted by Worboys on 26 July 2007 and another from a woman who was sexually assaulted in 2003.

Having examined the Met's review, the IPCC has concluded that steps have been taken to address the concerns raised, but more needs to be done if public confidence in the police's response to reports of rape and sexual offences is to improve.

The IPCC's recommendations included that:
- The Met should provide information online and in leaflet form which sets out what victims of sexual offences can expect from the police during the reporting, investigation and court case, along with information about making complaints if the service they should expect is not met.
- There should be a requirement for victims to be updated regularly, by a named contact, in an agreed way at a time that suits them.
- The Met needs to work more closely with the voluntary sector, which has a crucial role working with victims to promote public confidence in the police. Third party reporting should be made available on a more formal basis than it currently is, and the training given to front line officers should be quality checked by independent observers from the voluntary sector.

It was noted that the Met had already altered its procedures and training, and significant changes had been implemented. Following its investigation into the handling of the Kirk Reid case the IPCC concluded that there was a case to answer for five officers, including senior officers. The report was currently with the Met and the IPCC awaited their proposals for disciplinary action. Deborah Glass, deputy chair of the IPCC published a report in 2010 and gave the reasons why only three, albeit senior officers, had a case to answer and said that the Met had agreed to arrange a misconduct hearing for

'Officers C, E and F.'[2] So far as I can identify, the last information publicly available was in 2012 when a Met spokesperson was quoted as saying: 'The matter is ongoing, therefore it would be inappropriate to discuss it further'. A FOI answer[3] at around the same time also suggested that the matter was still pending. If so, is delayed justice in fact no justice?

Whilst there are the up-to-date ramifications of Worboys to report, nevertheless for both continuity and consecutive reasons it would be appropriate to now include the IPCC findings on Reid dated 28th June 2010 when they told us that:

A superintendent and two inspectors are to face a Full Powers Misconduct Panel, following an investigation by the Independent Police Complaints Commission (IPCC) into the Metropolitan Police's handling of the case of Kirk Reid. The IPCC's independent investigation found that:
- there was a sustained failure by senior supervisory officers to give the investigation the priority it required and to get a grip on the longstanding pattern of offences committed within a single borough.
- investigating sexual assaults was never a priority on the borough
- supervisory officers felt under pressure in relation to performance and targets set by the centre.
- a lack of resources allocated to the investigation and the constant change of heads of department contributed to the failings.

Kirk Reid attacked lone women on the A24 corridor and near to Balham and Tooting underground stations. In March 2009, he was found guilty of 27 sexual offences and the Met has linked him to a possible 80–100 other sexual assaults between 2001 and 2008.

The investigation into this series of offences, known as Anflora, was carried out by officers from Wandsworth Borough, whose Sapphire Unit was set up in 2003, until January 2008, when a decision was made to allocate the series to the Specialist

---

2.   See http://www.ipcc.gov.uk/sites/default/files/Documents/investigation_commissioner_
     reports/kirkreidcommissionersreport.pdf

3.   See http://www.met.police.uk/foi/pdfs/disclosure_2012/march_2012/2011040001830.pdf

Crime Directorate (SCD 1) of the Met. Within three days of this re-allocation, Reid was arrested. He was then charged and ultimately convicted and imprisoned.

As Reid had come to the attention of the police in 2002 and 2004, the Met conducted an internal review of their investigation into Reid, and when the internal review had concluded, referred their handling of the case to the IPCC in January 2009.

An IPCC Senior Investigator examined the review. Eight officers, ranging from detective sergeant to superintendent rank, were interviewed…and asked to account for their actions and decision-making. The investigation concluded that a superintendent…has a case to answer. It has also concluded that two detective inspectors…have a case to answer.

The final IPCC report was passed to the Met in December 2009 with a request for the Met proposals for how they intended to deal with potential misconduct matters. These proposals were received in May 2010 and agreed in June 2010. A chief superintendent and a detective sergeant received formal words of advice.

It is also part of the IPCC's remit to identify good practice and the investigation found that a number of junior officers showed commendable investigative skills. The IPCC has recommended that the crime analyst whose work led to Reid's conviction should be commended.

IPCC Commissioner for London, Deborah Glass, said:

The failure to take a serial sex offender off the streets of London years earlier is a shameful chapter in the history of the Metropolitan Police Service. When considered alongside the failings in the case of John Worboys, their overall effect on the confidence of the victims of sexual offences in the police response cannot be over-stated. That is damaging not only for victims, but for the many dedicated officers who have worked hard to make a difference…

So by June 2010, eight officers were to face various levels of discipline and the IPCC concluded that the onus was on the Met to demonstrate that the changes recommended and supposedly implemented had indeed made a real and tangible difference. The report used stern words so let's consider the respective outcomes at the Met and IPCC. Sadly, bearing in mind our contributor's story, one can only conclude that neither the Met nor the IPCC learnt a great deal, if anything. Our contributor, you may recall, was actually arrested for harassment following two rape allegations by her while her appeal (post-2010 and the Worboys and Reid cases) to the IPCC was rejected. Perhaps, like the Met before them, the IPCC needed a bigger picture with the dots in bold type or even joined up for them.

However, the wider insult to all victims of rape, the IPCC and indeed the Government's wish to increase confidence in police forces, is the Met's punishments for incompetence. In the Worboys case, as we saw above, a detective constable and a detective inspector were to be disciplined — they received written warnings while the rest of those identified by the IPCC received 'words of advice'. Even Kirk Reid must be laughing because the IPCC recommended that a superintendent and two inspectors should face gross misconduct proceedings. In fact, the superintendent was promoted and given words of advice. The detective chief inspector is now a superintendent and was given a written warning as was the detective inspector, whose rank remained unchanged. Really harsh stuff, eh?!

I believe these punishments are the Met disrespecting the IPCC. I actually feel sorry for the respective IPCC commissioners who carried out these investigations because they have been a largely a waste of their time and, far from increasing confidence in our police forces, their work has highlighted the Met's disrespect, disbelief and disregard for victims of rape. Further, from our contributor's experiences, it seems that that attitude extends to the IPCC. In fact it seems that some police officers disrespect many citizens.

However, I'm delighted to report the chapter remains open, no thanks to the Met's determined investigations in other rape cases but entirely due to the courage and tenacity of two of Worboys' victims. The women argued in court that the Met had violated their human rights by the inadequate and flawed investigation that followed their original claims of rape. On 28th February 2014 they obtained judgement in their favour under Articles 3 of the Human Rights Act 1988 (inhuman or degrading treatment). This broke new ground, and opened the way for compensation. It is also particularly interesting to readers because, while there are major differences, *Chapter 8* tells of another example of a new precedent being set by a court against 'because we can'-style policing. This case opened the way for individual police employees to be charged by their victims (i.e. not solely by the CPS). So, thankfully, times may be a-changin' — but will these judgements make the Met and other forces more conscientious, mindful of their obligations, take rape victims seriously and act more competently? All good questions and only time will tell but the police can at least no longer do, or in the case of rape not do, quite what they like and are likely to be hit where it hurts (in the pocket!).

It's interesting to speculate whether the Met and others will be asked to provide compensation to victims outside the confines of the Worboys case. Hopefully, including those attacked by Reid and other individuals. With this in mind I took a few minutes to look into tort law and sketch a few inexpert thoughts about the rights, obligations and the remedies applied by courts in civil proceedings. Tort cases sometimes take place on behalf of multi-client claimants/plaintiffs. They need to establish that the defendant:

- was under a legal duty to act in a particular fashion — which seems to have been established above;
- breached this duty — which, in the case of two victims, also seems to have been accepted by the courts;
- consequential to which the claimant/plaintiff suffered injury, loss or damage.

So let's hope that the police do pay a price, that it's sufficient to get their attention and that they change their responsiveness and style. It would help if negligent officers were automatically sacked and that my corresponding plea for 'zero-tolerance' (*Chapter 22*) are thought to have merit. However, I expect that the police will fight the claims for damages every step of the way and resist changing their worrying, not-our-responsibility tactics. Indeed the Met has already argued, in effect, when defending its Worboys inaction that the appropriate interpretation of human rights law was that they were not required to investigate rape properly, and if there was an obligation it had not been breached. That is what you might call having your cake and eating it.

One thing *is* for sure — rape victims right across the country will continue to bottle-up the abuse they feel until there are major changes and, again, I'm back to the need for both serious legislative improvements to police responsibilities and to the teeth and status (and responsibility) of their 'watchdog'. *Chapter 21* contains a number of suggestions to get deliberations started. I thought it was already obvious but clearly the police's responsibility needs to be enshrined in legislation that each police force *is* required to protect its citizens including under the Human Rights Act. Why else, e.g. would the Met use 'Total Policing' as a motto? But in fact there is more expert opinion on record suggesting that indeed the Government does need to provide wider legislative protection for victims. Keir Starmer former director of public prosecutions suggests that 'Britain's criminal justice system fails the vulnerable and that we need a Victims' Law'.

To put Starmer's suggestion into context I need to explain that HMIC is already concerned about the whole issue of rape and sexual abuse and established a Rape Monitoring Group (RMG) to compare *reported* rape from regional force to regional force in England and Wales. The RMG wrote a special report, key extracts from which are paraphrased below.[4]

Police data on adult and child rapes recorded by 43 police forces are published together for the first time today. They will help the general public to understand the extent of rape offending in their area and to look at how their force is responding alongside other forces.

The number of recorded rapes, of both adults and children (under 16 years), has steadily increased since March 2008. In the year (to March 2013) there were approximately 6,000 recorded rapes of children and approximately 10,000 recorded rapes of adults.

In September 2013, HMIC hosted an event for police and crime commissioners to discuss HMIC's approach to monitoring forces, with practical examples of how data can be used to assist in setting priorities and identifying who is accountable for improving services to victims. PCCs asked for more data on rapes across all

4. It can be viewed in full at http://www.hmic.gov.uk/publication/
rape-monitoring-group-digests-data-and-methodology-2014/

forces, and today HMIC, on behalf of the RMG is publishing data showing how many rapes were recorded by the police in each force, and the outcomes.

The chair of the RMG, HM Inspector of Constabulary, Dru Sharpling, said on behalf of the RMG members:

> Rape is one of the most serious violent crimes and the impact on victims can be devastating. It is absolutely crucial that the police and wider criminal justice system has all of the information available to ensure that victims are being believed and the police are following through investigations.

> We will be seeking to improve on these data sets and will publish information at regular intervals to encourage and maintain performance improvements across England and Wales.'

These words sit uncomfortably with the Met's investigations into the Worboys and Reid cases and their response to the IPCC's recommendations. There is the Met's RMG digest[5] but nowhere could I find any indication of what it was doing to improve its response to, or detection of, rape crimes, nor could I discern any clear policies being introduced to encourage victims to come forward.

Reverting to the HMIC report, I could not find any comment upon the competence, thoroughness or integrity of the police in carrying out this doubtless harrowing work, or constructive suggestions about future steps to improve performance. In *Chapter 18* I explore HMIC more closely and explain that, regardless of the topic, too frequently it seems to react to what the *police* tell it and ignore what victims experienced and have to contribute.

Keir Starmer (above) seemed to have a better grasp when he wrote in *The Guardian* on 3rd February 2014 about how those who have suffered sexual abuse tend to be treated:[6]

---

5. See http://www.hmic.gov.uk/wp-content/uploads/2014/01/metropolitan-rmg-adult-and-child-rape-data-2012-13.pdf
6. http://www.theguardian.com/commentisfree/2014/feb/03/britain-criminal-justice-system-victims-law-public-prosecutions

The focus on the criminal justice response to victims of personal violence and abuse, particularly where it is of a sexual nature, is increasingly intense. The [Jimmy] Savile revelations were just the start of it. Last week's report by HM Inspectorate of Constabulary (HMIC) ... on the inconsistency of approach to rape allegations across different regional police forces, the recent drop in the number of prosecutions for rape and domestic violence, and the fact that there has not been a single prosecution for female genital mutilation (FGM) only add to the concern.

He went on to describe some of the difficulties for victims who, like most people, would resist telling a stranger about 'our very best sexual experience'; so that it takes 'real courage' to come forward when raped. In his view the nature of the criminal justice response dictates the likelihood that anyone will.

Undoubtedly, things have improved ... In my five years as director of public prosecutions, I met and dealt with many individuals who were committed to improving the lot of victims. But having reflected on my own experience, both of representing victims and as DPP, and having listened to many victims, their representatives and their families, I'm afraid I have reached some pretty unpalatable conclusions.

Starmer cited a lack of confidence in the system which he supported by the fact that none of over 200 victims of Savile who spoke to Operation Yewtree came forward during Savile's lifetime often through fear of not being believed or that the criminal justice system would prove ineffective. There are similar problem with domestic violence or female genital mutilation (FGM).

Next, there is the problem that even if a victim does pluck up the courage to come forward, too often they are met with a number of assumptions about how 'real' victims behave. The task of the police and prosecutors in assessing the likelihood that a victim will be believed in court is not easy. But until recently, based on their experience of what actually happens in courtrooms across the country every day, police and prosecutors adopted crude tests such as whether the victim reported the crime swiftly to the police, whether the victim was able to give a coherent and full account first time, whether the victim had returned to the perpetrator, and whether the victim had been affected by drink or drugs ... This tick-box exercise flushes out the model victim, but it does so at the expense of other real victims who are often vulnerable to crime precisely because they are unable to trust those in authority...

Starmer concluded by emphasising that even if victims do come forward there are later disincentives including the way they are treated in court. Bad experiences such as having to face those they have accused or being described as liars and that, even when a case is sensitively handled, the adversarial system does not always serve victims well. He proffered the example of a serious sexual offence against a child. The girl, 'who had suffered greatly in her short life and who found relations with adults very difficult,' agreed with everything put to her by prosecution or defence. Hence, he concluded:

> From a victim's point of view, our justice system is hardly fit for purpose. No doubt individual failings by police and prosecutors provide part of the explanation. But to suggest these shortcomings are the core problem is complacent...A more radical review of our criminal justice arrangements is long overdue... What is needed is a fundamental rethink, leading to a specific and legally enforceable Victims' Law, alongside a real and radical shift in attitude and approach. Perhaps we could start by retiring the description 'criminal justice system' and conceive instead of a criminal justice service fit for victims.

Comment

I haven't asked, but I feel sure our contributor would agree she made mistakes not least by returning to her ex which may have reduced her credibility in the eyes of the police. However there can be no excuse for the initial protracted and ineffective investigation and lack of protection the police offered before her return. Nor would it appear this police inadequacy towards sexual abuse is limited to this contributor. I expect they'll tell us that lessons have been learnt, but they always say that whenever an event proves what the little people have been telling things to those with deaf ears for years. So, I applaud those who brought the Worboys case to a civil court. They may not have won real justice, that is long gone. But they have some compensation. May many more have the courage to follow suit.

CHAPTER 5

Covering-up Procedural Errors?

David is the name we'll give this contributor who explains his first-ever experiences of the police while trying to protect his daughter from protracted harassment from her 'ex' who we'll also give a pseudonym to. We'll call him Iverson. Iverson effectively concluded his failing marriage by cashing a joint endowment policy without his wife's knowledge, re-mortgaged their jointly-owned house pocketing £50,000 of the equity and left many debts and household bills unpaid. Amongst Iverson's creditors was David who had loaned Iverson money to avoid repossession of the couple's home. Iverson disappeared leaving his wife to resolve many issues not least of which were a barrage of demanding phone calls, letters, callers and bailiffs. A year later she was at her doctor's receiving treatment, medication and counselling for post-traumatic stress disorder and pleading by phone to Iverson to redirect his personal and business mail as it was harassing, distressing and exacerbating her PTSD. Iverson took no action.

David helped as best he could through the next four years but the harassment and distress brought on almost daily by Iverson's mail, including bank and card statements, took its toll on his daughter. There was no forwarding address, so returning the mail to sender just generated more mail, threats and demands. The Post Office declined to help and after about 750 such provocations and no attempt by Iverson to stop the pain, David's daughter asked him to find a way to halt the mail. David wrote to the police and the Post Office for help and guidance. The police ignored the letter completely. The Post Office told David that the addressee, but only the addressee, should visit any Post Office, provide identification and complete a mail re-direction form. The Post Office could offer no alternatives, particularly as Iverson's address was still unknown.

David wrote to the chief constable asking why his letter requesting police assistance had been ignored and a week or so later a police officer visited David's daughter who explained her stress-related illness and the distress and harassment the mail generated and that it had continued for over four years. The officer said that no criminal offence had been committed, the matter was 'civil' and the police were not interested. The officer's emailed summary of the visit got facts wrong and left both David and his daughter convinced that the police were disinterested but also unhelpful and a waste of space. Nothing that has taken place since has brought either to revise their opinion.

David contrived to meet Iverson to ask him face-to-face to re-direct Iverson's personal and business mail. Iverson agreed and promised a copy of his redirection instructions. Iverson was still keeping his address secret so, after three weeks of inaction, David asked Iverson's brother to forward a letter to Iverson reminding him of his promises, in spite of which his mail continued to be delivered and make his ex-wife ill. Consequently, redirection was now necessary within the next couple of weeks, failing which David would write to the police and financial regulatory bodies drawing attention to the fact that Iverson was fraudulently using a false address for his personal and business mail. Nevertheless the mail continued to be delivered but David did receive a letter from Iverson's solicitors saying that David's letter was unhelpful and unnecessary and that his client was making arrangements to redirect his mail. But the mail continued unabated.

Several months later David found an on-line method of searching electoral rolls by name, paid a small fee and, now after nearly five years, found Iverson's home address. As a step towards recovering his debt, David wrote a 'Notice of Proceedings' letter warning of legal action if the debt was not repaid within the following month. David's daughter also took advantage of knowing the address and wrote her 'ex' a 'Cease and Desist—Notice of Proceedings' warning pointing out that for five years Iverson had persistently ignored her countless requests to re-direct his mail and left her to face his extremely distressing mail and creditors. She pointed out that Iverson's inaction was in contravention of their divorce papers that recorded 'And Upon the husband agreeing and undertaking to the court that he will redirect his post'. Her letter also alleged that Iverson's inaction was psychological harassment and as such a violation of the Administration of Justice Act 1970, section 40 and the Protection from Harassment Act 1997, section 3(2). She also told him that his manipulation of her psychological status and the impact of his behaviour is a violation of Article 3 of the Human Rights Act 1998 and as such she was entitled to seek retribution in a civil court or tribunal. Iverson redirected his mail the next day. The police could probably have achieved that result over 12 months previously, nevertheless the main issue was finally resolved and David's daughter now had the opportunity to live her life free of harassment.

The dispute would probably have died a death at this point but within a week Iverson complained to the police that David and his daughter were *harassing him*. The police concurred and emailed David a criminal police information notice (PIN) advising David that he risked arrest if he made further direct contact with Iverson. In the same email the constable also warned that David's daughter should not pursue her course of action.

David wrote a complaint to the chief constable seeking an explanation and asking 12 pertinent questions pivotal amongst which was whether, under malicious communications legislation was he not liable for the offence if he had or believed he had reasonable grounds for his letters. An inspector, writing on behalf of the chief constable, answered three of the 12 questions but ignored all reference to the Malicious Communications Act and the reasonableness of David's letters. Accordingly, David wrote to the Independent Police Complaints Commission (IPCC) who acknowledged the complaint by return but, following the standard police complaints system procedures, forwarded the complaint to the Professional Standards Department (PSD) of the police force for investigation.

The same inspector who had replied on behalf of the chief constable acknowledged the complaint as if he were part of the PSD. Over the course of the next 12 months there were some email exchanges but no satisfactory explanation, resolution or closure. In fact there was a gap of several months when the police seemed to have shelved the matter—explained later by the fact that the file had been lost between the inspector's domestic policing department and the PSD. After 13 months of pressing the police for an answer David wrote to the constituency MP who proved very helpful and expedited the PSD through a senior police officer. After 14 months, the PSD delivered its conclusion: there was insufficient evidence in their investigation report, which they enclosed, to uphold the complaint and that David was now at liberty to appeal to IPCC.

The same inspector who had handled David's initial complaint to the chief constable and had seemingly appeared to be part of the PSD also wrote the PSD's investigation report and was consequently, in effect, investigating and reporting on himself. The report exonerated all actions by the police, ignored 14 or 15 police PIN-procedural errors and included five obvious fabrications and up to 27 errors and omissions. Some of the omissions were convenient, notably any reference to the Malicious Communications Act. However the report did include a statement by the PC who had issued David with his PIN recording that, when making his harassment complaint, Iverson admitted that he had not redirected his mail for five years due to illness. Clearly the police had failed to check backgrounds and history, as is required by procedures, and with the PC's gullibility in mind, the numerous procedural errors and fabrications, David confidently sent his appeal to IPCC with 26 supporting documents proving credibility, omissions, inaccuracy and shortcomings.

David was amazed to hear from the IPCC that the police had acted appropriately and had been 'proportionately' helpful. The IPCC's case officer ignored the inconvenient facts which prompted David to write to the IPCC's Internal Investigations Unit complaining:

> '[T]he heart of this appeal was the inadequacy of the PSD investigation but the tone of your review was totally police-orientated. You avoid mentioning/exploring several important, some pivotal, shortcomings that my appeal raised with their report and consequently I wish to initiate the IPCC complaint procedure.'

The following is a summary of the remainder of the claims in David's letter:

(a) He justified or alluded to the reasonableness of his correspondence eight times in the context of the Malicious Communications Act and provided copies as proof, none of which had been addressed;

(b) He identified nine clear PSD errors in their investigatory report and provided documentary proof of each, asking, 'How can justice be properly served if the IPCC/watchdog just passes over everything without comment?';

(c) He questioned the accuracy of the PSD statement that 'the complainant declined to agree to the process'. The PSD had unilaterally and without consultation elected for an informal investigation whereas David contended that the police, particularly their PSD, could not be allowed to falsify the facts to suit their case;

(d) The PSD investigation failed to question the credibility of Iverson's claim that he could not visit a Post Office to re-direct his mail for five years and the gullibility of PC X in this respect. The IPCC review ignored this uncomfortable fact;

(e) In the light of published procedures, David challenged the suggestion that it was not necessary for PC X to carry out background and due diligence checks prior to issuing his warning;

(f) He challenged their satisfaction that the police made proportionate attempts 'to assist you both', whereas David felt that whilst he did receive prompt help from the fraud office in 2xxx his pivotal letter dated dd/mm/yyyy, asking for help and providing supporting evidence, had totally ignored references to the investigating officer stating that they were 'satisfied that these matters would not have impacted upon the final decision made by the IO in this case' and ignored the fact that had the report presented *all* the facts to DI xxx, the officer 'signing-off' the investigation, his decision might have been different; and

(g) David said that the errors, omissions and credibility issues in the PSD report collectively led him to question the wisdom of allowing the police to investigate themselves. Inspector Z was not only the officer handling the issue through 2xxx/2xxxx but had correspondence directed to the PSD routed to him (although not part of the PSD) and he also wrote the final investigatory report. David asked how he could be objective and be seen to be objective.

David quickly received a firm rebuttal when the IPCC case officer (note not the IPCC Internal Investigations Unit) replied:

> ...I am satisfied that I have provided you with sufficient rationale for my decision in my outcome letter to you. I do not consider it proportionate to reiterate this

to you now. I understand that you are unhappy with the decision of the IPCC;
however I will advise you that IPCC decisions are final. If you wish to seek to
challenge this, I would advise you seek legal advice.

The IPCC response brought David to conclude that an initially minor
issue that the police could have dealt with via an apology had mushroomed
and was now not only a question of police objectivity, even-handedness,
accuracy and integrity but raised the question whether the PSD/IPCC system
is fit for purpose. He was intending to explore the possibility of legal aid to
fund a judicial review when events took an unexpected turn.

A friend brought David's attention to questions regarding PIN procedures
that the House of Commons had debated. *Hansard* records that a Sussex
MP had been issued with a PIN and was challenging it both because it
inhibited his work as an MP but also, more relevant to David's complaint,
because police procedural requirements had been ignored. Consequently he
followed the procedural shortcoming revelations revealed in the minutes of
the Joint Committee on Parliamentary Privilege after their meeting on 28th
January 2014.[1]

That committee not only took the view that the police's action was a
contravention of Parliamentary privilege but, relevant to David's complaint,
that the police had contravened Association of Chief Police Officers (ACPO
and their own PIN guidance procedures. The MP's PIN was rescinded a
couple of weeks later with an apology because Sussex police had breached
Parliamentary privilege. The police pleaded ignorance of Parliamentary
procedures. The Parliamentary Privileges Committee also required that the
chief constable set up a review of how PIN procedures had/had not been
observed in the county.

David consulted the procedures governing how and when PINs should be
used and issued.[2] It was clear that these had not been adhered to and David,
in the absence of information regarding the PIN review, felt it prudent to
re-complain to the temporary chief constable, who was now responsible for
implementing Parliament's wishes, drawing attention to how David's original

1.   See http://www.parliament.uk/documents/commons-committees/Privileges-
     Committee/2014-01-28-Corrected-transcript-rev.pdf

2.   See http://www.acpo.police.uk/documents/crime/2009/200908CRISAH01.pdf

complaint had not only not addressed numerous procedural errors prior to the issue of his PIN but additional omissions within the PIN and indeed afterwards (14 or 15 in total). He also stressed that the ACPO procedural guide included provision for actions that 'were reasonable and lawful' and that his efforts to save his daughter's harassment and stress and to recover his debt fell into that category. Furthermore, he quoted the police code of conduct. David also pointed out that the police had broken the required level of confidentiality required by it when the issuing officer referred to David's daughter's conduct in David's PIN and that he wished this new complaint to be considered within the PIN procedural review required by the Parliamentary Committee of Privileges.

David took the opportunity to stress that the PSD had never investigated his complaint—it was an officer from domestic policing who had been responsible for the case, for the PSD review and for the investigation report—i.e. he was investigating himself but made over 27 mistakes in his report and David claimed 'fabricated' five statements that were quite untrue yet easily checkable. The response David received from the PSD was that 'in certain circumstances a recorded complaint does not have to be dealt with under the Police Reform Act, when it's called disapplication. Your complaint was considered repetitious ... before the decision is made to dis-apply it, I am writing to request if you have any further written representations.'

David wrote a few days later that he saw no benefit in duplicating the (six page and thus extensive) details already supplied but re-iterated that the police failed in their duty to follow ACPO guidelines when issuing PINs. As review was to be set up. David's re-complaint was on the instructions of Parliament addressed to that review body and included new information of the numerous but specific procedures ignored by the police. David told the PSD that he would not therefore categorise his letter as duplication or repetitious. He pointed out that the police should be guided by ACPO inspired procedures and had a duty of care not only to follow the procedures but to properly investigate complaints ... all to no avail as the following extracts from the PSD reply indicate:

> [Y]our complaint will not be investigated on the grounds it is repetitious ... The complaint you made about being issued with a PIN was dealt with under our

reference…following an investigation into this complaint, you appealed to the IPCC against the investigation but your appeal was not upheld.

The evidence you have provided regarding the chief constable appearing before a Parliamentary committee…has no relevance to your specific complaint.

After reviewing the handling of the complaint I am satisfied the decision that this is repetitious is correct because we have already investigated this matter and you have not provided sufficient grounds that would cause me to re-consider my decision.

Your appeal is therefore not upheld on this point.

After considering all the information available I have now made a decision about your appeal. I have not upheld your appeal [Police bold type].

The appeal body for this decision rests with our department…and your only recourse, if you disagree with my decision, is by way of a judicial review.

With regard to the PIN review I am not in a position to supply you with the information you requested but you can apply for details of how many PIN notices were issued by Sussex Police in accordance with a freedom of information request, details of which will be found on our website.

This decision now concludes the matter. Please note the Police Reform Act governing complaint procedures does not afford you a further right of appeal against this decision.

Before drawing the PIN procedural shortfalls and the police's disdain for the Parliamentary Privileges Committee findings to attention, David decided to separately enquire what details the PIN procedural review was investigating. He learnt that there are two separate parts to the review:

- focusing on current policy and any amendments that need to be addressed in content and application; and

- carrying out reviews in conjunction with the College of Policing, thereby addressing issues that affect legislation and therefore need to be implemented nationally. This review to cover the Harassment Act as a whole not just PINs.

David also enquired specifically whether the review would include any attempt to review PINs issued by the police over the last five years for procedural non-conformity and learnt that the review was not concerned about such irregularities or for members of the public who had been wrongfully 'labelled' by a PIN. Consequently, David wrote to the chair of the Parliamentary Standards Committee in September 2014. The committee had instructed a PIN review take place so David pointed out these major shortcomings in their report.

Meanwhile the assistant detective chief inspector of the PSD wrote to David in mid-September 2014 saying, amongst other details, that he had applied the standards of the procedures and policies in place in 2012 and not those of the new, updated polices. He was satisfied that the complaint was dealt with properly *at the time*. If they were to re-investigate now, it would cause injustice to the officers involved who, having been subjected to a public complaint for 15 months, had been officially informed that the matter had been finalised and that there would be no further action. It would therefore not be fair or proportionate to re-open the investigation into the complaint now and by comparing the actions of the officers to the requirements of a new policy that was not in existence at the time of the incident. In conclusion, the letter stated, 'I can confirm that I have no intention of re-opening your complaint of 2012.'

David remained convinced that this police force had failed in its duty of care a total of some 50 times given that their investigation report included 27 mistakes and five untrue statements and that there were 14 original PIN non-conformities and a further five revealed when the PIN procedural review was published. So David wrote to all this police force's MPs and in due course learnt that the HAC would carry out a short oral study of PINS on

13th January 2015.[3]

Amongst those giving oral evidence was the retired chief constable whose evidence included admissions that he had said he was surprised to subsequently learn that 75 per cent of the PINs issued under his guidance were 'used in inappropriate circumstances' and that he had made no effort to monitor the force's use of them. Further it was shown that, compared with much larger forces, the number of PINs issued under his watch seemed disproportionately high. David was gratified to read these revelations and intends to use the information through the chair of the HAC to press for an apology from the police force in question and a long overdue and frequently rejected investigation into the officers involved in his injustice (which include allegations against a senior officer).

Comment

There is one saving grace for recipients of a PIN, it will not show up on a Disclosure and Barring Service (DBS) check as it is not a criminal sanction; it is a notice of advice, usually valid for 12 months. Although not applicable to this case, for comparison a police caution for any offence *will* be disclosed on an enhanced DBS check (but not the standard one). The enhanced search is for certain types of employment such as working with children or vulnerable people. While none of this was applicable to David, nevertheless he felt a PIN is, in effect, *the police* finding him guilty, and no doubt others, unilaterally, without even enquiring as to the circumstances or ensuring they adhered to correct procedures.

---

3.   The minutes of the subsequent meeting can be viewed at http://data.parliament.uk/
      writtenevidence/committeeevidence.svc/evidencedocument/home-affairs-committee/police-
      information-notices/oral/17580.pdf

CHAPTER 6

Incompetence, Error or Cover-up?

We'll call him John. He wrote to tell me his story about how the police responded to domestic violence and what followed. The Met's procedures were dubious, leaving questions over the validity of a police caution, the uncomfortable experiences with the duty solicitor called-in by the Met, a local newspaper's change of resolve after talking to the police, the possibly coincidental but nevertheless suspicious harassment by a Met officer, and questionable IPCC 'adjusting' of evidence — in short a story that brings forth numerous questions about our justice system. John's story starts with him explaining that he's a white middle-class male now approaching 60-years-of-age. Aside from concerns about police becoming over-zealously politically correct, he never had any issues with them until 2009 when an Eastern European friend, who we'll call Oksana, telephoned the police to say that her mother-in-law had just tried to murder her.

This was the trigger for the events that followed, but Oksana's initial call-out and what happened next is not John's main concern. The main issues come later in his story as often seems to be the case for those who fight what thy perceive to be an initial injustice. Apparently, as John learnt later, Oksana and her husband had been arguing in their bedroom when Oksana's mother-in-law entered the room. Oksana felt threatened and tried to leave the room intent on calling the police. However, the husband thought Oksana was going to attack his mother and restrained his wife. But 'mother' thought Oksana was attacking her son and tried to pull Oksana off at which point Oksana began screaming. Mother put a pillow over Oksana's mouth, Oksana struggled free, scratching her husband's back in the process and made him bleed. She got to the phone and called the police.

The police attended promptly but after some cursory questioning, arrested Oksana assuming she was drunk. She was in fact perfectly sober although she does have an East European accent. Her sobriety was confirmed an hour and a half later when a police surgeon passed her 'fit for interview'.

She was detained for the rest of the night but obtained permission to ring John from the police station and asked what she should do. John advised a legal representative be present when she was interviewed and told her to ask for and trust the duty solicitor. He says he subsequently had cause to regret this advice.

After five minutes of private conversation with Oksana, the duty solicitor advised her to accept a caution for assault. The duty solicitor seemed to know that her husband did not want to press charges, presumably from the private discussion the police had with the solicitor prior to the formal police interview. The solicitor's notes recorded that the 'victim' (husband) might not give evidence that would, John believed, leave the police with little choice but to issue a caution or forget the incident. John also believed that the solicitor would have known that the police rarely bring charges without the support of a 'victim'. Consequently, in discussion with John a little later, Oksana thought that the duty solicitor was biased towards the police and taking the easy way out. However Oksana accepted the caution and emerged from the police station next morning cautioned for causing actual bodily harm (ABH) to her husband.

John was appalled as it was clear that the police had made no effort to investigate what had happened at the house and the solicitor appeared to have made no effort to defend Oksana. Although the caution would have no practical effect on her life, John says he was left wondering how many young peoples' career prospects had been damaged by undeserved cautions such as this. Consequently John set out to contest it.

Clearly this was a domestic violence call-out and it is the police's often difficult job to resolve such situations. However, it seemed to John that they did not handle this one well. A pillow over the mouth would trigger the survival instinct in all of us and it wouldn't matter how we managed to get it removed. But none of this seems to have occurred to these officers and sadly their poor response is not uncommon according to the 2014 HM Inspector of Constabulary's report entitled 'Everyone's Business: Improving the Police Response to Domestic Abuse'. Fundamentally that report says that the police response to domestic abuse is not good enough and must be improved. It goes on to say about the police in general that:

[HMIC], following an inspection of all 43 police forces in England and Wales, was commissioned by the Home Secretary to inspect the police response to domestic violence and abuse. The report found that while most forces and police and crime commissioners have said that domestic abuse is a priority for their areas, this isn't being translated into an operational reality. HMIC is concerned to find that, despite the progress made in this area over the last decade, not all police leaders are ensuring that domestic abuse is a priority in their forces — it is often a poor relation to other policing activity.

HMIC found alarming and unacceptable weaknesses in some core policing activity, in particular the quality of initial investigation undertaken by responding officers when they are called to a scene. The report also identifies that officers may lack the necessary supervision, knowledge and skills effectively to tackle domestic abuse, and some have poor attitudes.

HM Chief Inspector of Constabulary, Mr Tom Winsor added:

Domestic abuse casts a truly terrible blight on the lives of very many people, and can have tragic consequences. In too many police forces we found there were serious weaknesses in services, which are putting victims at unnecessary and avoidable risk, and failings in some core policing activity...

Domestic abuse is not only about violence; it is about fear, control and secrecy. It is essential that the police make substantial reforms to their handling of domestic abuse, including in their understanding of the coercive and psychological nature of the crime as well as its physical manifestations. They must create the conditions so that victims have the confidence to call for help, in the knowledge that they will be believed and kept safe. Domestic abuse is a volume crime, and a serious one. The police must accept that and act on HMIC's recommendations for urgent and material improvements.[1]

John continues his story by suggesting this was a case where nobody deserved a caution. It began when Oksana's husband mistakenly thought Oksana was about to attack his mother. In the days before the police were encumbered by targets a neighbourhood officer would probably have been able to sort it out over a cup of tea. The fact that all parties continued to live together for some months after this incident suggests it was a flash-in-the-pan sparked by misunderstandings. John believes Oksana cannot have been intoxicated as the attending officers alleged since she was passed fit for interview by the police surgeon less than two hours after the incident in the house and barely an hour after the desk sergeant had refused her access to her lawyer on grounds that she was very drunk. So John tells us that he and Oksana launched a complaint, which John believes immediately sent the police into cover-up mode.

The Met's Department of Professional Standards (DPS) failed to acknowledge John's initial emails of complaint. They responded only on about the sixth attempt when he'd copied it to his MP. The DPS then went to great lengths to persuade John and Oksana to agree to 'local resolution' of the complaint and as part of this resolution the police showed them 20 minutes of CCTV of the duty solicitor at the police station. They thought this an obvious attempt to get them to blame the solicitor rather than the police. This solicitor was clearly on familiar terms with the officers in the station, which prompted John to research how police could possibly influence how much a particular duty solicitor could earn through their scheduling of

---

1. There is an individual report for each police force and in the light of Oksana's experience in London I read the report on the Metropolitan Police with particular interest: see http://www. hmic.gov.uk/wp-content/uploads/2014/03/metropolitan-approach-to-tackling-domestic-abuse.pdf . It can be noted that for every 100 domestic abuse crimes recorded, there were 83 arrests in London. For most forces the number is between 45 and 90. Oksana's problems arose in 2009 when bonuses were available for senior police officers if their officers met Home Office targets for 'sanctioned detections.' In the 12 months to the end of August 2013 the Metropolitan Police recorded 50,263 domestic abuse related crimes of which 26% resulted in a charge. 19% in a caution and less than one per cent had an out of court disposal such as a fixed penalty notice for disorderly conduct. However, from the figures it is clear that the Met attend about 1,000 cases a week and it could be argued that they appear to be generally intent on arresting someone, or at least that targets create that incentive.

interviews. John said he found this a worrying concept and we return to CCTV recordings and his alleged duty solicitor reservations shortly.

One point of his complaint was upheld. A police sergeant who administered the 'Anything said in the interview might be used in court' caution before her official interview failed to ensure Oksana understood it. However, the police again tried to blame the duty solicitor by saying that it was the solicitor's job even more than the sergeant's, to ensure that Oksana understood it. John says he understood that the sergeant would be disciplined but the Met failed to uphold the rest of their complaint.

They appealed to the IPCC on a number of points, one of which was upheld and the appeal as a whole was classed as upheld, even though the majority of individual points had not been upheld. For good reason later in his fight for justice, John became sceptical about the IPCC and decided this solution was arrived at because it made the IPCC's statistics look better.

After about a year, the police expunged Oksana's caution, which John believes to be a rare event indeed as a caution does not have any legislated validity timeframe. It is normally for life even though not a criminal conviction. It will be entered on the Police National Computer (PNC) and used as evidence of previous misconduct if or when any subsequent problems arise. In fact, if you already have a caution it is likely any further trouble will automatically require a prosecution and the case to be heard in court. Furthermore, fingerprints can be taken and also recorded. For those employed in some occupations (teachers, NHS employees, children's carers, vulnerable adults, the police, security employees, even voluntary services) where a Disclosure and Barring Service (DBS) check[2] or clearance is necessary from time-to-time, DBS may be required to disclose the caution which could have serious ramifications for employment prospects. A caution for any offence will be disclosed on in an *enhanced* DBS. The enhanced search is for selected types of employment such as working with the vulnerable.

Whatever, offenders need to be aware of the significance of a caution and its potential effects and to provide their clear informed consent if a caution is proposed. These subtleties are difficult if the suspected offender is, e.g. not native English-speaking. Furthermore the police are not permitted to induce/entice suspects to accept a caution and this is one of the responsibilities that

---

2.   At one time called a Criminal Records Bureau (CRB) check.

the attending solicitor should protect his or her client from.

Feeling aggrieved by their IPCC appeal, John and Oksana then spent an hour with the editor of a local newspaper telling their story. The editor told them he would approach the local Met for a police quote and their side of the story. John says the story then went quiet. When no article appeared, John asked the editor why he did not print it. He said the editor had decided it was 'not for them' but John believes the editor would have known this before he spent his time with them and suspects that the police have some influence over what appears in the local media.

John points out that it is unlikely to encourage women to report themselves as victims of domestic violence if they are branded drunk by the police and administered cautions without proper investigation. Thus John says that some sort of police cover-up was not unexpected. Consequently via the IPCC for Operation Elveden,[3] they reported their misgivings about whether the police had applied pressure on the editor but heard absolutely nothing although the investigation launched by Scotland Yard about three years previously was still ongoing. John tells us that in February 2014 the CPS reported that an ex-police officer from Surrey was to be charged and that to date 84 journalists and public officials had been arrested. John hopes that their worries were noted but were thought minor compared to the police's other investigations. And he agrees that his suspicions are minor details compared to the harassment that followed and whether this was co-incidental.

One evening during the later stages of the complaint, John popped out to the supermarket to buy some wine. He found he had left his card at home, put the bottles back on the shelf and set off home to retrieve it. He says he had hardly left the store when two uniformed members of staff came running after him from inside the store. 'One pushed me, ordered me to stop and demanded to look in my bag.' John assures us that he remained perfectly calm, he knew he hadn't taken anything and that there was nothing in the bag. Nonetheless he asked, partly out of genuine curiosity, what authority the person had to search him. The staff member pulled out a police badge. John was amazed and thought it must be a fake but when John tried to note the badge-number the man said he would call for reinforcements. John showed him that he had nothing in his bag and complained about

---

3.   The police investigation following alleged covert payments to police officers.

the manner of the man's approach at which point the officer threatened to ban John from the store. John subsequently discovered the man was a special constable and that the nationwide retailer in question makes a point of recruiting 'specials' as security staff. Finding John's bag empty the officer departed, quite unapologetic.

John lodged a formal police complaint against the officer and thought this might have been suitable for 'local resolution'. He admits to being extremely vexed by the police's style and actions with Oksana's case, he had concerns over the public interest and suspicions that the freedom of the press had been influenced and tells us that he saw this as a chance to get back at them. But what followed was instructive (and he rather suspects possibly not simply a one-off police tactic).

By then John says he had become familiar with police complaint procedures and at the police station said he wished, as was his right, to make a written statement. The desk-sergeant who handled the complaint refused to allow a written statement. The special alleged that John had refused to be searched and had behaved in such a threatening manner that he deemed it unsafe to proceed. He also insinuated that John had hidden stolen goods under his jacket although the store's employee's report confirmed that John had taken nothing. However the statement by the store employee, the special's colleague, who John felt was a scrupulously honest person, was presumably deemed insufficient by the police to resolve the dispute.

During the subsequent police enquiry, about three weeks after the incident, an independent witness came forward to support the special constable's allegations saying that he had been sitting in a parked car outside the store and witnessed the incident. The witness did not put his statement in writing but the police sergeant gave it great weight. As far as John could tell, the sergeant made no attempt to verify that the witness was present and John feels that, while not totally impossible, it seemed improbable that someone was waiting in an adjacent car at this moment and decided to make himself known to the investigating officer three weeks later. John says he is not even confident that the sergeant verified the witness's identity and thought it likely that the sergeant simply advised the special to get a friend to ring up and verify the incident. In fact the witness's version sounded just like the constable's version but enhanced to present John in an even worse light.

None of this troubled John at the time because he planned from the outset to appeal to the IPCC. He had evidence that the sergeant knew of John's request to make a written statement and the sergeant's refusal was going to initiate John's IPCC complaint/appeal. However he tells us that he was quite unprepared for how the IPCC would deal with this: the IPCC's casework officer simply ignored John's unequivocal wish to make a written complaint. That officer simply renumbered John's documents. John had sent in four documents numbered 1 to 4, with one supplementary document. Document 1 as submitted to the IPCC showed that the sergeant knew that a *written* statement was requested but the IPCC officer simply ignored this document and renumbered documents 2 to 4 as 1 to 3 and gave his supplementary page the number 4. John was dumbstruck but decided that, since his only course of remedy was judicial review in the High Court, even if he was completely sure of success, it would have been extremely time-consuming and potentially expensive and decided against going down that path.

The IPCC case officer did however make one mistake: he failed to protect the identity of the so-called independent witness when responding. John pointed this out to the IPCC in a fresh complaint adding that the special had changed his story and furthermore stop-and-search procedures had not been followed. Initially the special constable stated that he had produced his badge in order to calm John so that he could search him. Later and following John's complaint, the special's statement to the PSD was to the effect that when he approached John, John had behaved like a maniac and in such a dangerous manner as to prevent the special searching him. The special's second statement said that he had produced his badge simply to calm John and with no intention of searching him. This contradicted his previous statement.

The independent witness stated the same. The special also claimed he saw something bulging beneath John's jacket but that he wasn't able to get near enough to ascertain what it was. John complained that the special hadn't followed proper stop-and-search procedures in that he had not recorded the search with the police. John tells us that normally he would expect a second complaint about the same incident to be rejected but doubtless the IPCC did not want him revealing the name of the witness nor that they had let the name 'slip'. John thinks that the desk sergeant was surprised that the complaint came back to them but nevertheless the IPCC did not uphold the appeal.

John believes that if a retailer employs special constables as security staff there should be some means of ensuring that, should these constables invoke police powers, they follow proper procedures. There should be no suspicion that constables produce their badges, bully shoplifters into civil debt recovery schemes (which are lucrative for the retailer) while the police record none of this. Any lack of a safeguard could lead the public to see the police as being controlled by private interests.

At the end of his police complaints road, John asked his MP what he made of private companies employing special constables who in turn use police powers in such circumstances. The MP's assistant contacted the police who stated that the officer had produced his badge 'to calm the male'. John asked if his MP would submit a further appeal to the IPCC on his behalf because he thought that might add weight. The MP declined on the grounds that John had not been injured, nor was he out of pocket, although the MP failed to mention the issue of growing mistrust in the police. This was before Plebgate (*Chapter 9*) so John now wonders if it makes a difference to MP's when the mistrust problems get closer to home for honourable members.

When his MP wouldn't support a further appeal, John lost the enthusiasm to take the complaint further although he believes that there are issues that should be of concern to us all starting with the question as to whether we can trust the police or IPCC? If, as his experience seems to suggest, we cannot, what can be done? However, the issue that has surprised and concerned him the most is the actions of the duty solicitor and the potential for the police to influence the actions of lawyers. Collectively these matters have shaken his confidence in the Rule of Law.

He tells us that he's not a member of the legal profession and so has no vested interest but explains there are disadvantages in Government cuts to legal aid. He believes duty solicitors have an interest in concluding cases as quickly as possible. In this case the solicitor told Oksana categorically that if she didn't accept a caution she would go to court and that '*A caution is not a criminal conviction* but will be recorded' (John believes a distressed person only hears the first part). However, according to the police, the solicitor must have known at that time that Oksana's husband had declined to press charges and that charges where the victim does not give evidence are rare.

From the CCTV recording released by the police it appeared to John that the duty solicitor had come to the station in connection with another client and that Oksana had been 'squeezed in' before this other individual. The rules applicable to duty solicitors, at least at the time, allowed them to have more than one client at a police station at any one time but for clients other than the first there must be a colleague ready to take over at 45 minutes notice in case the police want to interview one client whilst the solicitor is busy with the other(s). If another solicitor takes over, the first solicitor loses the fixed fee, so John believes there is pressure on the solicitor to give the police the result they want in which case the police will more likely cooperate in scheduling interviews. A solicitor may only be interested in keeping a good overall rate of 'no further actions', whilst the police may value detections and sanctions more in some cases, so the possibilities for horse-trading are obvious. John says that he has raised the potential problem in various quarters and discovered that nobody is interested, so he's left wondering if there might be potential for further police and legal profession involvement.

Because of John and Oksana's doubts over the solicitor's neutrality, through that solicitor, as mentioned earlier, they requested that the police release a copy of the CCTV tape covering the pre-interview meeting between the solicitor and the police. He had to threaten court action to get a copy but when the discs finally arrived they found that three crucial minutes of the solicitor's meeting were missing. Letters to the police requesting the 'lost' footage have been ignored while his letter, sent registered post to Oksana's MP, accompanied by full authority for John to represent her, was also ignored. John suggests this only adds more questions and uncertainty as to the confidence we can place in the justice system. Oksana is now in her home country, which makes it difficult to pursue the matter further and, as also mentioned, John has lost the will to pursue the issues any further.

John points out that he's included references of their separate complaints to their respective MPs because neither was handled well. John's MP has been the subject of police investigation and Oksana's MP is a Cabinet minister. John says he's left wondering whether, for one reason or another, some MPs are afraid to take on the police unless of course it is one of their own who is on the receiving end of malpractice. John assures us he is not out of pocket, nor injured, and of course would still turn to the police if he were the victim of serious crime. However his respect for them and indeed the whole justice system is greatly diminished.

Comment

If it does nothing else, this contribution serves to alert readers to the importance of having a sharp lawyer at your side when 'discussing' matters with the police and wherever possible the value of recording any conversation with a police officer, however unexpected it is.

It is also of concern that a special constable working as a supermarket security officer as his 'day job' could assume the authority of a police officer without 'signing-in' with his supervising officers. Via a freedom of information enquiry, the Met told me that in such circumstances a special is allowed to move outside the store, show his special constable's badge and assume the authority of an on-duty police officer. The Met continued:

> A report of any such act must be made as soon as possible to the Borough/OCU Commander through the Special Inspector or MSC Liaison Officer. This power to put themselves on duty must ONLY be exercised in situations when it is in the interests of the public that police powers should be assumed. To clarify, the SOP allows for an MSC officer to place themselves on duty without being formally 'detailed for duty' by a higher ranking officer however if this occurs they must report that fact to the borough or OCU commander...

John points out that these events occurred during the Home Office's 'sanctioned targets' era, which motivated officers to err towards quantity rather than quality of arrests. The Home Office target system was concluded a year or two later but the use of local targets in London, and indeed in other police areas, has been reintroduced by chief constables despite Government policy. We address this issue in a little more detail in *Chapter 12*.

CHAPTER 7

1970s Stitch-ups

You might think policing in the 1970s was different to policing today. It was after all back in the days when virtually everyone thought the police always told the truth. However, some things haven't changed all that much particularly if you were 18 at the time as my correspondent, who we'll call Geoff, found. The sad fact is that you never forget being stitched-up and the experience can affect your negative judgement of and attitude to the police for the rest of your life.

Following a route he was quite familiar with, Geoff left a shop and was heading for home on his motorbike along a route he'd ridden many times, less than three miles of 30 mph restricted road. Riding perfectly normally, maybe just a little quicker than the rest of the car-traffic, but certainly not recklessly, dangerously or speeding through a built-up area, and not accelerating until the road 'opened' up and offered a long sweeping left bend. Knowing the that there were no houses either side there, he did open-up the bike and hit the bend at around 60 mph, hanging off the left side trying hard to emulate his motorcycle racing hero. Job done, he straightened the bike up, eased the throttle off and cruised for home.

All of a sudden he heard a police siren and looking in the mirror saw a police Ital with its blue lights on following his route but way behind. 'Can't be for me as they are so far away,' thought Geoff, but being cautious he pulled to the side, put the bike on its side stand and removed his crash helmet. The driver hand-braked the Ital into the kerb just in front of him — 'Nice touch,' thought Geoff.

The passenger got out looking like he was fit to explode and greeted Geoff with, 'What the hell do you think you're doing!' The policeman then proceeded to exclaim that they had 'clocked' Geoff around the bend at over 70 mph and asked what he would have done if a child had run out from one of the schools. Geoff kept quiet.

This only served to make the angry policeman even more so. Geoff quietly explained that he had already passed the middle and grammar schools before he'd picked up speed so no child would have been at all likely run out from there, beside which it was half term and they were all on holiday. This seemed too much for the police officer to comprehend and he reached for his note-book. He asked Geoff where he had come from, where he was going and went over the bike with a fine toothcomb, seeming as if he was trying hard to find fault with it. Geoff says he was informed that he was going to be reported for dangerous driving and would likely be prosecuted for it. The police left and Geoff continued home.

Time passed and eventually he found himself in front of the magistrates who asked if he wanted the case dealt with there and then or to go to the Crown Court . He chose to have it dealt with there and then. The 'angry' policeman gave his 'evidence' but it was so far as Geoff was concerned mostly a pack of lies. The police claimed to have followed Geoff for three miles, right from where he'd told them his journey started, before being able to stop him. Further they invented a story about Geoff undertaking a bus, crossing a bridge so fast that pedestrians 'leapt out of the way fearing for their safety' and that he initially ignored the blues and twos. Geoff refuted all of this but being a rather long-haired teenage motorcyclist he wasn't surprised when the magistrates accepted the police version of this story, fined Geoff £100 (a lot of money at the time) and put four points on his driving licence.

But it was the 'story' that really angered Geoff because, had he had any idea that it would be mostly fabricated, he would have had legal representa-tion because if they'd followed him the whole distance as claimed, why had they not caught him at the traffic lights he stopped at? If Geoff had 'under-taken' a bus as alleged there was only one location where that is physically possible—where the one-way system is divided/arrowed to position right-turning traffic (mostly buses) into the right hand lane and left turning traffic (Geoff and others) into the left hand one. However, had it really happened there that is hardly 'undertaking' in the meaning of the phrase but, just to satisfy himself, he had not missed seeing something the size of a bus, he called into the bus depot a few days after the court case and established there were no scheduled buses on that road at that time.

It is much more feasible that the police were parked in a turning just off the sweeping left bend Geoff had found so enjoyable, clocked him speeding (which would have been a 'fair cop') and followed him for the next 400 to 500 yards. The rest it seemed to Geoff was made-up, simply because they could.

No division between the traffic police and criminal police investigators will ever repair the lifetime's lost trust this sort of fabrication established but were traffic policing, including speed cameras, a separate entity, at least the consequential damage would have been focused on the traffic arm.

Another correspondent related to me a slightly more perturbing sequence of events from that same era (though I guess it could have happened anytime given bad will on the part of the police). Christopher we'll call him was involved part-time in the antiques business. From time-to-time he would park his van, which had his name painted on each side, in town. One day, out of the blue, and even though his vehicle was on a stretch of road without restrictions (those were the days!) and not interfering with traffic, he received a summons in the post alleging 'unnecessary obstruction' of the highway. This is a charge which requires no evidence of actual obstruction or inconvenience and, as he was advised after consulting a lawyer, it was legally impossible to counter it. He complained to his local force who after some prevarication wrote to say the complaint had been considered and rejected.

The gist was that not only had his vehicle been singled out but that the officer in question was connected to him through their mutual membership of various local organizations, teams and social events, and that the prosecution seemed to have been brought as a grudge in relation to some past disagreement. The officer having recently joined the police, Christopher felt that this was no ordinary (and certainly not a fair) cop, but one rooted in some kind of payback or game in which a rookie officer's mettle was being tested by colleagues egging him on to catch out an acquaintance.

If that were all there were it might be only slightly more worrying than the 'urban myth' about traffic officers playing 'snooker'.[1] But during the period whilst the complaint was with senior officers something frightening occurred. One evening two experienced constables sidled-up behind Christopher as he was walking to his van (this time parked well off the road) and nudged him in the direction of an alleyway. There, whilst one officer acted as lookout, the other took Christopher out of sight into the recess of a shop doorway and fronted-up to him saying, 'I hear you've complained about one of my

---

1. Stopping cars in the same colour sequence: see http://news.bbc.co.uk/1/hi/uk/422651.stm

mates'. Then followed a warning to the effect that if the friend got into trouble there would be reprisals. Christopher was told the police could 'nick' him any time of day or night because they could always find something wrong with any vehicle, or failing this that someone had obstructed them (a reference perhaps to the scenario described elsewhere in this book whereby police provocation is turned on its head if a citizen stands his or her ground). Fortunately, Christopher remained calm and was not wrong-footed. But he dare not formally protest again, wondering if, as a result of his earlier complaint, the entire force now had his card marked.[2]

Years later Christopher made a career change that involved him working alongside the police as a youth justice worker. He tells me that he has recognised the signs of dubious police accounts of arrests on various occasions.

Moving to modern times, Rowena Mason writing in the *Guardian* newspaper on 3rd November 2013 endorsed the resentment traffic police generate:

> BBC presenter Ester Rantzen claimed she and her late husband Desmond Wilcox were the subject of police lies after he was stopped by a traffic officer while speeding. She said the officer wrote down that her husband had said: 'I am the well-known celebrity producer Desmond Wilcox and my wife Esther Rantzen is a TV celebrity. Don't you know who we are?' 'Of course we would never say anything like that,' she is reported as telling Sky News' Murnaghan programme. Rantzen said they did not take the matter further because they did not think they would have much chance against the word of a police officer: 'There's a few of the rotten apples in the barrels where this just comes as second nature to them.'

Comment

The devil is in the detail. If the police get it wrong, ultimately the respect they enjoy (or used to enjoy) becomes irrevocably eroded. One poor experience can last a lifetime. Even small instances of police misbehaviour need to be recognised and dealt with for what they are, minor forms of corruption. Otherwise they tend to grow and that way, however grand it may seem to say it, lies oppression and the slide into tyranny.

---

2. *Chapter 12* describes instances of police officers acting in a such a way towards their own colleagues, especially whistle-blowers or internal complainants.

CHAPTER 8

More Stitch-ups and Cover-ups

The police's dogged determination to 'do' someone who we'll call Jason for something, anything, is only matched by his amazing fortitude and the resilience of his fight to obtain justice and to bring what has proved to be a succession of police employees 'to book'. It is a lesson to us all, particularly in these days of at least some questionable police activity. The story started six or seven years ago yet much is still unresolved. Here's a précis of events starting with the dispute that sets the scene for all that follows.

A couple of days before the main trigger, the police responded to a call from Jason who requested help getting an unwelcome visitor to leave the family home. The police were indeed helpful but the unwelcome visitor returned a couple of days later whereupon Jason again called the police to assist with his removal. An officer (who has since attracted considerable notoriety) attended and the individual left, but later that evening returned, this time uninvited and with a second officer, and demanded entry into Jason's home. When asked to leave the officers threatened Jason with arrest for obstructing an officer and Jason responded by calling 999. The operator told Jason that they would certainly send an additional officer to help but that, since the first officers had a lawful right to be there, the additional police would be assisting the attending officers, not Jason.

Shortly afterwards, Jason complained to the police about this alleged abuse of police powers. The PSD, investigating its colleagues, rejected Jason's complaint. Jason appealed to the IPCC who listened to the 999 call recording and overruled the police, finding that the attending officer had exceeded his authority and they recommended disciplinary action. No disciplinary action was ever taken because the officer was involved in a separate major incident and retired before the police could consider it in Jason's case.

A couple of years later, the police did write formally apologising to Jason for their officer's conduct, but long before the apology Jason's problems escalated dramatically and he found himself thrust unwillingly into both the limelight and vanguard of improving British justice. With the earlier officer's incident behind him but not perhaps beyond the police's memory, Jason was caring for his growing family and quietly pursuing his career when he started to become concerned that an on-line sexual predator was grooming his teenage daughter. This is not as over-reactive as it may sound. The murders, subsequent investigations and trials relating to Holly Wells and Jessica Chapman in August 2002 were thoroughly reported by all the newspapers and added child sexual exploitation, paedophilia and internet grooming to all parents' legitimate worries through the 2000s. Indeed those concerns are still valid. Jason's reaction was particularly understandable because, following the subsequent abduction and murder of Sarah the *News of the World* ran a campaign to draw attention to and find remedial legislation to improve the protection of children. The newspaper and other concerned individuals were rewarded when the Home Office and National Society for the Prevention of Cruelty to Children (NSPCC) concluded an investigation and heralded a pilot scheme that passed into legislation a short while later.

Alerted by all this exposure, Jason took a large file of relevant information to the police at his local station and told them of his concerns. Given the Home Office, NSPCC, media and general activity and publicity, it is extraordinary that the police reaction appeared passive. Doubtless they will protest that vigorous inquires were afoot but, if that was the case, they failed to keep Jason abreast of their enquiries, nor did they then, indeed they have never, examined the daughter's computer. So again not unreasonably, Jason telephoned the police station to enquire as to their progress and whether his daughter was now safe. With amazing foresight and fortuitously, Jason recorded his calls because, equally extraordinarily, the police sent two officers to arrest Jason for harassing, aggressive, shouting phone calls (it's not the only time you'll read similar false accusations) to a member of police staff. They hauled him from his house in handcuffs in his dressing gown. A gross over-reaction for harassment even were it true, however, as we will see, the charges were a complete fabrication and only increase suspicions of police incompetence possibly of corruption.

George Monbiot, writing in *The Guardian* described events and tells us 'Justice is impossible if we cannot trust police forces to tell the truth. From Blair Peach to Ian Tomlinson, there is only one remedy for police officers found to have made false statements: sack them. [1]

My précis is as follows (with some names, dates and locations deleted):

> After Jean Charles de Menezes was shot …commissioner … Sir Ian Blair, claimed
> that de Menezes 'was challenged and refused to obey police instructions'. A state-
> ment by the police claimed his clothing and behaviour gave grounds for suspicion.
> An account that De Menezes' relatives believe originated with the police suggests
> that he was wearing a heavy jacket, that he fled from the officers when challenged
> and that he vaulted over the ticket barrier into Stockwell London Underground
> Station. None of this is true. Similarly, misleading stories surrounded the killings
> of Kevin Gately, Blair Peach, Richard O'Brien, Shiji Lapite, Roger Sylvester,
> Harry Stanley, Mikey Powell and others killed by the police.

Monbiot continued saying that the problem appears systemic and widespread: 'We can't trust the police to tell the truth. The issue is not confined
to killings. Here's a story that has received less attention, but involves a chain
of alleged falsehoods that almost deprived an innocent man of his liberty':

> In xxx (date), [Jason], who lives in xxx [location], discovered a long series of
> messages exchanged by his 13-year-old daughter with someone who appeared as
> if he might be grooming her. The messages were sexually explicit. At one point
> the person proposed staging a kidnap and whisking her away. [Jason] went to
> the police. He presented them with an 86-page dossier.

When he wasn't satisfied with the action being taken, he phoned xxx (location) police station five times to try to speak to a senior officer to complain,
and to find out why, in his view, the investigation seemed to have stalled.
Then a series of remarkable things happened.

> Two plainclothes officers arrived at [Jason's] house at seven in the morning, when
> he was feeding his baby, to arrest him. Among other charges, the police claimed
> that he had been harassing the commander's secretary.

---

1. 12th April 2011, See http://www.theguardian.com/commentisfree/2011/apr/12/
police-truth-blair-peach-tomlinson

The police later dropped the enquiry into alleged grooming on the basis that there was no evidence to prove the case, but perversely took Jason to court armed with a signed witness statement written by the civilian recipient of his telephoned enquiries. However, inexplicably, the police had not passed the inconvenient fact to the CPS that Jason had, fortuitously for him, recorded the calls. The recordings, coupled with the civilian employee telling the she wasn't clear about what had been said, brought about Jason's acquittal. They did however bring about Jason's first of several private prosecutions. This one alleged the commander's secretary was trying to pervert the course of justice.

In *Chapter 19* we explore how the CPS handles the vast majority of its prosecutions. Where a police employee is concerned, also recounted in that chapter, the IPCC is often instrumental in initiating the CPS involvement but for various reasons the CPS does not have a good record of prosecuting police employees. In view of the number of, we'll call them 'irregularities', surrounding the case, Jason initiated a 'managed' IPCC investigation, an achievement in itself. However the IPCC cleared all police officers of wrongdoing and consequently did not present the file to the CPS. Consequently Jason presented his case to be allowed a private prosecution before magistrates.

As you read accounts of several other contributors' experiences, you will note how some form of diversion or intimidation seems to occur at some point whenever a civilian challenges the police. In this case a member of Jason's family was handed a threatening letter. The police have consistently refused to investigate this event.

Not to be intimidated, Jason successfully fought against a CPS application for discontinuance of his private prosecution and the court set a plea hearing for the following month. However the CPS then sought to stop the prosecution by offering no evidence but the judge stayed the case and opened the way for Jason to challenge the CPS attempt to stop the case, via a judicial review in the High Court. However, the CPS did achieve a two-year delay but in due course accepted that the prosecution should proceed because it met evidential and public interest tests. Nevertheless, they refused to run the prosecution themselves so Jason took up the challenge personally and got a High Court consent order signed.

While legal wrangling continued regarding whether the commander's secretary should be prosecuted and if so by whom, Jason found himself with another battle on his hands. The *Daily Telegraph* summarised it well when Martin Evans on 15th Aug 2012 reported that:[2]

> [X]xx [name and rank deleted for security] and xxx [name and rank deleted for security] were summonsed to appear before xxx [location deleted for security] magistrates' court to face a string of allegations related to an arrest they made on a man suspected of harassing a colleague in September 2xxx [date deleted for security].

They explained how former aircraft engineer Jason, aged 40 claimed the officers turned up at his house at 6.30 am, smashed down his door with a battering ram in front of his terrified family, before handcuffing him and dragging him to the police station. The full background to the case includes how, frustrated at what he considered was a lack of progress in the investigation, Jason made a number of phone calls to his local police station and was subsequently accused of harassing a civilian police worker and how when he refused to let the officers into his home, they broke down his door and forcibly took him into custody. After being cleared of all charges he applied for permission to bring a private prosecution against the arresting officers:

> The summons issued by [a district judge] stated that the two officers were accused of trespass and an attempt to inflict grievous bodily harm on the home owner … [It] said: 'You were on the property as a trespasser and you threatened to smash down a glass-panelled door which the homeowner was holding closed. … You threatened and used a battering ram to support your threat of violence. The occupants were caused fear for their personal safety. You wilfully failed to perform your duty to such a degree that it amounted to an abuse of the public trust which had been placed in you.

It also alleged that the officers carried Jason away without lawful authority and effected an unlawful entry to his private home using unlawful violence 'to carry out this kidnap.'

---

2.   See http://www.telegraph.co.uk/news/9477981/Police-officers-in-court-as-man-brings-private-prosecution.html

> It is extremely rare for a summons to be issued against police officers as part
> of a private prosecution…Criminal cases are usually brought by the CPS, but
> people can pursue their own actions under the Prosecution of Offences Act 1985.
> Both police officers, who remain on full duties, are due to appear before [the]
> Crown Court…[3]

It cannot be a coincidence that different people, when standing up to the police, find themselves involved in 'distractions'. Jason had already received a threatening letter but, later in his search for justice, he finds himself in a disagreement with a court security guard at a magistrates' court. The guard alleged Jason was shouting and threw a punch that resulted in Jason's removal from court. Jason points out that video and audio evidence proves the allegations were fabricated but nevertheless he was found guilty of assaulting a court security guard. Jason believes it is relevant to mention the security guard in question was also the individual who controlled the court and adjacent street CCTV recordings and that some footage was not disclosed to the court. When asked why all the CCTV recordings that were initially available weren't disclosed, the guard stated: 'I gave you what I thought you might need'. Subsequently the video evidence has been destroyed (which may be common practice). However, knowing now what you've learnt about Jason, readers will not be surprised to hear the case will be going to appeal and consequently is not concluded.

Then there's the alleged questionable conduct of a senior officer that also alarms Jason. As worrying as much of the above is, it is even more disturbing to hear that this officer has been responsible for conducting investigations into alleged police corruption in Jason's case for over three years. Obviously an officer, particularly a senior one, should be open-minded while investigating such allegations but someone from the force leaked an internal email to Jason where the investigating officer refers to Jason in derogatory terms: not terminology that an objective investigating officer would use and likely prejudicial for others reading his message. Jason complained to the force's PSD but his colleagues investigating the complaint cleared this officer of any wrongdoing. Jason appealed to the IPCC. The IPCC upheld his complaint and requested 'management action' in relation to the officer's unprofessional

---

3.   Despite a search I have been unable to trace the Crown Court proceedings or their outcome.

conduct. Bearing in mind the IPCC is quite powerless as we see in several other examples elsewhere in this book, the force is unlikely to do more than offer 'words of advice' or some similar innocuous punishment. But the IPCC decision regarding the officer's conduct leaves the objectivity, direction and thoroughness of three years of police investigation into alleged internal corruption outstanding—so what odds on justice?

An update on the commander's secretary was provided by Tom Harper in *The Independent* on 18th October 2013[4] where he noted that: the police were '… facing fresh embarrassment after a citizen won the right to launch what was thought to be an unprecedented private prosecution of a police employee for perverting the course of justice, i.e. to bring criminal charges against a civilian worker alleged to have made false claims in a witness statement, raising fresh questions about police conduct—days after Plebgate' (*Chapter 9*). As further described by Harper:

> Ms xxx, who is the secretary to the xxx borough commander made a police statement alleging that Mr xxx called her ten times over two days and made her feel 'upset' and 'harassed'. The father-of-three then decided to bring a private prosecution against her, alleging that the witness statement was false … The bizarre case erupted in 2xxx when [Jason] , who lives in xxx, passed the [police] an 86-page dossier of evidence that he claimed showed a relative had been the victim of a crime. Frustrated by a lack of progress, he says he phoned xxx police station five times to try to speak to a senior officer and establish the status of the investigation.

During the calls, Jason had spoken to Ms xxx. Three days later, officers arrested him at home on suspicion of harassing their colleague, relying on the allegedly false witness statement, After he was cleared he reported the matter to the IPCC. However, Deborah Glass, deputy chair of the IPCC, decided that a 'proportionate and appropriate outcome would be a reminder to *police* officers to keep 'accurate and detailed notes.' Jason launched a private prosecution of Ms xxx, and the CPS took over the case in November 2xxx. The CPS later tried to drop the case, leading Jason to launch a judicial review.

---

4. http://www.independent.co.uk/news/uk/crime/private-citizen-wins-right-to-prosecute-met-police-worker-8890313.html

CPS lawyers *subsequently* conceded there *was* 'enough material to provide for a realistic prospect of conviction' and that it *was* in the public interest for the prosecution to proceed. However, the CPS stated that '

> In this case we do not consider there is a particular need for the CPS to take over the prosecution.

[Jason] was quoted in *The Independent* as saying,

> This has been a long and stressful battle. The failure of public institutions like the IPCC and the CPS forced me to take this unusual route. The proper place for this matter to be adjudicated is before a jury, not in a back office.

Consequentially and hardly surprisingly following the above catalogue of revelations, Jason's MP called for the Home Secretary to conduct a public inquiry stating that he had '… rarely come across a case where so many public bodies tasked with the delivery of justice [had] failed an individual in this way'.

Comment

The initial dispute was resolved when a court found Jason not guilty but, although extended now over a number of years, it is disappointing not to be able to record the conclusions to what has multiplied into several consequential but unresolved disputes between Jason and the authorities.

CHAPTER 9

The Fallout from 'Plebgate'

On, or at least shortly after 19th September 2012 a new colloquialism entered the British vocabulary — 'Plebgate'. The word and the subsequent fallout, still not fully resolved, were initiated by a 45-seconds exchange at Downing Street's security gates. The police on duty alleged that Cabinet Minister and Government chief whip Andrew Mitchell MP called them 'F… ing plebs' when asked to re-route himself and his bicycle through an alternative gate. 'Pleb' is defined in the *Oxford English Dictionary* as an informal derogatory noun meaning 'an ordinary person, especially one from the lower social classes'. Mr Mitchell denied using this word but admitted swearing at the police and for not treating the police with appropriate respect. He apologised for both a short time later but a month after that resigned his Cabinet post.

As will be explained, Sir David Normington and the Royal Society for the Encouragement of Arts, Manufactures and Commerce (RSA) have done a first-class job of throwing light on some dark shadows. Parliament and the Home Affairs Select Committee (HAC) have explored the then current issues in commendable detail. However, few emerge from the Plebgate affair with their credibility intact. Many of the events were a breach of trust by the institutions involved and damaged public confidence in them, while some of the individuals involved had their lives changed, possibly irredeemably:

- the Met took over 12 months and spent huge sums of money concluding their investigations under 'Operation Alice';
- some police officers were found corrupt and disciplined and one, in a criminal court, was jailed;
- other officers used the affair to misrepresent their federation and the content of a meeting with Mitchell;
- the Police Federation[1] itself was found to have inappropriately attacked politicians and the chief inspector of constabulary and to

---

1. The Police Federation of England and Wales is a staff association for all police constables, sergeants and inspectors. See www.polfed.org

have managed its affairs such that sweeping changes were essential. Senior managers invited an independent review of the federation, but on receiving an RSA report and under pressure from within, they resigned in April 2014;

- Mitchell initially addressed the police without appropriate respect and in a civil court was finally said by the judge not to have told the truth about saying 'pleb' or some such word;
- the IPCC was called upon to carry out a second investigation following their first report's dubious conclusion changes;
- the Association of Chief Police Officers (ACPO) seemed to be offering little leadership or guidance to its chief constables and many criticisms in the Normington report can also be levelled at it. House of Commons members suggested ACPO is badly constituted and pointed to West Midlands federation officials' cases, where various chief constables failed to uphold justice, instead requiring conclusions in a related IPCC report be revised; and
- even the three PCCs, who may not have been in post when the incident actually took place, but in August 2013 when the adjusted IPCC report was issued, weakly and unimpressively rushed to the defence of local senior officers.

The following is a summary of the multi-layered events that followed the original confrontation between Mitchell and officers. Someone claiming to be a member of the public wrote their version of the 45-seconds incident which was published in the *Sun*. That person turned out to be a police officer. On 24th September a second newspaper published a story based on leaked details of the police incident log, which Mr Mitchell asked the IPCC to investigate since it appeared that a Met officer did this. The Met commenced an investigation and, a couple of months later, Downing Street's CCTV recording was appraised and appeared to contradict several officers' statements and the police log. In fact the recording showed no members of the public were close enough to have heard the exchanges. However, under pressure from the media, on 19th October Andrew Mitchell resigned his Cabinet post.

Twelve months later further discord erupted when, with no police report or conclusions yet available and themselves now under pressure, the Met said their conclusions would 'take as long as it takes'. The IPCC was supervising the investigation and felt it should 'take as long as is necessary.' At this point Lord Macdonald QC (Director of Public Prosecutions, 2003–2008) told the BBC that the public and Mr Mitchell both 'deserved closure' and that 'the police have now spent 12 months investigating an incident that lasted 45 seconds'. He stressed that

> …this is a Cabinet minister forced to resign. If it turns out to be the case that the police are completely exonerated—fine, excellent, let's have that result. If it turns out that evidence against Mr Mitchell was fabricated, that is an exceptionally serious situation which we need to grapple with, sooner rather than later.

Lord Macdonald was speaking after the media reported three members of the public and five police officers as arrested but before any charge(s) or disciplinary action had been decided upon. It was also reported that this protracted investigation had cost £237,000 at 30th September 2013.[2]

Meanwhile, a second police integrity allegation was arising after three officers from the Police Federation requested a meeting with Mr Mitchell in an effort 'to clear the air' over what was said during the Downing Street encounter. The meeting took place at Mr Mitchell's constituency offices in Sutton Coldfield in October 2012. Fortunately, as it turned out, Mr Mitchell recorded the meeting because, subsequently, the HAC established the federation's prime reason for requesting the meeting was about cuts to police expenditure. The trio were attending as federation representatives opposing these cuts. One officer agreed their whole campaign at the time was about the cuts and that following the meeting the trio gave misleading statements to the press primed by their media agent. So rather than clearing, or even simplifying, the issues this meeting complicated things and took the federation officers' views into the public domain.

The situation deteriorated when, in August 2013, the IPCC issued a 'final' report focused upon their investigations and conclusions of the Sutton Coldfield meeting and in particular what the federation officers had subsequently told the press. As presented, the IPCC report contained a single set

---

2. See http://www.independent.co.uk/news/uk/crime/cost-of-andrew-mitchell-plebgate-investigation-reaches-237000-8849788.html

of conclusions to the effect that the three officers had no case of misconduct to answer in spite of the senior IPCC investigator saying, in his evidence to the Home Affairs Select Committee, that this did not reflect his opinion. His opinion was (and remained) that a case for misconduct had been made out but he understood his report was required to record the decision of the senior officers in each of the three police forces involved. Consequently his draft report had been altered to reflect their decision but Chief Inspector Reakes-Williams reiterated to the Home Affairs Committee that he still considered the three federation officers had a case to answer in respect of misconduct and the discredit they brought upon the police service.

The deputy chair of IPCC later gave evidence to the HAC focusing on the federation officers' actions, their statement to the press and the IPCC report. She told it that, bearing in mind that the Met's investigation was essentially into the initial allegations of conspiracy stemming from the Downing Street incident, the IPCC could not anticipate the extent of their involvement in this later, federation officers, development. She told MPs that when she saw the draft report it inappropriately had two conclusions.

Furthermore she was unhappy with the misconduct conclusion because it was really a case for gross misconduct. She thought the draft report demonstrated that the senior IPCC officer had a different view to the junior officer's opinion. The questions the senior officer posed were, she thought, about right but she did not completely agree with his analysis of the evidence. Deborah Glass went on to report that she had met with the investigating officer and his deputy on 31 July 2013 to discuss the report and the need for it to have one set of conclusions, but she explained that she was subsequently absolutely astonished when the 'final' report concluded there was no case to answer.

The three federation officers then gave evidence to the HAC. The record of both the questions and evidence presented by the witnesses are contained in the committee's report, 'Leadership and Standards in the Police: Follow-up' (3rd November 2013).[3] In summary, the HAC criticised evidence given by the officers because the committee found it to be misleading, possibly deliberately so, and lacking credibility. In the view of the committee, the answers they gave were contradictory, inconsistent and provided little or no insight

---

3.   See http://www.publications.parliament.uk/pa/cm201314/cmselect/cmhaff/uc756-i/uc75601.htm

into their actions. The HAC decided to refer two of the three officers to the IPCC and to recall them both on 5th November 2013 to apologise for misleading the committee. They also reserved the right to recall the third officer should they find that he too had misled the committee.

The apologies provided by the three respective chief constables were welcomed by the committee, although the committee criticised decisions made by two of their number not to reassess whether their officers should face a misconduct panel and one chief constable for seeking to correct some earlier evidence. A West Midlands officer was criticised for attempting to access the IPCC's misconduct investigation report prematurely and the committee regretted absence of leadership by all three chief constables.

The committee believed that ideally the IPCC should have carried out an independent inquiry in this case but was short of resources and called for further resources to be allocated to it in order that cases that had an impact on public confidence could be investigated quickly and thoroughly. Nevertheless the committee emphasised that the lack of an IPCC enquiry in no way excused the conduct of the three federation officers or the failure of the three police forces to undertake a proper investigation. The committee chair thought the matter hugely damaging to the public's perception of the police officers involved, the Police Federation and the force itself. He pointed out that the committee had referred the officers to the IPCC and welcomed their announcement to make a fully independent decision on this investigation. The chair said, 'It is vital that the public see that where police officers make mistakes, they will be held to account. The narrative of what we have seen could rival any great work of fiction. At every point and at every level, instead of being transparent, we have uncovered a process that obstructs the truth. If this can happen to a Cabinet Minister, what hope is there for anyone else?'

Two of the three federation officers appeared before the HAC on 5th November 2013. One apologised for unintentionally misleading the committee in his earlier evidence and reported 13 complaints had been lodged against him during his service with the police force but none of them had been upheld. The IPCC were to investigate largely because federation police officers were thought to have misled and obstructed MPs and because the conclusions in the IPCC initial report were altered by their respective chief constables and consequently did not reflect what the IPCC investigating officer believed.

Backtracking slightly, on 6th October 2014 the High Court had ruled that the three chief constables had not prepared a final report on the disciplinary issues posed by the three federation officers. Consequently on 3rd November 2014, after re-assessing the cases, the IPCC confirmed it was to investigate those officers. That investigation remains outstanding at the time of writing but nevertheless one cannot but wonder what system of checks-and-balances allows the only police watchdog currently available to be overruled by chief constables while simultaneously failing to 'flag-up' that the report had been altered and to insist, as the *independent* policing authority, that the report be revised to clearly express the IPCC's views. This sequence of events confirms both the lack of true independence of the body that polices the police and that the police forces' senior management are incapable of dealing with and reviewing their own errors. It also poses the question of where were the respective PCCs? And one wonders who pays for the consequently necessary second IPCC investigation ... the chief constables from their salaries, the federation from its (seemingly huge) financial reserves or the poor old taxpayer?

Reverting to the Met's investigation dubbed 'Operation Alice' into the original Plebgate row in Downing Street, we learn from the Met's investigation team that 'On 19 December 2013 officers from the Diplomatic Protection Group (SO6) arrested three police constables from the DPG on suspicion of being involved in the possession and distribution of obscene images via mobile phones'.

On 1st January 2014 the RSA published its final report on their independent review of the Police Federation. The RSA declares itself to be an enlightenment organization committed to finding innovative and practical solutions to today's social challenges and commendably the Police Federation had asked the RSA to carry out a review of their organization. Work started in May 2013 under the chairmanship of Sir David Normington. The work was concluded in September 2013 with an interim report published in October 2013 and a final report on 1st January 2014.[4]

---

4.   https://www.thersa.org/discover/publications-and-articles/reports/
     police-federation-final-report/

Amongst the quite critical findings in the report are:

> We have also been given evidence of bad behaviour within [the federation], including poor treatment of staff at HQ and the targeting of representatives in social media, at conferences and elsewhere simply because they hold a different point of view. If the federation wants to be respected and listened to in the future, this has to stop.

The report also states:

> The politics of personal attack and shouting has proved to be a wrong-headed response and more of the same would have resulted in an even less optimal outcome.

It was to have a significant impact generating a revealing Parliamentary debate, a Home Affairs Committee meeting and, I suspect, much turbulence within the federation and its membership. However, chronologically, on 10th January 2014 PC Keith Wallis pleaded guilty in court to misconduct in respect of lies about MP Andrew Mitchell and emailing his nephew to arrange support for his false claim. On 6th February 2014 this Met officer was jailed for 12 months. In the following months, further Met officers were disciplined as a result of Operation Alice and three dismissed for gross misconduct.

On 13th February 2014 Mr David Davis (MP for Haltemprice and Howden) (Conservative) addressed the House of Commons and moved

> That this House notes the Independent Review of the Police Federation conducted by Sir David Normington and calls upon the Government to take action to implement the report's recommendations and to reform the Police Federation.[5]

The debate explored many matters of universal concern. The following selection is intended to stimulate more thorough exploration:

---

5. Contains public sector information licensed under the Open Government Licence v3.0. For the debate see http://www.publications.parliament.uk/pa/cm201314/cmhansrd/cm140213/debtext/140213-0002.htm#14021362000001

- In 1918–19 strikes caused a similar low perception of the police following which a pay increase was implemented but the police forbidden both membership of a trade union and the right to strike. The Government effectively established the Police Federation in place of a union. For many years the federation was a constructive force behind British policing, raising the police reputation to the position it ought to hold. Regrettably, the federation today is a bloated and sclerotic body, and has acquired the worst characteristics of the worst trade unions that we thought we had seen the end of in the 1970s.
- ACPO officers have not led from the top and many of the criticisms in the excellent report could also be made of ACPO but the debate needed to focus on the federation although ACPO is badly constituted. It should have led firmly and, in the West Midlands cases, various chief constables were perhaps not as strong in upholding justice as they should have been.
- The House made an effort not to become too focused on the Andrew Mitchell case believing that the Normington report records that the Mitchell case is just one illustration of the flagrant and endemic bullying and harassment that often goes on among the federation's own members.
- Fiona McElroy, a former principal private secretary brought in to help the federation achieve reforms, was fired; her deputy also left the federation in outrage at her treatment.
- The federation had been bringing defamation cases against people who disagreed with the police's version of events. There is no downside for a police officer when they pursue a libel action backed by the enormous resources of the federation. Action against the press, who must hold the police to account, is utterly against the interests of a fair and free society while action taken against members of the public insulates the police from criticism and from being held to account for what they do. Such actions should not take place. There are two recent examples of the federation's appetite for litigation: one [officer] sued a burglary victim

after he tripped on a kerb outside his garage; while another sued a burglary victim after falling over a drain on his property.

- The purchase of large quantities of food and alcohol on (federation credit) cards is apparently not uncommon. Indeed the accounts showed a provision of £2 million in a tax dispute with Her Majesty's Revenue and Customs to meet any liability, at a tax rate of 40 per cent, suggesting £5 million in claims have been made on perks, perhaps unjustifiably claimed as a proper expenses.
- If correct, some newspapers said that federation officials treated officers' memorial services 'like a drunken jolly, getting drunk on federation credit cards. Their drunken excess upsets families every year'. Similar allegations had been heard about the behaviour of federation officials at conferences, at which bar bills of hundreds of pounds were again being charged to federation credit cards.

Early in April 2014, as though their list of troubles were not sufficient, the federation was faced with an additional problem when its chief executive left following reports of internal wrangling, criticisms about its part in Plebgate and subsequent events. Also, in April 2014 lawyers acting on behalf of PC Toby Rowland, the officer actually on duty at Downing Street's security gates on 19 September 2012, submitted a claim for up to £200,000 in damages from Andrew Mitchell for the distress, humiliation and upset PC Rowland had suffered. At about the same time Andrew Mitchell placed a libel action against the *Sun* newspaper and Toby Rowland's claim for damages.

On 16th May 2014 the HAC published its findings after discussing the reform of the federation. It used the headline 'Era of bullying and secret accounts must end'.[6] The Rt. Hon Keith Vaz MP, chairman of the HAC said:

> We were shocked by the scale of bullying that we found at the federation's headquarters. It rivals any popular soap opera. It is disgraceful that any chairman should have been hounded out for championing the long-overdue reforms set out in the Normington report. Only a new national chair, elected directly by the federation's rank-and-file members, will have the authority to implement these changes in full.

---

6. For the full minute see http://www.parliament.uk/business/committees/committees-a-z/commons-select/home-affairs-committee/news/140516-pol-fed-rpt-pubn/

He went on to say that the federation needs complete financial transparency to remove all suspicion about so-called 'No. 2 accounts'. Federation funds should serve the members and the public directly, not the organization itself leading to a suggestion that members should receive a rebate on their subscriptions which have accumulated into 'unnecessary' reserves of around £70 million. 'Our police service is the best in the world but its reputation has been extensively damaged by the federation suffering a sustained period of self-inflicted harm. I hope that, with these reforms, it can move forwards to become, once again, the powerful and respected voice that our police officers, and the country, expect and deserve. The following points further summarise the HAC's findings:

- bullying is endemic in the higher echelons of the federation;
- both the late Paul McKeever and the outgoing chair, Steve Williams, have been subject to systematic campaigns of abuse which have no place in a professional organization;
- the federation has a clear duty to speak up for its members and to engage with national policy changes which affect the police but, as McKeever had noted, some of its political campaigns have been too personalised;
- hiring radio 'shock jock' Jon Gaunt was a serious error of judgement which damaged, not enhanced, the federation's reputation;
- the dysfunctional relationships at federation headquarters have seriously undermined the organization's ability to speak with a powerful voice on behalf of its members;
- the HAC called for the immediate election of a new national chair, by all the membership;
- the federation's £70 million reserves were disproportionate to its operating costs and the excess should be returned to members immediately as a rebate on subscriptions;
- at a local level, while some smaller branches struggle financially, others have accumulated reserves which add up to around £35 million, some of it in obscure 'No. 2' accounts;
- a new funding formula, with subscriptions going straight to the centre and being distributed to branches, would remedy this; and

- the HAC called for full transparency of all the federation's accounts, at both national and local level.

Shortly afterwards, on 21st May 2014, Home Secretary Theresa May addressed the federation at its annual conference in Bournemouth and confirmed much of the HAC's views.[7] Her main points are as follows (paraphrased):

- This is a time of great difficulty for policing with the Leveson Inquiry, the appalling conclusions of the Hillsborough independent panel, Ian Tomlinson's death, the sacking of PC Harwood, an inquiry by an independent panel into the murder of Daniel Morgan, the first sacking of a chief constable for gross misconduct in modern times, the investigation of more than ten senior officers for acts of alleged misconduct and corruption, allegations of rigged recorded crime statistics, the sacking of three officers after Plebgate, worrying reports by the inspectorate about stop-and-search and domestic violence, the Herne Review into the Met's Special Demonstration Squad, the Ellison Review into allegations of corruption during the Stephen Lawrence investigation and further allegations the police sought to smear Stephen's family and another judge-led public inquiry into policing.
- Then there is the role of the federation itself, which as Sir David Normington said, needs changing from 'top to bottom'. We've seen accusations of bullying, lack of transparency, questionable tactics, infighting, huge reserves worth millions of pounds, and a resounding call for change from members—with 91 per cent saying things cannot go on as they are.
- The Normington review found a lack of transparency and openness in the affairs and finances of the federation. It found only limited accountability. It concluded the federation was unable to promote good behaviour and professional standards. Police officers had lost confidence in it and the federation had lost its

7. See https://www.gov.uk/government/speeches/home-secretarys-police-federation-2014-speech which contains public sector information licensed under the Open Government Licence v3.0.

ability to influence and represent members. As the report said, 'We have encountered some [fed leaders] who are more interested in fighting internal battles and protecting their own positions.'

- It is vital that the federation implements every one of the 36 Normington recommendations. But since that review was concluded, that is not what happened. Federation staff had been forced out and amidst allegations of bullying and victimisation. Instead of embracing the reform, some members have reverted to the worst kinds of behaviour exposed by Sir David Normington.

- The candidates who put themselves forward to replace Steve Williams have to choose the status quo or change to make sure the federation becomes once more the authentic voice of policing.

- If the federation does not make significant progress towards implementation of the Normington reforms the government will not let things remain as they are.

- The federation was created by Act of Parliament and it can be reformed by Act of Parliament. 'If you do not change of your own accord, we will impose change on you.'

- It is not acceptable that the federation is sitting on vast reserves worth tens of millions of pounds. 'I can announce today that federation funding will be stopped altogether from August. Instead, the money will go into a new fund to accelerate the introduction of Police First—a new scheme designed to attract the brightest young university graduates into the police.

- 'I want federation representatives to earn the right to represent their members. So in common with changes made elsewhere in the public sector, I plan to change the law so that officers will have to opt in to join the federation. This will mean that officers no longer become members by default. I also plan to change the law so that officers who have chosen to become members also have to opt in to pay full subscription fees.'

- 'I want to make the federation more accountable. That means, today and on an annual basis thereafter, the Home Office will use its existing legal powers to call in the federation's central accounts and will bring forward proposals to make the Police Federation subject to the Freedom of Information Act.

On 27th November 2014 Mr Justice Mitting rejected Andrew Mitchell's libel case against the *Sun* newspaper saying: 'I am satisfied at least on the balance of probabilities that Mr Mitchell did speak the words alleged or something so close to them as to amount to the same including the politically toxic word 'pleb'.' The judge added that Mitchell's had exhibited 'childish' behaviour and that his account was contradictory to the CCTV footage. Later PC Toby Rowland said, 'I am delighted to hear my innocence, my reputation and my integrity as a police officer has been recognised. I hope now that a line can be drawn and everyone can be left in peace.'

Comment

It is encouraging to note that the Home Secretary appreciates the catalogue of problems posed by the police of late. Consequently, this author is a little more optimistic that remedial policies may be forthcoming, but would be more comforted if firm remedial proposals were available.

The Police Federation revelations were an unanticipated consequence of the short confrontation at the gates of Downing Street. The self-implementation of the recommendations will be worthy of note if achieved and helpful to both the public and members. However it will not be self-achieved if the federation allow, or force, staff committed to change to leave. Consequently the extent, methodology, implementation and timescale as well as how much external pressure will be required remain very much up in the air.

The IPCC is the independent body that polices the police. However, as recounted here and elsewhere in this book, it has largely lost the trust of those members of the public who have experienced its work. Consequently, in the light of the excellent work of the RSA at the Police Federation, perhaps as an initial step towards improving the independence, performance and trust in the IPCC, the Home Secretary might like to invite a similar investigation by the RSA into the IPCC.

Finally, where were the relevant PCCs responsible for the above police forces when needed and why did they not stand up to be counted?

CHAPTER 10

Harassment in Sussex

As an MP you cannot choose the make-up of the people you represent, but will probably feel fairly confident about the fairness and impartiality of the police force that serves you and your constituents. However, that assumption, at least so far as this chapter is concerned, would be misplaced because you might find the forces or law and order seem to be stacked against you (as did Andrew Mitchell in the previous chapter). I cannot ask Tim Loughton, MP for East Worthing and Shoreham, for his contribution because his case is still ongoing. However, the background and, certainly to my mind, bias of the local police force requires that his story be summarised to acquaint readers who are seeking to learn about police integrity and British justice with it.

As we have seen from an earlier contribution, an unsolicited communication that the recipient is unhappy with can be deemed to be harassment and warrant punishment. An extraordinary attitude in these days of Sussex's unresolved serious cases including: the murders of Katrina Taylor, Karen Hadaway, Nicola Fellows, Billy-Jo Jenkins and Valerie Graves; alleged conduct of officers in relation to the Jimmy Savile scandal; a Chichester kidnapping; a Hove teenage gang robbery; and a bank robbery. This is to list just some issues that you would think were the focus of a financially hard-pressed police force.

Junk mail is always unsolicited, harassing and never make me anything but unhappy, but one just lives stoically with these trials and tribulations. Just as the particular MP in question and his staff soldiered-on when they received a regular stream of abrasive communications from a constituent over a number of years. Tim Loughton's mistake was not to lodge a harassment complaint with the police because the complaints about local services generally (but ironically including the police) were often offensively worded, odious to Mr Loughton and upset his staff.

More detail on the background to the first part of this story is best served by reproducing Tim Loughton's own account as recorded in *Hansard* for 13th March 2013 (see later). However, I must first explain that, extraordinarily and perversely after a stream of abuse from this constituent for a number of years, the police interviewed Tim Loughton in August 2012 under caution after he had sent his constituent a single email. The police then spent six months (and large sums of money*) investigating him. They dropped their investigation in February 2013. The full story can be gleaned from his speech in the House of Commons from which I have paraphrased extracts:[1]

> Tim Loughton (East Worthing and Shoreham) (Con): I am very grateful, par-
> ticularly to you personally, Mr Speaker, for this opportunity to raise a matter in
> the House that relates to a criminal investigation that has been conducted against
> me by Sussex police over the past six and a half months before being dropped,
> but which has implications for all hon. Members and how we communicate with
> our constituents.
>
> I am sure that I speak for all hon. Members when I say that we all appreciate our
> constituents—it is one of the reasons we do our job—but I doubt that there
> are many hon. Members without a tiny minority of constituents who either by
> design or default try to make our lives hell. A very few think they have a divine
> right to be gratuitously rude to MPs or other figures in the public eye, and some
> think they can be offensive because of their own political allegiances—although
> I have never had that problem with my own opposition locally, with whom I
> have always had a constructive relationship—and others have personal issues
> that make them obsessive.
>
> I am referred to as 'an arrogant, lying, racist arsehead'—one of the more moderate
> terms of endearment that [this constituent] uses—and am likened to the perpe-
> trators of the holocaust. The cabinet of Y council in my constituency is referred to
> as 'the Führer council'; a council official is an 'ugly pig-faced fascist'; a constituent
> is condemned as 'a paedophile'; and another who is now suffering mental health
> problems as a result is taunted with the phrase, 'Let's hope his **** shrivels up and
> drops off whilst he is suffering a horrible death at the hands of a nasty disease.'

1. This story contains Parliamentary information licensed under the Open Parliament Licence
    vi.0, but I have taken the liberty of substituting crosses for some words that some readers
    may find offensive. For the unabridged version or to see the reply by the deputy leader of the
    House of Commons see http://www.publications.parliament.uk/pa/cm201213/cmhansrd/
    cm130313/debtext/130313-0004.htm#13031374000001

Let me give a more graphic idea of what I am talking about. [this constituent] has recently posted a photo-shopped image of me taken when, as a Minister last year, I was visiting a school in east London in support of the City Year charity, except that now I have Nazi insignia on my jacket and I am toting a smoking gun in a playground full of screaming, fleeing children ... Despite complaints to Sussex police, these remain on the web.

Last year, [this constituent] engaged in almost constant complaints against the local ... district council, in respect of which he was a tenant of a council house and had an allotment. The most prolific issue was on account of his losing his allotment because of complaints about his abusive behaviour against other allotment holders and his using human excrement on his compost heap. After a court case, which he lost, the council placed [him] on their 'customer of concern' list ... but [he] complained the council should deign to refer to him as unkempt.

After failing to get satisfaction from the council and after one of his regular abusive visits to one of my street surgeries, he wrote to me. I investigated and sent an e-mail back to my constituent, saying that given that the dictionary definition of 'unkempt' is 'untrimmed, dishevelled and rough', the council's description — not mine — struck me as 'eminently accurate'... Within hours of receiving my e-mail, and before phone calls to my Westminster office and a foul-mouthed tirade at my researcher, [the constituent] contacted the police claiming that I was guilty of an offence under the Malicious Communications Act 1988. A few days later, I was contacted by a detective inspector from the police requesting a meeting to discuss a 'sensitive issue'. I responded immediately, saying that I was happy to help in whatever way I could, and 48 hours later a discussion of a 'sensitive issue' became a 90-minute recorded interview under caution ...

I was presented with a disclosure document that had given rise to the interview, in which xxxxx had claimed that the single email that I had sent him qualified as a malicious communication because [he] feels that the references made against him within the email are of a racist nature and that the email contains insults of a grossly offensive nature.'

I was happy to help the police with their inquiries. It is absolutely right that all MPs should be treated no differently from any of their constituents, notwithstanding the occupational hazard facing us and others in public life that we are more high-profile targets for vexatious complaints. I have no problem with the fact that the rather embarrassed custody sergeant had to go through the formalities before the interview, asking whether I could read or write or had mental health problems; the answers were yes and no in that order...

At that point, anyone with any common sense could have seen that there was no basis to the case that had been advanced by a serial complainer, well versed in making malicious and vexatious complaints. The case could have been terminated at that stage. It would have satisfied the procedures that sprang from the Macpherson report, under which alleged race incidents should be taken seriously and should be subject to at least an initial investigation. However, there was no remotely racial side to this case... Equally insidious, though, are the forces of political correctness that seem to have been brought to bear in this instance, which can do so much damage to good race relations and social harmony and which too often triumph over common sense. In this case a full-blown investigation ensued, lasting six and a half months. I had contact with at least six separate officers who were involved, and a file was then sent to the Crown Prosecution Service in December. All my Westminster office staff were interviewed, as well as a former secretary... We trawled the archives for all copies of previous correspondence... [whilst the constituent] continued to prejudice the case or be seen trying to influence the outcome.

When I put in my own complaint to Sussex police about some of these blogs being grossly offensive, my complaint was not taken up, and instead X was warned to take down some of his posts and went quiet for a while, but only a short while. When I pointed out that I had made a formal complaint of my own and that the blog could provide material evidence, it transpired that the police had failed to take copies of the blog entries before they disappeared. They had lost their own police evidence and subsequently had to come to ask me if I had taken a copy, which, fortunately, I had.

Eventually the Crown Prosecution Service decided there was no case to answer and informed the police. A further two weeks later, on 26 February, when the investigating chief inspector returned from his holiday, my secretary—not me—was eventually told I was in the clear. That came as a huge relief, after this whole case had been hanging over me and my family since August of last year …

How did this happen, and could it happen again, if not to me, then to any other hon. Member? …I gave the chief constable a list of questions in advance, to try to get to the bottom of exactly how I had been subjected to such an intensive, and intensively wasteful, use of police resources. Yet without going into detail about that confidential meeting, I was treated by the chief constable not only as if I was the subject of ongoing criminal investigations, but almost as if I had actually been charged and found guilty. It was as if 'Plebgate' runs well beyond the confines of Whitehall. I was given a prepared list of one-sentence answers, effectively saying the investigation was dealt with in an exemplary way. The chief constable is apparently happy that everything was handled properly, so clearly the same thing could happen again and again to me or anyone else.

What had the police done to determine that [my constituent] actually is of [ethnic or foreign] origin, and what specifically had caused offence to such a retiring violet? Who had authorised the investigation to carry on for this long? How many officers had been involved in the case, and how much had it cost? All these questions were met with a stone wall. To get any further, I would have to submit freedom of information requests to my own local constabulary. Well, that I have done, as well as submitting requests to the CPS and making a formal complaint about the way the investigation was carried forward, the incompetence with which it was handled by the police, and the failure of the chief constable of Sussex to exercise a modicum of common sense and instead support the system …

Risk aversion has replaced common-sense judgments as certain senior police do not want to do anything that might jeopardise their career with head office. The Association of Chief Police Officers 10-point decision-making model has been junked. An inquiry process that should be justified, accountable and proportionate has been ignored, and investigations have been stepped up to a higher authority and ultimately the CPS for fear of making a decision that might reflect badly.

If this can happen to an MP, it can happen to any of our constituents. It is no way to run a police service...

The bigger question for this House and for hon. Members—I am delighted to see so many of them here this evening—is how do we deal with the small minority of constituents where a robust reply is the most appropriate? Outside this Chamber, unprotected by parliamentary privilege, as my case starkly demonstrates, we now risk a feel on our collar from a police force pandering to political correctness and unquestioningly taking the word of someone intent on lodging a vexatious and malicious allegation...

What if you, Mr Speaker, were innocently to refer to someone as 'well kempt' whose religion demands that he should be fully bearded—would that be racist? Even more unlikely, what if you were to praise someone famous for being proudly gay and out only for the celebrity involved to be very much heterosexual—could you find yourself under criminal investigation for some form of inverted homophobia? Where will it all end, Mr Speaker? Are we to be issued with a manual of words and phrases that we can or cannot use? Perhaps we need a whole new section in *Erskine May*. Will this House and hon. Members in future be muted in speaking their minds, ironically at a time when the public and the media criticise politicians for not saying what they really mean more and for hiding behind obfuscation and spin? It is no longer good to be straight, Mr Speaker—oh dear, I may have done it again!

Following the debate in question, Tim Loughton sent an unmarked copy of *Hansard* to his constituent to inform him that he would no longer be acting as his MP as the constituent had made this position untenable. This was done under Parliamentary privilege as advised by the clerk of the House of Commons. However, and unbeknown to Loughton, the constituent reported the debate to the police as a 'hate crime' and complained that sending a copy of *Hansard* was 'harassment'. Extraordinarily, the first Loughton knew about these complaints was when the police contacted him to serve a police information notice (PIN) in late August 2013—because the *Hansard* communication was unsolicited and caused the recipient distress. Confirmation of the PIN was sent through the post on 4th September 2013.

However the police also, finally, awoke to the fact that the constituent had, to use Tim Loughton's words, been 'harassing, bullying, stalking, trolling and abusing' him and his staff over a protracted period and also issued the constituent with a PIN, presumably for harassment. Nevertheless throughout all of this the constituent continued his running commentary of abuse on his blog, twitter and email sites without any known intervention by the police.

In October 2013, Loughton raised the matter of his PIN in the House of Commons as it was of concern to all Members of the House and a potential obstacle to their work and communications with constituents nationwide. After the debate the matter was referred to the House of Commons Privileges Committee who met on 28th January 2014 to inquire into the background, Tim Loughton's PIN and the issues around sending a copy of *Hansard*. They invited the chief constable of Sussex and Mr Loughton, amongst other expert members and attendees, to give evidence.[2]

My summary of the more general key points is as follows:[3]

- Sussex police's own guidance (adopted from the Association of Chief Police Officers (ACPO)) on how PINs should be used and issued was not followed. For example, there are three defences where someone cannot be served a PIN. Not only were those defences not offered to Loughton, but he was never under the impression — or had knowledge — that he was being investigated for harassment. Sussex police decided that there was a case of alleged harassment that they wanted to investigate, but they did not tell him about it. Loughton stressed: 'They did not ask me to defend myself, and they decided, on their own knowledge, that they would issue a PIN without my being able to defend myself.'

- Referring again to the ACPO/Sussex guidelines, it was pointed out that, 'In general, the issuing of PINs will not be helpful when dealing with entrenched disputes'. As noted, Tim Loughton and his staff had been receiving correspondence for a number of years.

---

2. The minutes are available at http://www.parliament.uk/documents/commons-committees/Privileges-Committee/2014-01-28-Corrected-transcript-rev.pdf

3. The text contains Parliamentary information licensed under the Open Parliament Licence vi.o.

- Mr Merrett, retired assistant chief constable of Sussex Police, told the committee, 'A PIN seeks to advise people as to their conduct and behaviour so that they have information that someone else believes that their act or acts may be causing harassment or alarm. They are designed to act as a means of crime prevention, and to enable the police to support policing and to keep the peace. They are often an effective tool to bring to the attention of an individual that their behaviour has caused another person harassment, alarm and distress of some description.'
- Fiona O'Donnell asked ,'You said that the aim of the PIN was to try to de-escalate—to bring this situation to an end. Do you think the PIN has been successful in achieving that, or do you agree with what Mr Loughton said earlier: it has, in fact, exacerbated the situation?' The police denied any escalation, but they could hardly agree that they caused it under the circumstances.
- The police appeared to have no concept of the personal and consequentially family anguish, stress, alarm and harassment that their cavalier, indeed unlawful use of PINs caused law-abiding people generally. In Tim Loughton's and indeed any public servant's case be they an MP, councillor or planner, a PIN brings with it added ramifications as to how the police perform their job and communicate with the public.
- The police had allowed the constituent to continue his campaign of abuse after issuing him with a PIN thus showing both their misguided and ineffective policy, and in spite of all the rhetoric, their double standards.

On 6th March 2014, the Joint Committee on Parliamentary Privilege issued a follow-up report for the matter referred to the Committee on 9th October 2013.[4] The following is a précis:
- the central issue facing the committee was not that a PIN has been issued to an MP, nor that a member's communication with

---

4. See http://www.parliament.uk/business/committees/committees-a-z/commons-select/ privileges/news/first-report/ The text contains Parliamentary information licensed under the Open Parliament Licence vi.0.

a constituent had attracted a police warning, but that the action referred to in the PIN was sending a daily part of *Hansard.*

- The privilege of absolute freedom of speech in proceedings in Parliament is articulated in Article IX of the Bill of Rights, but this freedom does not extend to the publication of proceedings. That is governed by the Parliamentary Papers Act 1840 which provides that legal proceedings arising from the publication of a paper by order of either House of Parliament, or a copy, will be stayed on delivery of a certificate that such publication is by order.

- There is legal protection for the publication of excerpts or summaries of proceedings, when they are made without malice.

- The police claimed that the PIN was issued because of the action of sending *Hansard*, but the committee's analysis of the PIN, the complaint and police evidence led it to conclude the PIN was in fact motivated by his speech to the House.

As the Joint Committee on Parliamentary Privilege said: 'The fundamental purpose of affording absolute privilege to proceedings in Parliament is to protect those proceedings, so that the democratically-elected representatives of the people can engage in free and fearless debate on issues of public concern.' If people consider there could be adverse consequences from saying what they really thought, even in Parliamentary proceedings, they would be less likely to speak out — the so-called 'chilling effect'. The committee accepted the contempt was inadvertent. It noted that the protection of the 1840 Act meant the PIN was 'an empty threat'. It considered it would be appropriate for the PIN issued to Tim Loughton to be withdrawn (still a matter for the police).

> We are not qualified to judge whether it would be appropriate for the police to issue a further PIN in relation to the other behaviour referred to, although we note it would presumably be based on the actions of unknown persons and on letters which they themselves have said they do not suggest were sent by Mr Loughton. The [county police] should inform the committee of the decision that they make and the reason for it. We will not consider this matter closed until they do so.

As far as reference to Tim Loughton's sending *Hansard* in any future PIN is concerned, the committee saw no merit in a PIN which explicitly stated that the act complained of could not be the subject of any prosecution, and the police actions in relation to the sending of *Hansard* were so clearly related to the content of the document that no rider could avoid the repetition of their previously inadvertent contempt.

During the inquiry it became apparent that Loughton's words in the House had also given rise to a matter recorded as a complaint about a racist incident. The committee warned that:

- if... members' know their words in the House could be recorded as potential crimes, there would undoubtedly be a chilling effect, and interference with the freedom of speech in the House; and
- considered that the recording of such a complaint in this case was not a contempt because no one outside [the county police] service was aware of the action taken, and therefore it could not be said to interfere with the functions of the House or its members.

In conclusion, the committee noted that each case must be judged on its own merits, but:

[W]hile we have exercised restraint in this case, given the novelty of the circumstances, we would regard future attempts to restrict members' freedom of speech in the House through PINs as a serious contempt. Moreover, we would deplore any attempts to circumvent either the freedom of speech in Parliament or the protection of the 1840 Parliamentary Papers Act by resorting to technicalities. Mr Loughton's purpose in sending Hansard was to give notice that he would not deal with his constituent again, and so we consider a repetition of the incident is unlikely. If a Member were to misuse his or her position, and misapply public resources, by repeatedly using Hansard as a means of intimidation, we expect that the Parliamentary Commissioner for Standards and the Committee on Standards would be prepared to investigate and take action.

However the committee did not consider further action necessary in the case, subject to an appropriate response from [the county police]. Nonetheless, it deplored their inability to recognise that freedom of speech in Parliament, and the ability of members to carry out their functions without unfounded legal threats, are themselves part of the law which the police should uphold.

On 14th March 2014, two statements were issued to the press, the first by the police's temporary chief constable who said, 'I am writing to confirm our actions in light of the report published by the House of Commons Committee of Privileges last week. Following due consideration and taking the advantage of legal advice, I can confirm that [the police] accept the findings… in full. We have decided to remove the PIN that was issued to you last September and please accept this letter as formal notification. The police database will be updated to reflect this.'

I apologise on behalf of [county police] for the contempt of parliamentary privilege, which arose out of the service of this PIN and for the inconvenience this has caused to you. This was an inadvertent error. All notices were served in good faith and issued to treat all parties equally and fairly in a serious and very difficult situation. I have asked for a review to be conducted within the force, which will tie in with the Commissioner's contact with the College of Policing, on the use of PINs within [the county]. The review will be led by a detective superintendent and will report within two months. I would welcome your contribution to this review and will be happy to share the findings with you, when complete.'

Tim Loughton responded with his own press release:

I am relieved and pleased that the new management of [the county police] have acted swiftly to acknowledge that they were in breach of Parliamentary privilege, which is an important safeguard of free speech in our democracy, and that they failed to follow their own procedures in the use of PINs. But I am also angry that so much police time and taxpayers money has been wasted on this shambolic and clearly nonsensical investigation, which has caused great damage to confidence… The early departure of the former chief constable affords an important opportunity for the police to re-establish that confidence… across the county that [the police] can tell the difference between victims of abuse and perpetrators of abuse and protect us appropriately.

This whole sorry saga has wider implications for the use of PIN notices and the way police deal with harassment cases beyond our county boundaries and I have accepted the invitation of the temporary chief constable to contribute to a review into their use to be carried out with the help of the College of Policing. I have received many letters from people across the country who have also been the victims of inappropriate use of PINs, including former police officers, and clearly this is an area that needs to be urgently addressed along with the way police follow their own guidance when issued by ACPO. Consequently I will be raising these issues in Parliament and the chairman of the Home Affairs Select Committee has expressed his interest in investigating this too. Many questions remain about how [the police] allowed this situation to get out of hand to the extent it did and I will therefore be submitting a full complaint to the IPCC but I am pleased that in the meantime I have been given a full apology.

Subsequently, as we read in *Chapter 5*, the HAC did indeed take oral evidence on PINs on 13th January 2015. The (retired) chief constable was amongst the witnesses. He confirmed that 75 per cent of the PINs issued on his 'watch' were inappropriate and that he had no monitoring role, although his replacement was improving the situation.

Comment

I note from the statement that Tim Loughton intends to appeal to the IPCC as to the conduct, double standards and ineffectiveness of the police's investigation although I also understand that of late rather more objective and constructive discussions have taken place between him, the new (temporary) chief constable and the police and crime commissioner. Nevertheless I believe this story shows how easily the police confuse victims with perpetrators even with several months' of investigation. What can anyone say!

CHAPTER 11

The Government Does Know

This book contains several examples of reports prepared in close proximity to Parliament and thus Government. As reported in the preceding chapter, Tim Loughton MP initiated a debate in the House of Commons encompassing police ignorance of Parliamentary privilege and their circumnavigation of ACPO procedures. The latter cannot have escaped the Home Secretary's attention nor can the report prepared by the Home Affairs Select Committee (HAC) on the IPCC (summarised in *Chapter 21*), and nor can Andrew Mitchell MP's resignation from the Cabinet. So there can be no doubt that the highest echelons of Government are aware of a general problem and probably appreciate a need to re-think the whole pre-court justice system structure. That begs the real question as to whether the job is too big for a Government to tackle and, if it is not, why haven't they started?

To reaffirm that the vast majority of those in the Palace of Westminster appear to be well aware of the problem, the following extracts from the Lords debate following the Queens Speech on 15th May 2012 are pertinent:[1]

Lord Maginnis of Drumglass:[2] To ask Her Majesty's Government when it is appropriate for the Home Office to intervene directly in matters of police discipline and incidents of police corruption, and whether current delegated arrangements are proving adequate.

The Minister of State, Home Office (Lord Henley): My Lords, the police are expected to maintain the highest standards of professional behaviour at all times. Where there are allegations of misconduct or corruption, the most serious cases are investigated by the Independent Police Complaints Commission. As the name

---

1. This chapter reproduces extracts from the Lord's *Hansard* and as such contains Parliamentary information licensed under the Open Parliament Licence v1.0.
2. http://www.publications.parliament.uk/pa/ld201213/ldhansrd/text/120515-0001. htm#12051582000026

suggests, the IPCC is independent of the Government and the police to ensure that investigations are impartial. The Government do not intervene in any individual cases. The Government consider that these arrangements are adequate.

Lord Maginnis of Drumglass: My Lords, does it not all boil down to the fact that the coalition Government have no real concept of hands-on responsibility or of timely decision-making and believe that by delegation they can wash their hands of responsibility? Are the Gary McKinnon and widow Hofschroer cases, respectively awaiting justice for ten years and three years, not examples of a Government who could not care less?

Lord Henley: My Lords, the noble Lord makes a number of points. First, I make it clear that this is not just a matter for the coalition Government; it is a matter that goes back to the 2002 Act which brought in the IPCC. I think all sides of this House agree that there should be an Independent Police Complaints Commission and that it should be independent. It can be independent of Government only if Government cannot intervene. It would be quite wrong for my right honourable friend the Home Secretary to intervene in individual cases. It would surely undermine the IPCC's independence if she tried to second-guess its decisions. The noble Lord went on to mention two cases. Gary McKinnon has nothing to do with any allegations of police corruption because his case is purely about extradition. The case of the Hofschroer family is, as the noble Lord knows, a matter that has gone to the IPCC. It is a matter for it to produce its decision and if those involved in that case do not like that decision, they can then take the appropriate action in the courts.

Lord Maginnis of Drumglass:[3] My Lords, in so far as I intend to pursue in more detail the issue that I raised earlier at Oral Questions, I want to make it clear that I am not anti-police. Concurrently with my first employment as a schoolmaster, I became a special constable and served for seven years. Later, as an Army officer, I had responsibility for joint planning and liaison with the police, and that during our troubled times in Northern Ireland. While I was an MP, I was parliamentary

---

3. http://www.publications.parliament.uk/pa/ld201213/ldhansrd/text/120515-0002.
htm#12051510700072

adviser to the RUC. I feel no need, however, to make similar ameliorating comments about my attitude to our virtually invisible and ineffective Home Office.

At the beginning of a new parliamentary year—I have seen 29 come and go here—one still waits with bated breath for some sort of signal that next year is going to be better. Such an expectation is difficult to sustain when one reads through the coalition's programme for business in 2012, particularly in relation to creating a fairer society. Everything I read there confirms my impression of those exceedingly well educated folk who occupy the Front Benches in another place but who seldom appear to have rubbed shoulders with reality. Ideas hatched in some intellectually gifted corner of the Palace of Westminster float through a maze of implementation levels that are ill defined, largely disconnected and often wholly inefficient.

It is some years since the noble Lord, Lord Reid, described the Home Office as not fit for purpose, yet we continue without respite to find it delegating responsibilities in a way that it seems to consider absolves it from any real decision-making role. Just try, as I have, to discover why a police constabulary appears to be inefficient or corrupt and you will get the answer that I got last November when I was told by the Home Office that it had not held 'aggregate data' on police since 2004. Why not?

One may be advised to speak to the Independent Police Complaints Commission. I have, only to be told that the fairly obvious injustice that concerns me was not within its bailiwick because my complaint overlapped with social services. I belatedly referred the issue to the Justice Department, but it could not intervene. I am referring to a case where a lady in her 80s was cheated out of her home. The Minister knows it well and over the past three years the Home Office has received hundreds—yes, hundreds—of communications through me about the matter. Successive Secretaries of State have been so concerned that none would meet me, despite the fact that Interpol was activated to pursue this elderly lady all the way to her son's home in Austria. Does anyone in authority care that social services and police in North Yorkshire have conspired in the persecution of Mrs Hofschroer and her son? Are details of dismissals, forced retirements and other shady and costly measures pertaining to North Yorkshire Police available to legislators in Parliament? No. Basic justice is distorted by the system, but I can see nothing to address this major issue in the Government's plans.'

Lord Laird:[4] My Lords, I have noted the gracious Speech and hope that in this parliamentary year things can be changed that should be. For example, I have become increasingly worried about a build-up of resentment over actual or perceived corruption among police forces the length of this country. I am aware that my good friend, the noble Lord, Lord Maginnis of Drumglass, is also particularly concerned about this topic. I want to underline that corruption where it exists is only among a very small part of the overall police service.

In this parliamentary year, the Home Office must take a firm grip of the methods it has to supervise existing forces and, if necessary, seek new regulations. The geographical area that I am concerned about today is south Wales, its police force and the independence and governance of its police authority until taken over by police commissioners. Because I am known for having an inquiring mind, I have for years received amounts of information from many in the southern parts of the beautiful country of Wales. It seems that systemic corruption by a section of the police has been going on in that area for many decades, at all levels and involving officers in all types of crime and the operation of professional standards. It has done much to damage the image of the police. The force has failed to comply with Police and Criminal Evidence Act and there is an apparent non-adherence to the terms of the 2003 Clingham case standards of proof in evidence, judgment for which was heard in this House.

I go as far back as 1987, with the murder of a Cardiff newsagent, a dreadful and tragic event, made all the worse when the men convicted served over 11 years in jail only to have their names cleared in court and be released. The 11 years in jail followed the first trial, in which the accused had their human rights violated by inappropriate methods of questioning and by not allowing them at appropriate times legal representation. Following the release of the unfortunate accused, no action was taken against the police known to have been involved in the frame-up,

---

4. http://www.publications.parliament.uk/pa/ld201213/ldhansrd/text/120515-0002.
    htm#12051599000033

and no apology given. There was just the bitterness of having the accused back in the community, with their lives, and those of their families, ruined.

This case from the 1980s may be dreadful, but is only one of many. There are the cases of Hewins, Clarke and Sullivan, the Darvell brothers, Jonathan Jones and many more, in which people were jailed who subsequently had their convictions quashed and were released back into the community. In all cases, the names of most of the police officers who set up the evidence that caused the convictions are well known. Some 20 officers are involved, but the believed ringleader, an inspector, has never been arrested yet. Much has been written about their actions, which gave them the opportunity for the named officers to sue the writers for libel—but, interestingly, they did not. Many journalists, including TV and radio programmes, have explored these cases, but no substantial official action appears to have been taken against them. Why?

As if all the pain and suffering were not enough, the cost to the taxpayers of investigations and trials was massive—funds that could have been spent in other areas of policing. I have examined myself the tops and bottoms of types of cases handled by South Wales Police. Now let us consider the police authority. As from 10 May, the current chairman, a magistrate and independent member, Mr John Littlechild, will have served continually since 1989. When complaints are made against the police, the authority, rather than acting independently to ensure that the force is monitored to keep it working efficiently and effectively and meeting all appropriate standards, seems to align with its friends against all comers. This includes Her Majesty's Inspector of Constabulary when it makes critical comments. For an example, see police authority minutes of 13 February. The authority in its standards and recording its business apparently fails to adhere to its own standing orders. For an example, see again the minutes of 13 February.

As recently as last night, at an Old St Mellons Partners and Communities Together group meeting, the sector inspector Nicky Flower withdrew her officers from taking part in the group meeting. She ignored written requests made to her and copied to senior officials last May to meet with all the village PACT panel members. This group has to date had nine freedom of information requests to provide documentation regarding information requested by residents on crime and anti-social behaviour incidents in the area, and the action taken. The residents are concerned at the number of burglaries, arsons and other crimes in the area. At two public meetings, there have been unanimous shows of hands for the information, which is still not provided, but which is freely given out at other PACT meetings in the same area. The number of crimes in the area reported to the Home Office is only a small fraction of the actual number, as claimed by the residents. They attend because in many cases they have been directly affected and suffered loss and cost. The chairman wrote last July for a meeting of the full panel, with the chief constable or the assistant chief constable responsible for PACT in person, due to dissatisfaction. The deputy chief constable stated to the panel members at force headquarters on 13 February that she had no knowledge of the requests but would have a meeting. This meeting has still not taken place.

Following the collapse of the £10 million Lynette White murder trial before Christmas, the chief constable, Peter Vaughan, claimed the loss of the IPCC evidence documents, saying that they had been shredded. He then went on to admit, on 17 January, to the Director of Public Prosecutions, that they had been found.

Comment

If there were *effective* bodies that policed the police we would be better served than is currently the case. A new Government must take a clean sheet of paper and figure out effective replacements for PSDs, the IPCC and (I would argue) PCCs—as well as giving them teeth.

CHAPTER 12

The Other Side of the Coin

The public are certainly not happy with the service they get from their 21st-century police forces in England and Wales, but few of us question whether the majority of police are happy with the work they do. All failings in the system are laid at the door of the police, but in truth not all the short-comings or the style of policing are necessarily the frontline officer's fault. There are many other factors both from within and external to our police forces — so we shouldn't (always) shoot the messenger.

While absolutely nothing excuses individual police officers from the alleged short-cuts, incompetence, bias and integrity issues reported here, much is traceable to Tony Blair's Government's target culture which should carry the blame for 'skews' in police methods, as well as the police's own frustration and the public dissatisfaction these have generated, at least until October 2012. The targets, or at least their make-up, were ill-conceived and changed not only what we see and get in the form of police services but also the internal priorities, workloads, paperwork, job satisfaction and management pressures the officers need to cope with from within their respective forces. There are also the added complications that other sections within the criminal justice system experience — the CPS, IPCC and more recently the PCCs do not all always appear to be on the same page as the police as we find out in *Part 3*, along with how these things adversely impact on police services.

As one friend explained, as a 'service' there were no Government set targets and the overall aim of the police was to provide a service to the local community whether this involved doing things that were not really police matters or that clearly were. In more recent years targets have necessitated focus onto core police activities and the positive discontinuance of anything outside of those set borders to the detriment of the whole community. This means that although we each have a 'force' that deals with just the set functions designated for that force and the subsequent removal of Governmental targets, even where they have been genuinely removed, this may not signal a return to policing for the good of the community.

In May 2008, Nick Allen explained the then switch in police tactics, the reasons and consequences in the *Daily Telegraph*[1] from which we learn that, in the context of considering the other-side-of-the-coin, it is safe to say that no one was unhappier than the police themselves with the ramifications of Tony Blair's target culture. The volume of sanctioned detections required being the game-changer and the fact that other essential police skills or the need to investigate a serious 'non-sanctioned' case, for example a murder or missing person investigation, the CPS electing not to prosecute, an offender dying or youth crimes all counted for nothing in the eyes of the Home Office and its sacrosanct targets. There was pressure from the Home office for each force to achieve its sanctioned detections each month — indeed the chief constable's bonus used to depend upon it. The forces target translated down the line to the PCs' responding priorities.

Nothing wrong in setting achievable targets — but it is the consequences of 'sanctioned detections' targets that led the police to focus time and effort on criminalising people. Anyone who can be 'done' in a few minutes to get the number of detections up got prioritised while relegating serious, more long-term issues to a lower priority. There was been widespread resentment to this artificial skewing of their focus at least among the lower ranks of the police while the public consequently saw the police as uninterested in problem-solving because they are focused upon nicking a student trampling a flowerbed. A PIN is, I'm guessing, a 'sanctioned detection' that got a Sussex PC a gold-star when dished out to Tim Loughton (and no doubt others) as recounted in *Chapter 10*. This and similar policies have progressively detracted from the general public's respect for the police, from police officers' job-satisfaction and contributed to increased complaints about the police.

Furthermore, one of the objects of this brainchild was to reveal under-performing police officers. Another laudable objective, but often it had the reverse effect. So it is good to report that, in October 2012, the Coalition Government launched a targeted consultation seeking views on '*A Revised Framework For Recorded Crime Outcomes*' and stopped setting national targets for police forces and paying a bonus to senior officers for achieving

---

1.   http://www.telegraph.co.uk/news/uknews/2052629/Police-punishing-middle-classes-to-hit-targets.html

those targets. However, as we see below that does not preclude police forces using local targets—which may ultimately be little different to nationally set targets. The Government published its consultation conclusions in March 2013[2] in which it maintained that the changes that about half the police forces were using on a voluntary basis pending legislation would (my précis[3]) strengthen police discretion so that the emphasis should shift from hitting targets to appropriateness and help to promote a more victim-oriented approach, focused on providing a better service to victims of crime by removing perverse incentives for forces to record and pro-actively pursue certain crimes on the basis of locally-set detection targets. The Government also thought it would further increase transparency in policing, and trust in national statistics, by providing the public with a richer picture of crime, and how it is dealt with in their area, this broader set of information can be used as a tool by which the public can hold the police to account. Also a basis for constructive engagement between communities, police, and PCCs. Later in the report the document also said the Home Office 'would replace the term 'sanction detection' with 'crime outcomes'.

I cannot see how splitting-up some existing categories of recorded crimes, adding new ones and changing the names used will reduce the time required by officers to record crime statistics. Indeed some information technology changes are required to accommodate the change, which is not reassuring although a reduction in the 'target culture'-style of policing would be encouraging even if it does not reduce paperwork. However, whether a locally set target will eventually take us back to the policing we used to 'enjoy' remains to be seen. I believe that unlikely but it might just be the first of several steps in the right direction. With or without targets it will take years for the consequences of the 'tough on crime, tough on the causes of crime' political dogma to work out the gulf between the public and the police. However it may help if we all remember that it was not the police's choice to have their superiors, motivated by bonuses, drive them towards more and more sanctioned detections—sorry, that should now read 'crime outcomes'!

There are many other police problems that impact on officers' working

---

2. See https://www.gov.uk/government/uploads/system/uploads/attachment_data/file/157796/consultation-response.pdf

3. Based on Parliamentary information licensed under the Open Parliament Licence vi.o.

lives: firstly staffing levels, second equipment, thirdly who responds and when there is a response, and finally the prioritisation of the many daily public calls for police help. Few readers will be surprised to hear that many forces have insufficient 'responders'. An insufficient establishment in the first place will be diluted by sickness, long-term sick, holidays, secondments, compassionate leave and training. These all add to the workload and the time available which those on duty have to respond to a call. Additionally, some non-operational cars or equipment can also hamper the force with the consequence that response officers are sometimes unable to address all calls to their satisfaction. They may even need to leave one call-out prematurely in order to respond to a more urgent one. It all increases the officers' frustration and reduces their job-satisfaction.

The response officers are rarely the public's initial contact. If you call the police via the 999 emergency service you will likely be put through to a police managed call-centre that could be miles from your town. You will be questioned by the operator, your location, your situation prioritised as 1, 2 or 3 and the telephone call concluded. If your situation is deemed by the centre's operator priority 1 the call-centre will ask by radio for the nearest available police response officer to attend straight away. Some of the very slow police reactions recounted elsewhere were likely the result of the call-centre giving it a priority 2 or priority 3 category and those police officers that were available were just simply too busy to allow lower priority calls to reach the top of the pile. Thus if/when the police do manage to attend they will likely meet a disenchanted, even irate, caller that extends the subsequent discussion as the police first have to calm/explain the situation before dealing with the original issue.

Then there are the resulting complications when the call-centres, themselves under target/time pressures, fail to record all the facts or make mistakes which further compounds the attending officers' difficulties and the time required to resolve issues. They are deemed ineffective by the public but it may well not be their fault and they are likely to be unhappy about a situation outside their control. But these shortcomings and frustrations are not beyond the control of more senior police officers who should be addressing such issues.

While not a daily occurrence, police offers would not be human if they failed to keep in the back of their minds the danger that their chosen profession can bring. Nicola Hughes and Fiona Bone were shot dead responding to a reported burglary in Greater Manchester in 2012.[4] We must not forget that we do owe many police officers a debt of gratitude for their selfless service, none more so than those who die in the line of duty.[5] This must bring an added pressure that, in times of peace, only the police and emergency services experience.

Aside from the dangers and frustrations of the job, a police officer has pressures on the parts of life that many of us take for granted—family, friends and a social life outside the police, the problems that stem from shift work's erratic hours, switching-off the job's tensions and the hostility that some citizens exhibit. These very difficulties weld the police into internal solidarity which sometimes ensures officers back-up each other in major situations and support each other by concealing infractions from the attention of seniors.

As I've reported earlier, for perhaps most of the ten years prior to 2012, the police had been under a great deal of pressure to meet artificial targets 'dreamed-up' by the Home Office. Those pressures may be diminishing in some forces, although in other forces the chief constable may see fit to replace them with his or her own targets. Targets brought the quantity verses quality dilemma into focus and, because the target is numerically set, it is quantity that wins out. Consequently whether they agree or not, officers were, and maybe still are, required to arrest lots of minor delinquents rather than pursue fewer but more serious criminals. That reduces job-satisfaction but also the pursuit of numbers can be a pressure to use a few short cuts, only resisted by each officer's character, how each reacts to the pressure to perform and the workload placed upon him or her.

The BBC brought this into focus in the Metropolitan area on 4th April 2014 when home affairs correspondent Danny Shaw reported that the Met has a 'culture of fear'. This he said existed due to 'draconian' performance targets. A report into the force by the local Police Federation confirmed this and described some targets as 'meaningless' and 'unrealistic' whilst others

---

4.   As reported, e.g. by the Guardian at http://www.theguardian.com/uk/2012/sep/18/
     woman-police-officer-killed-manchester
5.   See the most up-to-date information including officers local to your area at http://www.
     policememorial.org.uk/index.php?page=annual-roll-of-honour

were 'disguised' by senior officers.

Scotland Yard denied claims of a 'bullying culture' and said it made 'no excuses' for valuing performance. John Tully, chair of the Metropolitan Police Federation, described some targets as 'questionable' and said the report painted a 'devastating' picture. He told BBC's *Today* programme that officers who missed targets were put on a 'hit list' and some faced potential misconduct proceedings.

One officer had told the federation that he had to arrest at least four people a month and carry out ten stops-and-searches, one of which must have a positive outcome.

The report, submitted to Metropolitan Police Commissioner Sir Bernard Hogan-Howe described how officers had hit 'rock bottom'. It followed a warning from Home Secretary, Theresa May that police performance targets were making a 'comeback' despite the fact that she had ended most centrally-imposed targets, because forces saw them as a security blanket. The report highlighted a number of stop-and-search targets, i.e. a:

- 20 per cent arrest rate for stops-and-searches;
- 20 per cent of stop-and-searches should be for weapons;
- 40 per cent should be for neighbourhood (property) crime; and
- 40 per cent should be for drugs.

It also identified targets set for one policing team in 2011:

- PCs to make one arrest and five stops-and-searches per shift;
- Met special constables to make one arrest per month and five stops-and-searches per shift; and
- police community support officers (PCSOs) to make five stop-and-accounts and two criminal reports per shift.

Assistant Commissioner Simon Byrne accused the federation of 'sensationalising', telling *Today* that it was the Met's job to bring down crime and since it had a 'more accountable way of doing things', rates were down by ten per cent. Danny Shaw also commented that:

As soon as the first bulletin about the federation report had been broadcast I was contacted by a former Met officer. He'd not been an active federation member—but had risen through the ranks to a senior position in the force. He told me the main reason he'd left was because of a 'pervasive' culture of bullying, with too great an emphasis on arrest and stop-and-search targets, to the detriment of neighbourhood policing. In fact, the report shines a light on practices that I'd heard about anecdotally for several years... Even taking into account the federation's role, to represent its members and highlight issues of concern, the findings make uncomfortable reading for an organization already under the spotlight...

I expect the Met and other police forces to motivate their employees by incentives for those that perform well while speaking quietly, constructively and privately with those who don't. It's not up to me, but over the course of my industrial career I found that few things motivate employees more than a financial reward and/or a public words of praise for a job well done. On the other hand, public humiliation is utterly demoralising and demonstrates that management, more than the individual officers, has failed. It also helps if those at the coalface know that staff or equipment shortages and other hindrances are at least understood by the higher echelons. They may not be able to do much about it due to budgetary constraints, but at least management can be seen to appreciate the difficulties a team is working under.

Given this unrest, it's hardly surprising if the police are disenchanted with reducing numbers of officers. The workload on police officers responding to public calls for help is considerable and it seems unlikely that Home Office cutbacks and the understanding of their chief constable do anything to take account of the reduction in police officers. The figures published for the year ending 31 March 2013 are as follows:

- there were 129,584 full-time equivalent (FTE) officers: a decrease of 3.4% or 4,516 officers compared to a year earlier which follows a decrease of 5,010 officers in previous 12 months;
- there were 6,537 FTE Minority Ethnic officers: 5.0% of total: no change on the year earlier;
- FTE police staff numbers stand at 65,573: a decrease of 2.8% compared to a year earlier;
- the total number of FTE police community support officers was 14,205: a 1.3% decrease; and.
- there were 19,011 special constables: 6.5% fewer than a year earlier.

Such reductions in numbers on an already hard-pressed force are going to do little to help morale.

The character of individual police officers will of course vary, as do all human beings across all walks of life. However, in the case of applicants to join the police, only those interested in 'getting the bad guys' will likely apply, which could be re-phrased by saying only those with aggressive tendencies will. Furthermore, those with a burning desire to catch 'bad-guys' may be tempted to do so 'by whatever means'. Thus there is a conflict between the pressure to perform well and to do so legally. Also applicants know that with the police uniform comes authority, which some are likely to find motivating.

There are also pressures imposed by society, some by politics and some by their superior officers—but pretty universal is the demand to get results. It is possible that only those who get results are considered for promotion. As we have discussed, Tony Blair's Government increased the pressure on getting quick results by introducing targets that unintentionally undermined police training and rekindled the traditional police culture of a few 'short-cuts'. So, rather than increase efficiency legally there is, in effect, a subtle pressure to over-reach powers in order to increase 'clear-ups' and reach targets.

Although pretty scathing, Scarman (Brixton riots, 1981), Macpherson (Stephen Lawrence/racism, 1999) and other sources of reform have made minimal impact on established police culture aside from a few short-term improvements and maybe some superficial changes. In fact, they probably brought about more changes outside police forces than within them. The ramifications of the latter enquiry rumble on with police subsequently spying on the family of murder victim Stephen Lawrence! Hardly a legal and commendable improvement. However, as a consequence the police on the streets see themselves under attack—in public enquires, by politicians, the public, the legal profession, senior officers and of late police and crime commissioners. Like all human beings, they fear changes and consequently consolidate their tight-knit groups with a culture of using those powers they do enjoy and of keeping outsiders from 'their world'.

Ironically, police documentaries like *Traffic Cops* shout out 'Look how good we are' and actually hoist-the-police-on-their-own-petard because they tend to over-egg crime-solving skills, which puts even more pressure on officers.

Is there similar pressure on officers who want to do a good job, get-on, be promoted but are not prepared to take 'short-cuts'? The pressure is probably considerable if they see colleagues moving ahead by occasional or maybe frequent use of short-cuts or dubious tactics and even greater if that officer ever contemplated whistle-blowing.

As mentioned a couple of times already, the police are a close knit group, often out of necessity, so whistle blowing will seriously harm their futures and the damage may extend far beyond likely getting the sack. One officer complained to her boss about sexual innuendo but was not taken seriously. Nevertheless the complainant endured a nine-month investigation into her own conduct and she was stopped more than 70 times while driving her car for 'suspected offences', including drink driving and assault. So a complaining police officer faces a dilemma. While not a whistle blower, one police officer was framed by racist 'colleagues' and although innocent was actually jailed. Imagine what treatment a whistle blower would get. The usual problem is gathering the evidence whether you are a whistle blower or seeking to defend yourself. Complaints require evidence, so some officers, rather than informing management of suspicions which would create problems, quietly seek corroboration of the evidence, but more often look the other way.

The annual *Crime Statistics* show that crime is reducing and the issues surrounding those figures are examined in *Chapter 17*. A reduction in crime could be fillip, boost morale and signal a job well done. But perhaps the crime figures are too remote from the daily events in a police officers' life, or maybe the higher echelons don't make enough of the apparently improving figures, or perhaps the sheer size of the police force is just too large for individuals to derive that sort of job-satisfaction from these figures. Or maybe the police know something we can only suspect—that the statistics are massaged. The next paragraph encapsulates the last two issues in one piece of news. A Met constable who reported (i.e. whistle-blew) concerns about the under-recording of crimes (for local and national crime statistics) initially faced serious disciplinary procedures instead of, as would have seemed more appropriate, commendation and being given a medal.

Little wonder the officer subsequently resigned as the following extract from the BBC News website explains (paraphrased):

A police whistle-blower who raised concerns about the recording of crime statistics has resigned. PC James Patrick said crime figures were manipulated and sexual offences under-reported by 22–25%. In a blog, PC Patrick said resigning had not been an 'easy decision'. He had previously faced gross misconduct proceedings, but these were downgraded after an outside force investigated the case.

In his blog, PC Patrick said that his resignation had arisen directly from his treatment 'as a result of making disclosures in good faith and in the public interest.'. He added: 'My experience led me to see just how flawed the whistle-blowing system is, how it fails, but also to firmly believe that no police officer should normally resign or retire while subject to any misconduct investigation; but the circumstances are such that I have no choice...

PC Patrick told MPs on the Public Administration Select Committee (PASC) that massaging figures to hit performance targets had become 'an ingrained part of policing culture'...He claimed that serious offences including rape and child sex abuse were being recorded as 'crime-related incidents' or 'no crimes' and he said he had found disparities between the number of reported burglaries and those finally recorded.

The Met Commissioner Sir Bernard Hogan-Howe previously said there was a 'truth' to PC Patrick's allegations. Following Patrick's resignation Scotland Yard made no further comment.

It is difficult to appreciate in this day and age but the Police Reform Act 2002 used to *deny* a police officer the right to make a complaint against other officers/staff within his or her force. This constraint is similar to earlier National Health Service constraints, however the NHS lifted the restriction allowing staff to air malpractice. The Public Interest Disclosure Act 1998 (PIDA) was intended to allow employees to make disclosures in the public interest. It overrides confidentiality clauses and was amended in 2003 to specifically include the police. However, that does not help any potential whistle-blower/complainant to cope with the aftermath of their disclosure. Thus additional legislation to impose a 'duty of candour' on every member of a police force, including PSDs, the IPCC, HMIC and the NCA is required, but additionally the associated practical help, possibly anonymity, is essential if we really expect employees to do their unpalatable duty and step forward.

Cathy James, CEO of the charity Public Concern at Work[6] also thinks that the current supposedly protective whistle-blowing legislation needs updating:

> Ministers and employers say it is vital for an open and transparent workplace culture, but ask the whistle-blowers and the story is starkly different: they are gagged in the NHS, arrested in our police forces and blacklisted in may industries. The findings demonstrate why speaking up in the workplace may seem futile or dangerous to many individuals. Employers are still shooting the messenger and overlooking crucial opportunities to address concerns quickly and effectively.

The IPCC has made an effort to guide police employees wishing to raise concerns about colleagues and practice.[7] However on reading their advice I was set wondering about what advice, help and encouragement the IPCC would offer whistle-blowers because they seem anxious to divert complaints, incidents or the action of other officers back to the relevant force's PSD who are hardly impartial and, because of their proximity to the complainant this will possibly land the officer concerned in a lot of trouble. The IPCC actually says it '… would not normally become involved unless the conduct in question fell within the *mandatory referral criteria*', thus absolving themselves of all but the most serious issues. Officers may be better advised to follow the alternative IPCC suggestion and contact their federation representative but, again, their support is extremely weak in this context and encourages honest officers to keep their heads down.

To his credit, the Met officer referred to by the BBC report dated 24th March 2014 (above) did quite the reverse. PC Patrick contacted the chair of the House of Commons Public Administration Select Committee (PASC) who used Patrick's knowledge as a serving police officer to help the committee prepare their report published 9th April 2014 entitled 'Caught Red-handed: Why We Can't Count on Police Recorded Crime Statistics'. The committee were investigating whether crimes were being appropriately recorded by the police, looking at the factors which can influence police miss-recording of

---

6.   www.pcaw.org.uk
7.   See at http://www.ipcc.gov.uk/page/police-officers-how-raise-concerns

crime, and assessing whether enough has been done to ensure the integrity of crime data. The committee recorded that it was '... indebted to PC Patrick for his courage in speaking out, in fulfilment of his duty to the highest standards of public service, despite intense pressures to the contrary'. Bearing in mind the numerous examples of alleged police corruption and dubious integrity it is heartening to hear of such moral strength and commitment.

The PASC report stated as follows (my précis):[8]

[W]e recommend that the Home Office clarifies the route open to police whistle-blowers who have exhausted internal channels within their police forces. Police whistle-blowers should be free to refer their allegations to the IPCC, and should, while those concerns are pending formal investigation, enjoy immunity from disciplinary proceedings in relation to actions taken in order to raise those concerns.

We recommend that Her Majesty's Inspectorate of Constabulary should investigate the Metropolitan Police Service in respect of the treatment of PC Patrick and review the internal processes and procedures of the police for dealing with whistle-blowers... We have grave doubts that the Metropolitan Police Service has treated PC Patrick fairly or with respect and care.

Thank goodness someone has a wiser head than the Met. Pending Home Office clarification and assurances, I suggest whistle-blowers could contact their PCC stressing absolute confidentiality or by writing anonymously. Alternatively, and until such time as whistle-blowers are properly protected both in theory and in practice, it would seem that the PASC is receptive to information on dubious practices within police forces. Within it, the PASC requested the Met commissioner to invite:
- academics to review the Met's no-crime reports
- a public figure study how it responds to sexual offences; and
- change the standard for no-crime sexual offences to 'beyond reasonable doubt'.

Consequently and in the context that the public are invited to comment,

8. Contains Parliamentary information licensed under the Open Parliament Licence v1.0. See
    http://www.publications.parliament.uk/pa/cm201314/cmselect/cmpubadm/760/760.pdf

and while I'm stretching the PASC's request, I suggest concerned police officers draw attention to dubious practices by writing to that committee.[9]

Comment

The difficulties the police face weld them together which is commendable. However, I believe this strength will conversely be likely to lead to collective resentment for anyone who 'breaks-ranks' by trying to right wrongs. So the honest officers who consider whistle-blowing know it will almost certainly seriously damage their future beyond possibly getting the sack. Consequently, practical protective legislation is urgently required.

---

9. The address is Clerks of the Public Administration Select Committee, Committee Office, First Floor, 7 Millbank, London SW1P 3JA.
The Committee's email address is pasc@parliament.uk

CHAPTER 13

Incompetence or 'Screening-out'?

Returning home around 9 pm one February evening, this contributor, who we'll call Bill, was startled to see a dark figure standing in the shadows of his car port. It proved to be a uniformed police officer who was not only helpful and sympathetic but guarding the house pending the arrival of an out of hours glazier. Although double-glazed, the officer explained that the house had been entered earlier in the evening by breaking a vent at the rear of the property, squeezing through it and opening a larger window. Thereafter, the two burglars had come and gone by that route until disturbed by neighbours. The police had called the glazier, who indeed arrived soon afterwards.

The police officer asked Bill and his wife not to touch anything as the fingerprint experts were calling the next morning and asked that Bill prepare a list of missing items. Indeed, the fingerprint team arrived early the following day, but sadly reported there was nothing to help with identification.

Later Bill found a couple of electrical goods and a kitchen knife half-way up the back garden which he subsequently learnt had been abandoned by burglars when making their escape — nevertheless they got away with many smaller/high value items, principally irreplaceable family jewellery, valued at several thousand pounds. Also that morning, a plainclothes officer arrived to collect Bill's 'stolen' list and interview two neighbours who had witnessed the culprits. He sounded reassuring and left Bill with a contact name/telephone number and instructions to contact him with any additional information. At this point Bill felt the police had acted as helpfully, speedily and professionally as possible.

Bill made a point of calling on the two neighbours to thank them for their involvement and learnt one had been jogging and had been alerted by the sound of breaking glass. He'd looked over the fence, seen the burglars and called the police. The other neighbour, a student, had seen one of them standing at Bill's wife's dressing table with the bedroom light on. Both neighbours gave good descriptions of youths with hooded jackets with the tops pulled up. In one case the hood was dark green.

The next day Bill noticed a young looking builder up the scaffolding of a nearby house re-pointing a chimney. He called on both neighbour witnesses to see if they were available and could positively identify the builder. Neither was home so Bill phoned the police contact number he'd been given. After a long wait he asked for the detective but was told he was not available, so Bill left a message. Nothing happened so the following morning, Day Two, since the builder was again up the scaffolding, Bill called again, asked for the detective, left a message and waited for a return call. Nothing happened but he learnt that the call-centre he was talking to was 30 miles away and had no idea in which town his address was located. The next day, Day Three, the builder and scaffolding were gone.

Bill and his wife called at all the local jewellers and left descriptions of the stolen goods, but without any success in locating them. A couple of weeks later the detective called to say that they had heard of a youth who had been selling jewellery and had arrested him, searched his home but found nothing. Bill naturally asked about the missed chances two weeks earlier but was told the messages had not reached the detective. However, the detective was going to organize an identity parade and was about to visit the witnesses to agree their available dates. Bill learnt a week or so later that the jogger told the detective that he was not available for a couple of specified days as he was going abroad on business while the student was also unavailable at about the same time due to exams.

The police organized an identity parade and the two suspects, 16 and 15-years-old respectively, turned up. However neither witness arrived. One was abroad on business the other in the middle of an exam! Bill called to hear the result of the identity parade but was told of the debacle and says that he let the police know what he thought of their organizing ability. He asked when the next parade was planned for because he wanted to ensure the witnesses were, this time, available. The police told Bill that they would not be able to organize a second parade because that would be construed as 'harassing the suspects'!

The police dropped the case so Bill wrote a letter of complaint to the police detailing what he felt were their appalling communications and the fiasco of the identity parade, pointing out that two arrest and potential conviction opportunities had been missed.

Elsewhere in this book we learn a little more about the part call-centres play in policing our streets, see especially *Chapter 12*. In due course a police inspector offered an apology (which Bill and his wife refused to accept), declined to comment as to what disciplinary action would be taken and conceded that the jewellery was unlikely to be seen again. As he was leaving the inspector also said that convictions were unlikely to have brought significant punishment in view of the suspects' ages leaving Bill to ponder whether in fact the sudden lack of police interest wasn't more to do with workload management because he concluded that no-one can be that incompetent.

The house insurer met the claim in full after a visit from the loss-adjuster and several letters but nevertheless grandpa's tie pin and watch chain, grandma's rings, and Bill's mother-in-law's wedding ring could never be replaced.

Comment

It would appear that the police are content to exclude Joe Public from justice by walking away from a case or finding an excuse not to get involved, known as 'screening-out'. Designed to maintain a focus on viable investigations and more serious cases, it also serves to reduce police workloads. There is also the possibility in Bill's case that in view of the evidential problems once the identity parade faltered, the CPS said, 'Don't bother with this one'. Screening-out might go some way to contributing towards the discrepancies between the two sets of *Crime Statistics* presented each year as explored in *Chapter 17*.

CHAPTER 14

Metropolitan Corruption, The Untouchables and Operation Tiberius

Upon taking-up office as Metropolitan Police Commissioner in 1993, Paul Condon (Sir Paul Condon from 1994) vowed that his officers

> ...must be totally intolerant of racially-motivated attacks, intolerant of those who engage in racial abuse and intolerant of those who use hatred and violence as the tools of their political expression. We must be equally intolerant of our own colleagues who fail to reach the required standards. We demand exemplary standards from those we employ.

By 1998, Sir Paul was struggling to fulfil both his racial and his police integrity commitments. Following a judicial enquiry into the investigation of the murder of black teenager Stephen Lawrence it was clear that Condon's officers, some allegedly incompetent, had failed to bring Stephen's white killers to justice,[1] which brought the commissioner to attempt an apology to Stephen's parents. Had this been an isolated racial issue, the press, public and maybe the Lawrence family may have reluctantly accepted this failure but, although this was the highest profile Met race-related case, there were a number of others and the Met in general and its commissioner in particular were roundly criticised. Mrs Lawrence called for Condon's resignation. However, as we will see later in this chapter, efforts to resolve the Lawrence case became complicated as it was pursued alongside Condon's second priority—resolving malpractice, dishonesty and corruption amongst police officers.

Police malpractice can take many forms. It may be passive (e.g. accepting what's offered by a witness or failing to report a breach of procedures) but much of it may be active, positive or even aggressive. As we will see later in this chapter, the IPCC seems to accept that some passive malpractice is

---

1. They were brought to justice many years later following a change to the double jeopardy laws.

inevitable. The media tends to focus on the more aggressive corruption. Writing in 1998, BBC News Home Affairs Correspondent Graeme McLaglan reported the Met's new policy under the heading 'Police anti-corruption squad stepped up':[2]

> The police are to double the strength of a special anti-corruption squad targeting a hard core of corrupt officers in London. The team is being expanded to deal with the amount of information being received from former officers. The special squad of experienced detectives was set up secretly to deal with what the Metropolitan Police Commander, Sir Paul Condon, says are up to 250 corrupt officers in London. Traps were set to catch detectives suspected of stealing large amounts of money and recycling seized drugs.

McLagan explained that this happened after some of those under investigation confessed to corruption and began informing on other officers, so great was the volume of information flowing from this. One allegation was that officers stole £250,000, part of the proceeds of a security van robbery and there were claims that some officers seized drugs from dealers and sold them back to dealers. Corrupt relations between police and lawyers were also under scrutiny.

> The chair of the Metropolitan Police Federation, Mike Bennett, is quoted as saying that he did not doubt corruption existed and was concerned the investigation had not so far produced results:

> As a police federation we want the 250 people that the commissioner has mentioned publicly, arrested. We want convictions, not just discipline, and we want lengthy prison sentences as a deterrent…We are not getting that, the public is not getting that and we are no further forward than we were…

McLaglan wrote a second report, 'Condon's "crusade" against corrupt police'[3] in which he noted Sir Paul had mentioned that it was 'a crusade' for him, having inherited deep-seated problems of malpractice.

---

2.   9th May 1998. See http://news.bbc.co.uk/2/hi/uk_news/90028.stm
3.   15th December 1998. See http://news.bbc.co.uk/2/hi/uk_news/235284.stm

The approach included expanded use of undercover officers, unearthing dishonesty, working with the Criminal Investigation Bureau (CIB) at Scotland Yard ('The Untouchables')[4] and offering bribes to officers. The intention was to widened this to include 'integrity tests', using financial and even sexual inducements and other tactics to find out if an officer had racist or sexist attitudes (both of which Condon regarded as endemic).

McLaglan also reported how critics maintained that the Lawrence inquiry had shown the depth of racism within the Met, 50 officers having already been suspended and 20 charged as part of Condon's 'purge', whilst Condon hoped the new strategy would 'nip future corruption in the bud.'

> The last major corruption crackdown in the Met was in the 1970s when a team led by Sir Robert Mark [the then commissioner] investigated officers—mainly in the vice squad—accepting bribes from criminals. Scores of officers resigned or were sacked....The problem seemed to have been conquered but in recent years there have been more embarrassing cases.

> One 'bent' detective had been filmed for the BBC's Panorama programme accepting a £20,000 bribe. The officer was later sentenced to eleven years in prison on corruption charges. Several provincial forces were set to follow suit with forms of integrity testing.

Condon was succeeded by Sir John Stevens. Regardless of the commissioner in post during and from the late-1990s there has been an appetite to purge the Met of such matters. Yet, with the advantage of hindsight, those early attempts may have been largely unsuccessful.

Writing in *The Guardian*, Michael Sean Gillard and Laurie Flynn updated the outcome of Met's anti-corruption efforts in 'Corruption squad under fire.'[5] The following is my précis of the key points in that article:
- after six years the Complaints Investigation Branch (CIB) was subject of three inquiries, two internal and one by an outside force, prompted by complaints it used discredited methods such as entrapment, inducements, super-grasses, non-disclosure

---

4.   Since renamed the Department of Professional Standards.
5.   4th March 2000. See http://www.theguardian.com/uk/2000/mar/04/1

of information to the defence of vital documents, abuse of the evidence-gathering procedures and double standards;

- one solicitor compared aspects of the CIB strategy to the discredited methods prevalent in the 1960s and 1970s;
- the CIB, unable to sustain its efforts, was reassessing methods;
- seventy-five people had been charged with corruption offences, including 26 serving and eleven former police officers. Of the 26, there had been five convictions and one acquittal.
- Seventy officers had been suspended;
- the CIB had gained only seven convictions for major corruption: ;
- four high-profile court cases had collapsed;
- the CPS had decided not to proceed against 80 serving officers;
- of 70 officers still suspended, over two-thirds had not been charged and a significant (undisclosed) cleared internally.

The authors went on to explain that the results fell somewhat short of what was envisaged in 1994 when the anti-corruption drive was launched. Arguably, the CIB had always had a reputation for 'unconventional' methods, but it was now being undermined from within its own ranks.

Much of the CIB's work involved covert policing and the use of secret intelligence. A kind of 'ghost squad' it claimed to be on the cutting-edge. It's then head, Commander Andy Hayman was quoted as being keen to 'push the parameters' so as to be ahead of officers being targeted, including through surveillance and bugging of homes, offices, police vehicles and police stations. For example, in one case, cannabis to the value of half-a-million pounds had been in a flat and word passed to two Scotland Yard officers, who were caught red-handed on video trying to move the drugs. Once convicted each turned super-grass. A third officer, who was acquitted, alleged that he had been offered inducements to provide evidence: a reduced sentence, safe house, fresh identity and money. The CIB found itself denying that arrests were being made to justify speculation about corrupt officers or a secret blacklist of 'untrustworthy' officers.

Gillard and Flynn later wrote a book on corruption in the Met,

Untouchables: Dirty Cops, Bent Justice and Racism in Scotland Yard.[6] Amongst their disclosures were (paraphrased):

- the police can't be trusted to investigate their own;
- the police complaints system lacks independence;
- there is a the need to question cosy relationships between Scotland Yard and the media (a precursor to phone-hacking, etc.);
- cover-ups, double standards, miscarriages of justice and a 'phoney war' on corruption masked underlying problems;
- this had re-emerged in wars on terror and crime, with the same effects: prosecutions for misconduct, collapsed trials, bills for the taxpayer, victims left without justice and the guilty going free.

Although secret at the time, the Met launched an internal investigation into corruption in 2002 known as Operation Tiberius details of which were leaked to *The Independent* in 2014 when they emerged in a series of articles and case studies by Tom Harper,[7] showing corruption extending beyond the police. Harper describes how a corrupt detective chief inspector sold his car to a known criminal, who was a protected police informer. This was arranged by another corrupt officer — the informant's 'handler' — described as 'raping, blackmailing and encouraging the informant to facilitate the importation of heroin'. The report did not identify any action taken by the Met against the serving officer. Other examples include:

- the trial of a man charged with drugs-trafficking that collapsed after surveillance logs disappeared: Tiberius claimed that the police were paid to destroy them;
- collusion when detectives raided the home of a 'high-echelon' criminal believed to be involved in the importation and distribution of controlled drugs. Computer printouts revealed that two serving Met officers were in his pay. One investigating officer was approached by a corrupt colleague who told him not to pursue the

---

6. Initially published by Mainstream (2003) and later subsequently available as a Bloomsbury Reader (Kindle).

7. *The Independent*: 9th January 2014: 'Case studies: Operation Tiberius uncovers corruption in the Met'. See http://www.independent.co.uk/news/uk/crime/case-studies-operation-tiberius-uncovers-corruption-in-the-met-9050226.html

suspect as he was a 'nice fella' and he was expecting a big 'security contract' saying, 'If you don't touch him he'll help you.'

- a year later when the police began a separate inquiry into the same suspect there was a stabbing thought to be linked. The investigating officer recalled the corrupt one saying '… bad people go to the club' and asking if 'I knew who they were.' Tiberius noted the corrupt officer also had an 'ongoing sexual relationship with a female drug supplier' and was accessing police intelligence for her.

In January 2014, Tom Harper wrote a feature, 'The corruption of Britain: UK's key institutions infiltrated by criminals'[8] in which he claimed that the entire criminal justice system was infiltrated by organized crime. This according to Operation Tiberius, which had found that notorious criminal suspects had compromised multiple agencies, including HM Revenue & Customs, the CPS, City of London Police, HM Prison Service and 'pillars of the criminal justice system' including juries an lawyers.

Harper described the ramifications as 'serious and disturbing'. Additionally, the fact that none of the crime syndicates concerned had been seriously disrupted provided an insight into the effectiveness of their networks. Examples discovered by Harper after the leak of the Tiberius report include:

- a 'leading criminal' acquitted of importing cannabis after he allegedly 'bought' members of the jury, when a named police officer 'was involved in some way or another';
- concern about the ability of the one family to escape the law by penetrating the criminal justice system (as reported by a national newspaper). In 1998, the police appeared to have made a breakthrough when one family member was jailed for importing cannabis but the 'only reason the family had allowed this was to teach xxx a lesson for getting involved in crimes they had not authorised.'
- 'Witnesses terrified into silence, dodgy jurors, bent lawyers, bent policemen and bent CPS clerks—all part of the same cancer eating away at justice. A cure will not be easy to come by. Perhaps

---

8.   *The Independent*: 10th January 2014. See http://www.independent.co.uk/news/uk/home-news/
      the-corruption-of-britain-uks-key-institutions-infiltrated-by-criminals-9052617.html

we should begin by acknowledging that the patient is sick.' Tiberius disclosed that when the Met interviewed the journalist who wrote the story (after the murder of Solly Nahome, a money launderer credited as the 'brains' behind the particular criminal empire), the reporter stated one of her sources was (an unnamed) corrupt police officer.

- 'foul play' within HMRC, the body supposed to lead the fight against white-collar crime such as money laundering;
- in 2000 a key informant secretly helping Scotland Yard with an investigation into the importation of £10m of heroin by a Turkish gang. The deal went wrong, the informant was tortured in a cellar and 'an attempt was made to sever his fingers with a pair of garden shears'. His associate was also attacked and had 'three fingers chopped off with a machete'. The henchman, Tiberius alleged, who had committed the assaults was the son of a named Met detective, who repeatedly tried to impede police inquiries into the case. The man also had a corrupt relationship with a named detective sergeant based at Marylebone Police Station and suspected 'to have organized cheque frauds'.

Seemingly, according to *The Independent*, nobody had ever been prosecuted. The Turkish drug dealer was later convicted and told police he was an HMRC informant who knew of 'corrupt contacts within the police' and had a Cyprus-based customs officer as a handler who 'took money off him'

Again in January 2014, Harper wrote a further piece entitled: 'Exclusive: Scotland Yard's rotten core: Police failed to address Met's "endemic corruption"'[9] in which he described how organized criminals were able to infiltrate Scotland Yard 'at will' by bribing corrupt officers and suggesting that only a tiny number of police officers had been convicted. He described how Keith Vaz, chair of the HAC, had said, 'I am deeply concerned … It is vital that the police have the utmost integrity. The public must be able to trust [police] to do their job and ensure justice prevails.' He continued (paraphrased):

---

9. *The Independent*: 10th January 2014. See http://www.independent.co.uk/news/uk/crime/exclusive-scotland-yards-rotten-core-police-failed-to-address-endemic-corruption-9050224.html

The Met have made vast progress rooting out corruption in the force in the last
20 years but it would appear more may still need to be done. [I will] be writing to
the current Met commissioner to ensure allegations have been fully investigated
and to confirm he is satisfied corruption no longer exists'.

This time Harper instanced a range of concerns (again paraphrased):
- an allegedly corrupt officer in charge of a team investigating a
  gangland murder;
- officers said by Tiberius to be corrupt working on inquiries into
  organized crime, many resulting in compromised investigations
  and sometimes failed prosecutions;
- some relationships between Met officers and the criminal under-
  world being so close that in one case named police officers were
  identified as co-owning properties and racehorses;
- a statement from a sensitive witness found in the safe of a night-
  club controlled by 'a major crime family';
- uproar when an informant's role was uncovered among corrupt
  elements inside Scotland Yard;
- organized crime syndicates able to infiltrate the Met 'at will';
- a rogue detective inspector threatening an informant's handlers;
- the ability of organized criminals to target highly sensitive police
  witnesses and informants; and
- the Met's inability to tackle the corruption of police officers by
  organized crime syndicates.

He explained that one of the few successful investigations reviewed by
Tiberius was Operation Greyhound, a long-running inquiry that found
two detectives had helped known criminals hunt a money-launderer. They
had been paid £50,000 for among other things using police intelligence
databases to try and track down and entrap the latter. Scotland Yard was
quoted as saying

'The Metropolitan Police Service will not tolerate any behaviour by our officers
and staff which could damage the trust placed in police by the public.'

The same report also instanced 'botched jobs' (including collapsed murder investigations), rogue investigations firms and how gangs use secret networks of Freemasons to corrupt police (which had in 1988 led then Home Secretary Jack Straw to argue that all police officers and judges should declare membership of that organization, an attempt that failed).[10]

જી

In an attempt to assess the success or otherwise of the Met's 'purge' let us fast-forward a few years. Although it makes uncomfortable reading you may care to search for the Stephen Lawrence/MacPherson Enquiry of 1999, six years after Stephen was murdered in 1993. But it is even more revealing to leap to 2014 by which time it would be reasonable to think 20 years of Met anti-corruption effort would be paying dividends. However, instead we read revelations about its undercover officers infiltrating the Lawrence family in an attempt to discredit them.[11]

Metropolitan police officer Andy Hayman, mentioned earlier, was in charge of the Met's 2005–2006 (i.e. first) enquiry into phone-hacking. He subsequently resigned as assistant commissioner following the start of a review of his expenses payments and allegations about professionally improper relationships. It should be emphasised that Hayman has always denied any impropriety including also in response to questioning by the HAC (see below). The HAC reviewed and 'deplored' News International's attempt to 'deliberately thwart' the original investigation into phone-hacking in 2005–2006, but takes the view that the police set aside a huge amount of material that could have identified other perpetrators and victims. They published a report in 20th July 2011 on unauthorised tapping or hacking of mobile

---

10. Ten of Britain's 43 police forces refused to take part and the policy was dropped under threat of legal action. *The Independent*, 13th January 2014. See http://www.independent.co.uk/news/uk/crime/revealed-how-gangs-used-the-freemasons-to-corrupt-police-9054670.html

11. As reported by the BBC News 6th March 2014 http://www.bbc.com/news/uk-26466867 which, together with Stephen Wright's article in the *Daily Mail* on 6th March 2014 http://www.dailymail.co.uk/news/article-2575174/Lies-spies-cover-ups-corruption-sickening-extent-Stephens-betrayal-police-exposed.html makes a strong argument to the effect that the Met is pretty much unchanged.

communications,[12] together with the opening comment that:

> The committee criticises Andy Hayman's cavalier attitude towards his contacts
> with those in News International who were under investigation which, even if
> entirely above board, risked seriously undermining confidence in the impartiality of
> the police, and accuses him of deliberate prevarication in order to mislead the com-
> mittee. It urges the swift and thorough investigation of allegations that payments
> were made to police officers by the media, which will help to establish whether
> or not such payments may have influenced police inquiries into phone-hacking.

The following are extracts from the Parliamentary report that day:[13]

> 10. Mr Hayman claims to have had little knowledge of the detail of the 2006
> operation, and to have taken no part in scoping it or reviewing it; his role seems to
> have been merely to rubber-stamp what more junior officers did. Whilst we have
> no reason to question the ability and diligence of the officers on the investigation
> team, we do wonder what 'oversight', 'responsibility' and 'accountability'—all
> of which words were used by Mr Hayman to describe his role—mean in this
> context. (Paragraph 66)

> 11. Leaving aside the fact that his approach to our evidence session failed to
> demonstrate any sense of the public outrage at the role of the police in this scandal,
> we were very concerned about Mr Hayman's apparently lackadaisical attitude
> towards contacts with those under investigation. Even if all his social contacts
> with News International personnel were entirely above board, no information
> was exchanged and no obligations considered to have been incurred, it seems
> to us extraordinary that he did not realise what the public perception of such
> contacts would be—or, if he did realise, he did not care that confidence in the
> impartiality of the police could be seriously undermined. We do not expressly
> accuse Mr Hayman of lying to us in his evidence, but it is difficult to escape the

---

12. See http://www.parliament.uk/business/committees/committees-a-z/commons-select/
     home-affairs-committee/news/110720-phone-hacking-report/

13. See http://www.parliament.uk/documents/commons-committees/home-affairs/unauthorised-
     tapping-or-hacking-mobile-communications-report.pdf

suspicion that he deliberately prevaricated in order to mislead us. This is very serious. (Paragraph 67)

12. Mr Hayman's conduct during the investigation and during our evidence session was both unprofessional and inappropriate. The fact that even in hindsight Mr Hayman did not acknowledge this points to, at the very least, an attitude of complacency. We are very concerned that such an individual was placed in charge of anti-terrorism policing in the first place. We deplore the fact that Mr Hayman took a job with News International within two months of his resignation and less than two years after he was—purportedly—responsible for an investigation into employees of that company. It has been suggested that police officers should not be able to take employment with a company that they have been investigating, at least for a period of time. We recommend that Lord Justice Leveson explore this in his inquiry. (Paragraph 69)

The experiences described by our contributors in earlier chapters, most of which relate to the post-2010 era and many from the Met area, do nothing but reinforce apprehension as to police integrity at all levels. Collectively, they surely also confirm that little has changed.

Harking back, Metropolitan Police Commissioner Paul Condon urged intolerance to racial abuse, malpractice, dishonesty and corruption and of those police officers who 'fail to reach the required standards'. If standards have barely changed in 20 years, should we not be intolerant of not only the police themselves but of the procrastination of politicians who continue to rely on a powerless, ineffective, often ignored watch-dog with inadequate quality standards to police the police? But there are other points of view and we need to consider some of those and whether they convince us that standards are improving after all. *Chapter 15* looks at some of these.

Police Corruption Cannot Be Eliminated

Perhaps not co-incidentally bearing in mind the issues noted in *Chapter 14*, Parliamentary disquiet about phone-hacking and ever-mounting and often critical media attention, on 20th July 2011 HM Inspectorate of Constabulary (HMIC) was commissioned by the Home Secretary to consider instances of undue influence, inappropriate contractual arrangements and other potential abuses of power in police relationships with outside parties. The fact that the Home Secretary made such a request accompanied by an invitation to make recommendations about what needs to be done, speaks volumes. However, there were no overt requests to investigate police integrity in general, although, as can be seen below, subsequent HMIC reports do mention this issue. So, whilst a step forward, the terms of reference seem to be too media-focused. The public might have hoped for a more all-embracing enquiry.

Commendably, just six months later, in December 2011, HMIC published an initial report on its findings and recommendations concerning police integrity entitled 'Without Fear or Favour—A Review of Police Relationships'. This looked at '…the system of controls that seek to prevent and tackle relationships that create a conflict of interest and therefore a risk to police impartiality.' In other words, police relationships that can lead to the public not being treated fairly by the police. The review included relations with the media, disclosure of information, hospitality, gratuities, procurement, contracts and business interests. HMIC examined the data (where available) and systems to pro-actively seek out wrongdoing, and examined the work of governing bodies, corporate governance and oversight, training, intelligence and enforcement.

The inspectors, as skilled and experienced as they might be, could do no more than scratch the surface, certainly in the time available. They could hardly have expected to persuade hardened police officers to confess to improper conduct, nor could HMIC possibly unearth all examples of racial abuse, malpractice, dishonesty or corruption as described in earlier chapters. Instead they focused largely on 'systems', especially those related to media relationships. It is revealing to see HMIC make reference to there apparently being on occasions no appropriate mechanisms in place to help senior officers spot malpractice. So at least HMIC was trying to ensure some methodology exists, but it can only be wondered what the inspectors said to chief constables where systems were found to be lacking and what was said by those in charge and the Home Office said to the senior and other officers concerned.

In 2012, HMIC conducted a review to track forces' progress against the recommendations of their 2011 report. Their summary looked at instances of undue influence, inappropriate contractual arrangements and other abuses of power in police relationships with the media and other parties:

It found no evidence of endemic corruption in police relationships, but neither did it issue a clean bill of health. This revisit found that, while forces have made progress, particularly around putting in place processes and policies to manage threats to integrity, more needs to be done. HMIC also found that, 'The pace of change also needs to increase, not least to demonstrate to the public that the service is serious about managing integrity issues, which have retained a high media profile over the last year'[1]

So, at least as far as the media was concerned they found 'no evidence of endemic corruption' in relation to media relationships. Had HMIC been briefed to explore improper police/public relationships one wonders whether they would have delved into some of the public's complaints about the integrity of the police. Each PSD/DPS would likely have had plenty of material for the inspectors to consider and it can be suspected the answer might have been very different. Another day perhaps.

Since we have been looking with particular interest at the Met, I should quote the press-release by HMIC for the national team, Stephen Otter QPM:

The Metropolitan Police Service has made some improvements to how it identifies, monitors and manages integrity issues since HMIC last reviewed this in 2011 ... This reflects our findings across the whole of England and Wales, where we found that the police service is making progress in how it monitors and

---

1. The full report, including the specifics re individual police forces can be read at http://www.justiceinspectorates.gov.uk/hmic/inspections/review-police-service-integrity

safeguards relationships with the media, contractors and others. However, we are concerned that changes have not been implemented at a quicker pace. HMIC will therefore continue to monitor and inspect progress in order to provide the public with assurance that all forces are gripping these vital issues.

Again it would be interesting to know what, if anything at all, was said to the more sluggish chief constables by the inspectorate, Home Office and indeed the relevant police and crime commissioners.

It is good to know that there are concerns about police integrity and police relationships with the media but, as much as HMIC's and the Home Secretary's thinking deserves respect, the impression seems to have been left that this approach is not going to crack the problem of police fairness and malpractice. The relationship with citizens is far more difficult to monitor, particularly as long as there is no effective policing of police forces. HMIC can report and recommend on systems and maybe improve media relationships but this will do little or nothing to ensure ordinary members of the public are dealt with properly, equitably and with respect. Nor will these steps lift the confidence of the public in basic police fairness and integrity.

No doubt in an effort to reassure the public about the Met's current integrity, DCS Bonthron, head of its Department of Professional Standards, met with *The Independent's* reporter Tom Harper early in 2014. Writing in that newspaper on 19th January 2014, Harper gave an exclusive report following that meeting under the heading 'Police corruption cannot be eliminated admits head of special Met unit.'[2]

According to Bonthron, corruption inside law enforcement agencies is impossible to eliminate and the threat of organized crime infiltrating the force 'very challenging', although he denied corruption was endemic. Concerns raised by Operation Tiberius disclosed that some of Britain's most notorious crime syndicates were able to infiltrate the Met 'at will', leading to compromised murder investigations, leaks of intelligence and covert informants being identified. Harper quoted Bonthron as admitting that there will 'always be vulnerabilities when you have people in systems', but he had also

2.   The full report is at http://www.independent.co.uk/news/uk/crime/
     exclusive-police-corruption-cannot-be-eliminated-admits-head-of-specialmet-unit-
     following-independent-stories-9070682.html

claimed that Metropolitan Commissioner of Police, Sir Bernard Hogan-Howe, took corruption 'very seriously' saying 'We work very closely with other agencies ... whether it's a big HMRC job or ... the CPS feeling they are vulnerable.'

The following is a telling sample of other responses extracted by Harper:

- 'Organized crime by its very nature is very challenging. Has corruption gone away entirely? I don't think it has; you have always got vulnerabilities. Part of our role is to make sure the organization is absolutely doing the best it can to be corruption-proof.'
- 'We have had April Casburn[3] and we've got other cases coming through on that, and I publish the outcome of our disciplinary findings on the internet for the public to read.'
- 'If we have got something to go after criminally, we will go after it. It's not about being embarrassed. Look at Operation Alice about Plebgate (see *Chapter 9*), that was a full-scale operation that involved taking thousands of statements and working it through ... Earlier this month PC Keith Wallis pleaded guilty to misconduct in a public office after he fabricated an email, claiming to be from a member of the public who witnessed ... Andrew Mitchell insulting police officers during a row at the gates of Downing Street.'[4]
- 'The Met's DPS has 385 staff and spends £24m annually—around 0.7 per cent of the Met's total £3.3bn budget.'
- 'I am not saying we are completely free [of such things as interference by organized crime] but I think ... there are lots of checks-and-balances in place ... The organization is more robust.'
- 'Whatever action was taken [when some individuals were not prosecuted] ... a number ... went to court and were acquitted. But if you are going after them and ... not getting the evidence, the intelligence ... then you can't put them before a court.'

---

3. The first person to be prosecuted as part of the investigation into payments by journalists to public officials. A detective chief inspector, she was jailed for 15 months.
4. See *Chapter 9*.

- 'Historically, if you look globally at organized crime networks, they are a professional group. It's their job... It's about us getting into them and taking them apart.'

Operation Tiberius also details how corrupt former officers who understand the criminal justice system often left the force for paid employment with organized crime syndicates, helping them avoid prosecution (*Chapter 14*). But according to Bonthron:

- You can research anything on the internet, watch TV shows. Some of these are very accurate and people will think, 'I won't do this and I won't do that.' The criminal justice system is much more open than it was, but there will always be vulnerabilities.
- Sir Bernard Hogan-Howe has made corruption one of his key priorities and times have changed dramatically since the 1980s when police officers were allowed to retire on ill-health grounds rather than 'face the music... You can't resign if you are suspended. If you get served a notice that you are under investigation, you can resign before you are suspended.'
- The Met's investigation into the death of Daniel Morgan (a private detective found in a south London car park with an axe in his skull in 1987 amid claims he was about to blow the whistle on Met/organized crime links) was not up for discussion because of a Home Office, judge-led inquiry but was a significant case for the Met and due process. 'Everyone wants to know what happened.'
- The vast majority of Met staff find it deeply depressing when allegations of corruption emerge. Some 99.9 per cent 'are honest, law-abiding individuals and find it abhorrent and are absolutely appalled... One officer, one member of staff, headline news... and it discredits the organization'.

What did the Met say in 2002 for Operation Tiberius (*Chapter 14*) and countless times thereafter—that there is/was no corruption or that it is/was one individual? So it's not surprising to hear that the vast majority of the Met 'are honest, law-abiding individuals and find it abhorrent and are absolutely appalled' and that we all hope is true. I have gone to some length to protect, victims, perpetrators and some police forces from identification, but nevertheless rest assured that the Met heads up the police forces where contributors have recounted unacceptable 'goings-on', some seemingly over-looked by higher ranking officers. The spin is unconvincing, so well done and thanks (again) in particular to Tom Harper of *The Independent*.

Comment

It *is* unlikely that police corruption can be eliminated, literally speaking, but we could and should set zero as a target and recognise that '[If] the patient is sick first recognise the illness' in order to find a cure. Police forces need vigorous policing and standards need to be set far higher than those of today's IPCC. If an ordinary citizen is arrested for, say, shoplifting he or she can't resign the moment they become aware that the police are investi-gating. Perhaps it would help bring about justice if all the loopholes to police 'facing the music' were closed off so that retired, resigned, even sick officers are pursued. Rather than the situation as described by Bonthron, 'You can't resign if you are suspended', if you get served a notice that you are under investigation, you can resign before you are suspended. What a crazy system!

CHAPTER 16

It Doesn't End There

This brief chapter is intended to act as an introduction to later parts of the book which seek to provide a wider background against which the detail in *Part 1* can be set.

Part 2 deals with aspects of the pre-court or 'front end' of the criminal justice system together with references to further information.

Appendix 1 describes the system itself whilst *Appendix 2,* which is styled 'Further Examples of Causes for Concern: No Smoke Without Fire' contains a note of further instances of injustice, incompetence, malpractice or worse that I happened upon during the time I was researching this book. They were to numerous and detailed to include within the book itself without distracting from the narrative and typically do not involve items known to me personally. I have provided web links for those readers wishing to pursue them. I would add that any internet search is likely to provide similar reports or records using just a few key search terms around police discipline, integrity, claims or enquiries.

One person whose work has been to reinforce what I am saying is Paul Woods who maintains a website dedicated to charting prosecutions of and disciplinary proceedings against police, prison and court personnel who have been charged, convicted or proceeded against. He began his list in 2009 and I am grateful to him for allowing me to use it for reference purposes. It includes developments so far as these can be traced (which is sometimes difficult due in part to the often 'hidden' nature of police disciplinary proceedings and outcomes), but cannot always track those police officers or other public servants who retired or resigned to avoid disciplinary or other. It does of course include data from cases which do hit the headlines.[1]

Again, as I explain in the *Preface* my own reasons for changing some names of people, places and locations is that I have not set out to 'point the

---

1. See http://info.fmotl.com/PoliceListV27.pdf (last accessed 15 February 2015). The list is the copyright property and responsibility of Paul Woods rather than the author of this work.

finger' at individuals or to cause additional distress in what for them must be sensitive situations, but to emphasise, whatever the good points about our police forces, the sheer scale of the problem of police integrity and the apparent lack of will to do anything really constructive about it. These are the guardians of the law: what being able to compile such a comprehensive list as Paul has done demonstrates is how fragile that guardianship can be in certain instances.

Anyone with a genuine reason in discovering the underlying details in relation to anything included in the book, such as researchers or other *bone fide* enquirers, is welcome to contact me via the publishers when I can consider this and speak with the individuals concerned as it is largely their choice whether to share their experiences further.

PART 2

The System:
Some Strengths, Many Weaknesses

CHAPTER 17

Crime Statistics

There are two sets of official *Crime Statistics* produced and published annually. There are considerable discrepancies between them that gives rise to concern but, at least currently, they are congruent, both showing a reduction in crime albeit from widely differing base figures. However, because of the variations and methodology both are of questionable accuracy and neither is comforting or satisfactory. We will explore both in turn, starting with the Office of National Statistics' (ONS's) *Crime Survey of England and Wales* (CSEW). These may well be the more accurate and are certainly incurring less controversy than the heavily criticised Home Office/police generated figures. Whatever the reasons, these figures (which we will look at later) are likely to under-record the extent of actual crime because they amalgamate police recorded crime. No report, no record, no inclusion in the statistics. However, when looking at year-on-year comparisons, the statistics may well provide a reasonably accurate guide to the trend in crime rates.

The Crime Survey of England and Wales

This numerically more alarming survey by the ONS works on a different basis. It asks a sample of households across the country about their experiences of, attitudes to and perceptions of a range of crimes.

Also known as a 'victimisation survey', the sample is then extrapolated to generate overall crime estimates and attitudes across the UK. Some 46,000 interviews were conducted in 2011/12 but the sample size was reduced in 2012/13 when 35,000 adults contributed. The ONS says that it ensured a minimum of 650 adult interviews were conducted in each police force area. Additionally, about 3,000 ten-to-15-year-olds were interviewed (down from the previous 4,000).

The ONS survey tells us there were 26.4 million households in the UK in 2012. Of these, 29 per cent consisted of one person and about 20 per cent of four or more people. Thus to attend 46,000 homes (2011/12 figure) represents 0.17 per cent of households, seemingly a relatively small sample, but to reduce (by the best part of 25 per cent) the interviews to 35,000 (0.13 per cent) in 2013 appears to my untutored mind to be questionable, particularly since there is such a significant variation with the police figures. Since a CSEW respondent's information is taken at face value I would have felt more comfortable with a larger rather than smaller sample to reduce the multiplier effect of any interview misunderstandings.

The CSEW is a face-to-face survey in which people resident in households in England and Wales are asked about their experiences of crime in the 12 months prior to being interviewed. If they experienced crime, they are asked about the details, whether or not they reported any incidents to the police. The ONS considers the CSEW provides a more reliable measure of trends in crime than police recorded crime statistics as it maintains a consistent methodology and is unaffected by changes in levels of reporting to the police, recording practice or police activity (or inactivity). But it stresses that its CSEW estimates and police recorded figures should be seen as complementary, jointly providing a better picture of crime than could be obtained from either survey in isolation.

The CSEW findings for the year ending June 2013 do indeed provide an interesting comparison. Their key points are listed below with acknowledgement and thanks.[1] However, the headline figures for 2012/13 estimate 8.5 million offences (including 200,000 frauds but excluding 800,000 crimes against children). Falling crime figures are also a feature reported in the *Office for National Statistics Bulletin* for 2013 — being down by seven per cent. The key points are:

- an estimated 8.5 million crimes were experienced by households and resident adults in the previous 12 months, based on interviews with a nationally representative sample in the year ending June 2013. In addition, the CSEW estimated that there were 0.8 million crimes experienced by children aged ten-to-15 resident in the household population;
- the headline estimate for crimes against households and resident adults was down seven per cent compared with the previous year's

---

1.   The full survey can be viewed at http://www.ons.gov.uk/ons/dcp171778_331209.pdf

survey, the lowest over the history of the survey, which began in 1981, and is now less than half its peak level in 1995;

- the police recorded 3.7 million offences in the year ending June 2013, a decrease of five per cent compared with the previous year. This is the lowest comparative level since 2002/03 when the National Crime Recording Standard was introduced to bring greater consistency to crime recording;
- victim-based crime accounted for 83 per cent of all police recorded crime (3.1 million offences) and fell by six per cent in the year ending June 2013 compared with the previous year;
- other crimes against society recorded by the police (400,156) showed a decrease of eight per cent on the previous year;
- in the year ending June 2013, 230,335 fraud offences were recorded. This represents a volume increase of 21 per cent compared with the previous year and should be seen in the context of a move towards the centralised recording of fraud by the police;
- within victim-based crime, there were decreases across all main categories of recorded crime as against the previous year, except for theft from the person (up eight per cent), shoplifting (up one per cent) and sexual offences (up nine per cent). The latter increase is thought to be partly a 'Yewtree effect',[2] whereby more victims came forward to report historical sexual offences; and
- there were an additional one million offences dealt with by the courts in the year ending March 2013 (the latest period for which data are available), which are not included in the police recorded crime figures. These cover less serious crimes, such as speeding, which are dealt with no higher than in the magistrate's courts.

---

2.   Operation Yewtree.

Home Office Figures[3]

The headline figures recorded by the police for 2012/13 is 3.5million offences (excluding fraud). Reductions in crime are indeed recorded in the Home Office *Statistical Bulletin* for 2013, down by six per cent. While these figures may appear to be good news for politicians, the public and police forces alike, in fact they encourage crime if the reductions are in part due to under-reporting.

Unfortunately, since April 2011, police forces in England and Wales have moved away from recording fraud offences as a result of the implementation of Action Fraud as a single national fraud-reporting centre. While forces continue to investigate frauds following this change, they do so only in those cases referred to them by Action Fraud. Furthermore, data is not yet available on how many of these crimes are detected. By the end of March 2013 all 43 territorial police forces in England and Wales and the British Transport Police had transferred the recording of these offences to Action Fraud.

Therefore, to preserve consistency between the Home Office statistics and the ONS *Crime Statistics*, fraud figures have been excluded from the Home Office headline detections total. One wonders whether *either* set of crime figures is keeping pace with technology. There is growing digital activity facilitating ease of access to and dispersal of 'low-cost' goods. In some cases the goods may be stolen or non-existent but with minimal redress, police knowledge or record. Further as appears from some of the contributions in *Part 1* of this book, police forces manage their workloads by screening-out/ ignoring some reported, so-called minor, crimes or declaring them 'civil' offences and therefore outside the police remit, or by non-attendance or declaring something to be 'an incident' not a crime or by changing the name from a recordable to reportable crime. In short, there is a lot of room for reducing the true crime figures, which collectively across 43 police forces rather changes the Home Office figures.

Whatever police miss-reporting/corruption takes place, many crimes do

---

3. The crimes detected in England and Wales 2012/13 (2nd edition) as recorded by the Home Office can be studied in detail at https://www.gov.uk/government/uploads/system/uploads/ attachment_data/file/224037/hosb0213.pdf *Statistical Bulletins* are prepared under the National Statistics Code of Practice.

not seem minor to victims, but nevertheless the message is fairly clear — if the police take their time (one contributor spoke of three weeks) in getting to a crime scene, or declare it 'civil', or simply walk away from it, this screens-out and excludes it from the Home Office statistics.[4] Thus Home Office figures tend to under-record crime. We see confirmation of that possibility in *Chapters 18* and *23* ('Her Majesty's Inspector of Constabulary' and 'Police and Crime Commissioners', respectively) when HMIC investigated Kent's accuracy and methodology and found the figures inaccurate. Consequently, the computer cliché 'rubbish in-rubbish out' is brought to mind when weighing up the validity of the police/Home Office figures. Furthermore, could this be the start of an ever-tightening circle whereby the reported crime statistics appear to be reducing so government feels reductions in policing costs are not unreasonable, so the police take a few extra short-cuts, so fewer citizens bother to report crimes because they know nothing will be done, further depressing the statistics, which not only tightens the circle of crime but worse still criminals become even more embolden by the fact that they stand an ever-increasing chance of 'getting away with it'.

Mark Wallace writing for 'Conservative Home' on 16th January 2014 tells us that police crime statistics are fiddled.[5] He recounts one example, but with wider implications (and from an impeccable correspondent)(paraphrased):

> Climbing from her car for a few seconds to access a pay-and-display machine, she returned to find her handbag gone from the passenger seat. Obviously stolen, she reported it to the police, who said it couldn't be registered as a crime as she hadn't actually seen someone take it. The police explained that she couldn't have a crime number, but an incident number if needed for insurance purposes.

> Later that day, a Good Samaritan phoned her — they had found her handbag, emptied of cash and bank cards, while retrieving their football from shrubs in the park. With the evidence that she had been robbed, and that her bag hadn't walked off under its own steam, she rang the police again. OK, they conceded,

4. In that event I urge you to write a letter of complaint to your local police, copy to the IPCC, the relevant Police and Crime Commissioner (PCC) and the Home Secretary.
5. See http://www.conservativehome.com/thetorydiary/2014/01/an-overdue-confession-the-police-crime-statistics-are-fiddled.html

it was a crime but gave her a crime number for her street, one used for all the residents there rather using a new one each time something happened, thus saving on paperwork.

The process was clear—if possible, the police refuse to register crimes as having occurred. If the proof is indisputable, then they register them all under a number for the whole street—thus keeping the official statistics down.

This happened about ten years ago, so the process may well have changed since. But it is a *telling* example of how unreliable police statistics *can be*, and *as Wallace describes it* 'of some forces' willingness to manipulate the numbers'. It's good news that these failings are finally being confessed and confronted—for too long officialdom has been content to live a statistical lie, and to allow some parts of the police to operate in a manner which is essentially dishonest. Importantly, contrary to some media reports, this doesn't affect the fact that crime in the UK is *going* down. The *British Crime Survey* (forerunner of the *Crime Survey of England and Wales*), which in no way relies on such flawed police data-gathering methods and was set up specifically to bypass them, independently confirms this.

Then there are the differences between reported and recorded crime. The Home Office could iron out that subtle nuisance if it wished because a reported crime should become a recorded crime and not be influenced by what a police force is focused upon for the time being. Furthermore, those current differences can be multiplied by how the Home Office National Crime Recording Standards are interrupted by each force, by their actual recording practices and the efficiency of any audit that may or may not take place. The auditing should be external and take into account the number of letters of complaint recorded by the public (hence the importance of the public writing, writing and writing). There will always be areas for uncertainty, but never the under-recording of crime. It is perhaps a matter of opinion as to whether a case is in reality actual or grievous bodily harm, whether a fraud has been committed at the perpetrator's or victim's address or when domestic violence may or may not have taken place. In these 'grey' areas a police and crime commissioner (*Chapter 23*) can do much to earn public respect, even gratitude by calling the police's attention to their responsibilities if he or she receives relevant correspondence/information.

However, while many people are disinclined, I believe that it is every citizen's duty to report crime and again in my view they should have the right to insist that the police record and investigate each such report in the absence of a thoroughly valid explanation. The police will, of course, respond with pleas of 'cutbacks' or 'inadequate resources', but if we look at our small cross-section of contributions in *Part 1* there are not only non-attendances or protracted attendances and 'civil matter' excuses but examples of *gross* over-reaction, inordinately extended investigations and wasted resources that the police can still mount even with their reduced and supposedly meagre resources ... if they have a mind!

Most damning of all in relation to Home Office crime-recording is the written evidence, prepared 1st February 2013 that Dr Rodger Patrick, a retired detective chief inspector, presented to the HAC listing methods by which police altered the Home Office recorded crime figures. He also claimed that these methods are tacitly approved of by senior police officers, watchdogs and the Home Office itself! Dr Patrick's report lists several real examples of police dishonesty in each category but, in my view, as shocking as these admissions are, they do not cover the full extent of this form of police corruption. In fact I am not only disappointed that the report falls short in this respect but also in the euphemistic phraseology used (how else can one describe police altering numbers but as corruption). The extracts from the Executive Summary below include an explanation of the four categories identified and some worrying but perhaps unsurprising conclusions (paraphrased).[6]

> The research into the impact of Performance Management on the Police Service indicated that 'gaming' behaviours i.e. 'cooking the books' or 'fiddling the figures' was negating the potential benefits of the reform programme. The findings based on analysis of the performance data and official documents suggest the phenomenon is organizational in nature. It was also evident that the malpractice was managerially driven in a 'top down' fashion and had spread as a result of ineffective regulation and governance. Establishing the evidence for this assertion

---

6. The extracts contain Parliamentary information reproduced under the Open Parliament Licence v1.0. The full can be found at http://www.publications.parliament.uk/pa/cm201213/cmselect/cmhaff/494/494vw03.htm

involved the examination of a number of investigations carried out by the IPCC into incidents involving 'gaming' type behaviours. It was clear from the review of these investigations that the IPCC were unable or unwilling to identify and address the organizational deficiencies or hold chief officers responsible..

1. Categories of Police 'Gaming' Practices...

Cuffing: Under-recording of reported crimes, the term being derived from the magician's art of making objects disappear up the sleeve or cuff (Young, 1991).[7]

Nodding: Involving collusion between officers and suspects to confess to large numbers of offences, usually whilst in prison after sentence, in return for favours such as reduced sentences, access to partners, drugs or alcohol. The term is used to describe the act of a prisoner pointing out or 'nodding' at locations where they claim to have committed offences (Wilson *et al*, 2001, 63).[8]

Skewing: Involving moving resources from areas of activity not subject to performance measures in order to improve performance in areas monitored for control purposes (Rogerson, 1995).[9]

Stitching: Including a variety of malpractices designed to enhance the strength of evidence against a suspect in order to ensure the desired criminal justice outcome. Fabricating evidence or stitching someone up are forms of this behaviour.

In conclusion the report states that the IPCC appears unwilling or unable to identify the organizational nature of certain types of behaviours referred to it for investigation which enables senior officers, ultimately responsible for the standards their officers subscribe to, to avoid being held to account. 'However this criticism can also be levelled at all the bodies entrusted with the regulation and governance of the police suggesting that a wider ranging

---

7. Young, M (1991), *An Inside Job. Policing and Police Culture in Britain*, Oxford: Clarendon Press.
8. Wilson, D, Ashton, J, and Sharp, D (2001), *What Everyone in Britain Should Know About the Police*, London: Blackstone.
9. Rogerson, P (1995), 'Performance Measurement and Policing: Police Service or Law Enforcement Agency?', *Public Money & Management*, October-December 1995.

inquiry and more radical reform are required'.[10]

In its recommendations, it concludes that

> [C]loser external scrutiny of IPCC investigations is necessary and investigators
> need to be made aware of the organizational factors which manifest themselves
> in complaints, i.e. they are symptoms. In such cases the introduction of police
> commissioners, with the power to hold chief officers to account, could provide a
> conduit for their findings. The appointment of a non-police Chief HMIC and
> closer collaboration with the IPCC could also make the skills required to inves-
> tigate organizational failings more available to the IPCC. Legislative powers for
> investigating officers and sanctions penalising those who fail to disclose relevant
> information or obstruct investigations would reduce the reliance on the support
> of chief officers. Closer collaboration between the IPCC and the Police Federa-
> tion ... could help in the early identification of concerning organizational trends.
> Better protection for 'whistle-blowers' should also be provided ... The ACPO
> proposal to restrict the provisions of the FOI Act should be rejected.

Alan Travis of *The Guardian,* comparing the two methods for gathering
statistics, commented that.[11]

> The gold-standard 'national statistics' status has been withdrawn from police
> recorded crime figures following repeated allegations that some of the quarterly
> published figures have been subject to 'a degree of fiddling' ... The UK Statistics
> Authority said it had taken the decision as a result of 'accumulating evidence' that
> the underlying data on crimes recorded by the police may be unreliable.

He went on to say that this followed concerns over the integrity of the
police crime figures raised by the Commons Home Affairs and Public
Administration Select Committees and statements by HM Chief Inspector
of Constabulary, Tom Winsor (even though he had ruled out 'institutional
corruption' lying behind inaccurate recording). He explained:

---

10. See http://www.publications.parliament.uk/pa/cm201213/cmselect/cmhaff/494/494vw03.htm
11. *The Guardian* 15th January 2014, UK Statistics Authority withdraws gold-standard status
    from police figures, pointing to 'accumulating evidence' of unreliability'. See http://www.
    theguardian.com/uk-news/2014/jan/15/police-crime-figures-status-claims-fiddling

[P]olice recorded crime figures, which date back to the 19th century, are one of the two major measures of crime in England and Wales. The second yardstick, the *Crime Survey for England and Wales*, which dates back to 1981, is unaffected by the allegations and has consistently shown a fall in crime since 1995.

The Statistics Authority said the removal of the designation of national statistics would remain until the ONS, working with the Home Office, Her Majesty's Inspectorate of Constabulary and others, was able to demonstrate that the quality of the underlying crime data was sufficient to meet the needs of users.

[A]llegations have included claims that the Metropolitan police have understated sexual offences by as much as 25%. MPs have heard allegations that fiddling techniques have included downgrading offences to less serious crimes or persuading victims not to make a complaint, while in some cases crimes were only recorded if they were solved. Other incidents were kept completely off the books if an offender could not be traced, they have been told.

The inaccuracy of the Home Office figures has been endorsed by the Public Administration Select Committee (PASC) aided by a courageous police whistle-blower, as mentioned previously, that produced a damning report dated 9th April 2014 entitled 'Caught Red-handed: Why We Can't Count on Police Recorded Crime Statistics'.[12] I quote key extracts from the report (my précis).[13]

The chair of PASC was contacted by a serving police officer, PC James Patrick, acting as a whistle-blower, who had serious concerns about the validity of crime statistics. We are indebted to PC Patrick for his courage in speaking out, in fulfilment of his duty to the highest standards of public service, despite intense pressures to the contrary.

The introduction of the NCRS led to an immediate structural increase in the number of crimes recorded in the first two years of its implementation (2002–03

---

12. The full report can be read at http://www.publications.parliament.uk/pa/cm201314/cmselect/cmpubadm/760/76002.htm
13. This includes Parliamentary information licensed under the Open Parliament Licence v1.0

and 2003–04). Since this initial bedding-in phase, overall recorded crime levels have fallen in every subsequent year, at a faster rate that the CSEW suggests is credible.

There will be inevitable changes over time in how people report crime — what an independent review of crime statistics, written for the Home Secretary in 2006, called 'unknown and uncontrollable variability in the public's reporting of crime to the police'.

However, we have seen an accumulation of substantial and credible evidence — based on statistical analysis and on authoritative testimony from current and former police officers — indicating that:

- the PRC data does not correctly represent the rate of decrease in crime or the composition of crime;
- the erosion of police compliance with the agreed national standards of victim-focused crime recording has contributed to this; and
- monitoring and audit arrangements have been insufficient to ensure acceptable standards of data quality and integrity.

The consequential HMIC investigation is even more enlightening. Their *interim* report published 1st May 2014 confirms this statistical inaccuracy.[14] In summary it concluded that 13 of the largest police forces who collectively report 60 per cent of annual recorded crime, were failing to record 20 per cent of that crime. Thus about three-quarters of a million offences a year go unrecorded which in itself undermines Home Office statistics. Amongst the unrecorded crimes revealed were 14 cases of rape. HMIC's final report dated November 2014 has 33 paragraphs.[15] I have selected a small number of key points:

- Victims of crime are being let down. The police are failing to record a large proportion of the crimes reported to them. Over 800,000 crimes reported to the police have gone unrecorded

---

14. It can be read in full at http://www.hmic.gov.uk/wp-content/uploads/2014/05/crime-data-integrity-interim-report.pdf
15. For the report, see http://www.justiceinspectorates.gov.uk/hmic/wp-content/uploads/crime-recording-making-the-victim-count.pdf

each year. This represents an under-recording of 19 per cent. The problem is greatest for victims of violence against the person and sexual offences, where the under-recording rates are 33 per cent and 26 per cent respectively. This failure to record such a significant proportion of reported crime is wholly unacceptable.

- The position in the case of rape and other sexual offences is a matter of especially serious concern. The inspection found 37 cases of rape which were not recorded as crimes. The national rate of under-recording of sexual offences (including rapes) as crimes was 26 per cent, and the national rate of incorrect decisions to no-crime rapes was 20 per cent. In the case of rape no-crime decisions, in 22 per cent of cases there was no evidence that the police informed the complainant of their decision. These are wholly unacceptable failings.
- Even when crimes are correctly recorded, too many are removed or cancelled as recorded crimes for no good reason. Of the 3,246 decisions to cancel, or no-crime, a crime record that we reviewed, 664 were incorrect. These included over 200 rapes and more than 250 crimes of violence against the person. Offenders who should be being pursued by the police for these crimes are not being brought to justice and their victims are denied services to which they are entitled.
- In over 800 of the 3,246 decisions we reviewed, we could find no evidence that the victim was told of the decision to no-crime their report. Victims may be under the impression that their crimes continue to be recorded and investigated when they are not.

HMIC's inspection of crime data integrity intends to identify to what extent police recorded crime information can be trusted. The interim report was based on inspections carried out in 13 police forces and sets out emerging themes. The existing report looked at how the Home Office Counting Rules (HOCR) and National Crime Recording Standard (NCRS) are used—identifying serious concerns The report deals with a number of these: poor knowledge of the HOCR and NCRS, poor training, supervision or management and the pressures of workload, including overload.

That the Home Office/police 'statistics' are unreliable is now generally known, viz various news reports.[16] However, Peter Fahy, Chief Constable of Greater Manchester has been quoted as saying that it was not about 'fiddling' figures, but the way forces chose to categorise various types of offence due to a 'huge field of interpretation'.

Comment

In summary I conclude that the Home Office figures appear no better than an exercise in collating valueless information that few people believe in. I wonder how many police officers and Home Office staff would be released for more pro-active work were the figures dropped and we relied on the *Crime Survey for England and Wales*, although I would be more comfortable if CSEW could find a way to increase the size of their sample back to pre-cut levels and also to obtain some confirmation of their information particularly if they were to become the sole measure of crime levels.

---

16. See, e.g. http://www.bbc.com/news/uk-25022680

CHAPTER 18

HM Inspectorate of Constabulary

Her Majesty's Inspectorate of Constabulary (HMIC) inspects and monitors the 43 territorial police forces in England and Wales, sometimes referred to as Home Office-funded forces. HMIC has statutory powers to inspect and report on the efficiency and effectiveness of these police forces but only as an inspectorate, not a regulator. Regulatory authorities have powers of direction and intervention but inspectorates are unable to direct or to intervene.

It is for police and crime commissioners (PCCs) and the Home Secretary, as appropriate, to decide in the light of HMIC's conclusions and recommendations whether, and to what extent these should be the subject of their own powers of intervention. And therein may lie a problem — HMIC findings are, basically, to use my terminology *advisory*, as in essence are those of PCCs. If a chief constable doesn't concur with their opinions or chooses to ignore them, in the end only the Home Secretary can do anything about it.

But let's start with the basics. How many ordinary citizen's have heard of or know much about HMIC and the work it does? I'd not heard a great deal about it either until I started my research for this book. To the man in the street, HMIC seems to hide its light under the proverbial bushel. However, that is not a deliberate policy because when it does interface with others it makes a good job of its publicity, explanations and spin (paraphrased):

> Our core role is summarised in our statement of purpose:
> - Through inspecting, monitoring and advising, to promote and advance improvements in the efficiency and effectiveness of policing. We will do this independently, professionally and fairly, always championing the public interest, and we will explain what we do and why.
> - Inspecting policing in the public interest. The public want the police to succeed in their mission to keep people safe and secure. It is in the public interest that the quality of policing in England, Wales and Northern Ireland keeps improving.

- At HMIC, we monitor and report on forces and policing activity with the aim of encouraging improvement.
- By providing accessible information on the performance of forces, we allow their public, and peers, to see how they are doing. This will place pressure on those forces falling below average in aspects of policing to raise their game.
- We will always try to see policing through the public's eyes. We will use consumer 'watchdog' tactics, such as mystery shopping, and ask the public, in surveys, what they think about policing and where they want improvements.
- Our reports will be clear, jargon-free and designed to be accessible, measured, objective, statistically reliable and authoritative.
- We also continue to provide high-quality professional advice to police — using experienced officers and other experts, such as lawyers and accountants to identify the 'best practice', which all forces can aspire to. We will encourage operational excellence and, increasingly, a good deal for the public in terms of value for money.
- We carry out many force inspections and regulatory visits each week, through our network of regional offices, and publish our findings [at our website].[1] Our reports on broad policing themes and specific subjects — from terrorism and serious organized crime to custody arrangements — can all be found in the publications section.
- Much of our work relates to the mainstream police forces in England and Wales, together with the Police Service of Northern Ireland and British Transport Police. However, we also inspect other law enforcement agencies, including the Serious Organized Crime Agency[2] and HMRC.

Yes, HMIC sounds as if it is the body to ensure the police keep within the law and do their job honestly and effectively. And you'll be even more impressed with the publications section of HMIC's website (above) and its paper 'HMIC's Approach to Monitoring Forces: An Overview for the Public, Forces and Local Policing Bodies: September 2013'. Like me, you'll be surprised at the work they do behind the scenes — yet we still have the police forces we have.

---

1. www.hmic.gov.uk
2. See the note to the List of Acronyms at the start of this book.

So does more need to be done or is it that the approach needs to change? Perhaps local offices get too close to 'their' police forces, HMIC are asking the wrong questions, or the wrong people, or is there too much emphasis on efficiency? Do HMIC address the question of integrity sufficiently robustly, or is their publicity machine better than their performance or effect?

In an open FOI exchange in June 2013, it is worrying that only one member of the public (plus two police officers) contributed apart from the disaffected questioner! I hope that more than four people read this chapter and that most would like to see what Thomas P Winsor, HMIC wrote as the forward to his second consultation document entitled '2014/15: A Transition Year For HMIC's Inspection Programme':[3]

> The changes to policing in England and Wales over the last few years—which include the creation of police and crime commissioners, the College of Policing and the National Crime Agency; wide-ranging alterations to police terms and conditions; and huge advancement in the use of technology, by both offenders and officers—collectively amount to perhaps the greatest reforms to the service for many decades.
>
> Over the same period, the expectations of the average person on the street in relation to the amount and immediacy of the data about public services available to him or her have also changed radically. The public are accessing more information, through more channels, more quickly and easily than ever before.
>
> As the body responsible for inspecting and reporting on the efficiency and effectiveness of policing in England and Wales in the public interest, it is imperative that HMIC responds to and keeps pace with these changes. As a result, 2014/15 will see some major changes both to the scope and pattern of HMIC inspections, and to how we communicate the results of this work to the public.
>
> Perhaps the most prominent of these changes will be the introduction of a new, annual programme of all-force inspections (announced by the Home Office in a Written Ministerial Statement laid on Wednesday 18 December 2013). The

---

3. See http://www.hmic.gov.uk/wp-content/uploads/2014/01/hmic-inspection-programme-consultation-2014-2015.pdf

intention is that this programme will first report in its entirety in autumn 2015; however, fieldwork will begin in late summer 2014, and we will provide an interim assessment this November (more details on this are given on p.7).[4]

HMIC will develop and implement this programme alongside conducting our national thematic inspections (which in the last year have reported on and encouraged improvement in such vital areas as the use of stop and search powers, police integrity and how forces are meeting the demands of austerity), joint inspections, commissions from the Home Secretary and local policing bodies, and inspections of other national law enforcement agencies. This represents a huge amount of change and work in 2014/15, which will be a year of transition for HMIC.

To reflect this change, this consultation document is different to those issued in previous years. It contains an overview of all the inspections either continuing or already committed to over the period, but focuses consultation questions on two areas: a list of proposed new thematic inspections; and some specific areas of the all-force inspection programme (which will be the subject of much more consultation as work on its development continues).

As ever, my fellow HMIC board members and I thank you for your interest in reading about our proposed inspections, and for the invaluable input which your consultation responses have in formulating and developing our plans.

It is also surprising to learn the size of HMIC. In a FOI exchange, dated November 2013, the enquirer asked:

In my email of 9th October there is a description of HMIC staff structure of permanent core posts (civil servants) and flexible posts, often flexible and fee paid police officers. Please disclose, as of 15th October 2013, how many people are employed as permanent core posts and their individual paid hours per week. Please disclose, as of 15th October 2013, how many people are employed as flexible posts and their status as police (and confirm rank), police civilian, or non-police.

HMIC replied:

---

4. Author's note: i.e. p.7 of the consultation document.

With effect 15 October 2013 there were 74 staff in HMIC employed on a permanent or fixed term contract basis. Full-time staff are contracted to work 41 hours per week gross (that is, 36 hours per week excluding breaks) if their normal place of work is in London, or 42 hours per week gross (that is, 37 hours per week excluding breaks) if their normal place of work is elsewhere.

With effect 15 October 2013 there were 53 staff on secondment to HMIC from outside organizations. The majority of these secondments (50) were police officers, 2 were police staff and 1 was from a Government Department. With effect 15 October 2013 the majority of police officer secondments to HMIC were at Chief Inspector (15), Superintendent (21) or Chief Superintendent (9) ranks in addition to Detective Sergeant (1), Inspector (2) and Deputy Assistant Commissioner (2).

So we've got 127 people working in the public interest to assess police forces for their performances with neighbourhood policing, serious crime and in the fight against terrorism. HMIC prepares reports asking the questions that a citizen would ask and answers in accessible form, using its expertise to interpret the evidence. Furthermore it provides authoritative information allowing performance comparisons between forces to be made and uses its evidence to drive improvements in the service to the public. Couldn't apparently be better but it leaves unresolved the questions I alluded to earlier: why do we have so many outstanding questions about police performance, mistakes and integrity. And why does HMIC not report speaking to the public, nor have I heard anyone say, 'Do you know what, an HMIC inspector knocked at the door and asked me about the local cops'?

In fact, from reading some of the HMIC reports I conclude that it is solely talking to police officers and staff, who may indeed have grievances, but in the scheme of things these people are not likely to blow the whistle on some colleagues' major errors, dishonesty or management incompetence. Certainly HMIC finds shortcomings and recommends corrections and, while this work is important, it mainly gives the inspected department a thumbs-up which brings me to suggest that too much of HMIC's available resources are focused on routine inspections. Exceptions, repetitious problems, integrity issues and input from outside the police force should provide greater content.

HMIC does carry out special checks and reports at the behest of the
Home Secretary and PCCs. These are generally impressive and one particularly caught my attention in view of my scepticism about the accuracy of
police reported crime (see *Chapter 17*). Kent's PCC requested HMIC to
check the police crime recording in Kent, which was indeed found wanting.
Disappointingly, I did not see any follow-up reports on other police forces
reporting methods and accuracy but thought HMIC's Kent report was so
good it was worth providing a brief summary here.

The culture in Kent Police and its effect on crime recording practices

The April 2013 inspection identified that a target-driven culture had in the past
led to some officers in Kent pursuing crimes on the basis of how easy they were
to solve, rather than on their seriousness or impact on victims and communities.
The force had already identified some of these issues through its internal review
and was developing an approach which put greater emphasis on the quality of
service to the public, and less on meeting numerical targets ...

Until his retirement on 31 December 2013, Chief Constable Ian Learmonth was
very visible in leading the force through this essential change. Staff commented
positively about his leadership and the clear message that had been conveyed by
him about the importance of delivering a high quality of service in line with the
force's stated mission, vision, values and priorities.

But there is some evidence to suggest that not all chief constables are
as enlightened as Kent's over the target culture and that targets are alive
and well and being used in perhaps half the police forces of England and
Wales ... particularly the Met as outlined in *Chapter 12*. It's not HMIC's job
to enlighten these forces, but perhaps it should be addressing the accuracy
of the recording of crime and assessing whether the focus of these police
forces is skewed towards easy to resolve, less serious crimes. That would surely
be within HMIC's remit. There was also a report on the Met's methods of
handling rape cases (explored in *Chapter 4* and mentioned towards the end
of *Chapter 18*) which is of particular interest because of the discrepancies
between our contributors in *Part 1* and HMIC's findings and the absence

of any HMIC discussions with rape victims.

As I mentioned earlier, HMIC also responds to the Home Secretary who occasionally requests an investigation and/or report into matters that are of particularly serious concern. One example of this was HMIC's review to establish which police forces received allegations with regard to the late Jimmy Savile's behaviour prior to the launch of Operation Yewtree on 5 October 2012. HMIC was to establish whether any allegations were robustly investigated and whether police failings were established. In summary, HMIC reported 'Mistakes were made.' This gives no-one, least of all the numerous victims, any comfort whatsoever unless the forces in question sacked, disciplined or seriously censured the erring officers. So was discipline administered? Not to my knowledge, although there are still some officers being quizzed.

Quite apart from the Savile case there are thousands of victims of crime who will have an opinion about the investigation that followed their viola-tion. I would have thought victims of crime, both where the perpetrator had been caught and punished and where the case was unresolved, presented many opportunities for HMIC to get into the story behind 'customer' satis-faction/dissatisfaction. Further, there is a mountain of complaints to the IPCC about police performance and responses. One huge issue creating much public disquiet is the police failing to record complaints against them-selves which seems to be of no account to the police, their PSD and the IPCC—that leaves only HMIC. But I see no visible signs that HMIC is concerned, or particularly interested either.

Then there is the question of advance notice. I'm all for consultation and certainly HMIC has a host of 'partners' to consider as well as its wish to enjoy input from the public, but is it possible that the police force recipients get to much notice and are able to prepare for and brief their staff?

Needless to say, none of my nit-picking is covered by the department's annual assessment of policing in England and Wales for 2012/13. It is however a comprehensive (200+ pages or about 1.5 pages per employee), beautifully written informative text.[5] As they are so pertinent, indeed capture the whole purpose of this book, I have taken the liberty of extracting from the report ten key paragraphs, while recording my disappointment that, although the

---

5.   See http://www.hmic.gov.uk/wp-content/uploads/2014/03/state-of-policing-12-13.pdf

questions posed are quite appropriate, the report leaves others to propose answers (some of which I suggest in my own concluding chapter):

32. The greatest asset of the police service is its people—police officers and police staff. Despite this, in too many respects, officers and staff suffer frustration and must work around inefficiency and unnecessary bureaucracy, antiquated and malfunctioning systems and practices which belong to a past age, blunting their ability to serve the public which the very great majority are eager and determined to do. They—and the public they serve—deserve much better. The discharge of this essential obligation is part of the core skills of every manager in the police service, and should be seen as such.

33. As policing has become more complex, the need to ensure that police officers are properly trained is intensified. With increasing specialisation of police officers has, in some respects, come a reduction in the opportunities of police officers to acquire, use and develop the full range of core skills which police officers of the past often possessed. In particular, the knowledge of police officers of the substantive and procedural rules of criminal law and evidence is in some cases materially below the necessary standard. Police officers go to court far less often than formerly, and some have never been to court. It is important that police officers have a sound knowledge and understanding of the end-to-end process of the criminal justice system, so that they can have a proper appreciation of the likely consequences of their actions and failures to take action at the point of pursuing and apprehending those accused of crime. Knowing the rigour and meticulous forensic penetration of the weaknesses of a prosecution case, at first hand, would materially improve the ability of police officers to ensure that cases which deserve to be prosecuted are. The quality of the preparation of files for submission to the Crown Prosecution Service has been significantly failing, and for that reason cases which should have gone to court often have not, or have required appreciably more remedial work before the prosecution can proceed. In these respects, the public interest has been failed.

49. In the past, it was often said that the police is the last unreformed public service. It is certainly true that for many years the police service was not subject to major structural or institutional reform, and that such reforms as there were

were confined to incremental and gradual changes, maintaining largely in place structural and other features of the system which had been in place for many years. It may be that some in the service came to believe that it deserved to be insulated from fundamental and searching review, despite the fact that its workforce management policies and practices were becoming stale and discredited and had grown to work against the interests of the service, individual police officers and police staff, and the public in terms of the efficiency and effectiveness of the service.

77. It is very much to be regretted that the confidence of the public in their ability to trust the police has been so severely shaken by controversies which have recently achieved public prominence, and ones which have been the subject of public concern and criticism for many years. They include those concerning Hillsborough, Orgreave Colliery, the investigation of the murder of Stephen Lawrence and how police conducted themselves afterwards, the enforced resignation of a Cabinet Minister as a result of the actions of at least one dishonest police officer, the sexual deception of citizens who trusted undercover police officers, and others. Some — not all — of these cases remain open and unconcluded, but that has not stopped some commentators and others deciding them prematurely and without possession of the full facts. Others — such as the case of the murder of Stephen Lawrence — have reached the stage where a sufficient proportion of the facts are now known already to justify very severe criticisms and public disquiet.

78. Loss of trust in the police is corrosive to the heart of the British model of policing by consent by a predominantly unarmed service. Police officers require and depend upon the consent of the community, and with that consent comes co-operation and the provision of information. Neighbourhood policing is central to this, and it is from co-operation from the public at that level that the police obtain most of their information about crime and the potential for crime, whether it is in the roots of anti-social behaviour, leading to more serious crime, or for the purposes of counter-terrorism. It is therefore important that where trust has been lost or damaged, it is restored as rapidly and effectively as possible.

79. With the possession of considerable power comes the obligation not only to use that power so as to achieve just ends, but also to use it in a way which is conspicuously fair. In the context of police powers, fairness not only requires

adherence to the legal rules of criminal procedure, but also to the need to do so, and to be seen to do so, in a fair, courteous and respectful manner, consistent with the presumption of innocence and the rights of citizens not to be subject to violence—physical or verbal—by the agents of the state without lawful cause. In other words, the police must treat people with respect, as fellow members of the community of which the police are part.

80. This point is intensified when the police use their powers to stop-and-search people, since these are powers to deny a person his liberty and subject him to an invasion of his privacy and person. Such things must be done with care, and only on lawful grounds. The absence of such treatment inflames resentment and may damage or even lose the consent of the community to the manner of policing which is being operated for them and on their behalf. The public expects the police to know how to use the powers granted to them by Parliament in an effective and fair manner. HMIC's report in July 2013 in relation to the use by police of their stop-and-search powers found important shortcomings in their use, and made recommendations to ensure that police officers are trained in the lawful grounds for the use of these powers and in how they should be used fairly and effectively to prevent and detect crime.

81. I have been told by some retired senior police officers that low-level corruption was endemic in the police in the 1960s and 1970s, probably intensified by disgracefully low police pay at the time. And there were then also material levels of much more serious corruption, which eventually led to the enactment of the Police and Criminal Evidence Act 1984 providing for significant safeguards for suspects in relation to their treatment. Very considerable steps have been taken since then to extinguish corruption, beginning principally with the tenure as Commissioner of the Metropolitan Police of the late Sir Robert Mark, who devoted the greatest part of his time in that office to anti-corruption. Although in those years police evidence was usually accepted by courts and juries almost without question—whereas now there are real fears that it is treated with greater caution and deserving of no greater weight or respect than the evidence of any other witness—it is almost undeniable that the police today are far more honest and honourable than they were 30 and 40 years ago.

82. There is very probably no profession, trade, vocation or occupation which can validly claim that every one of its practitioners or members is scrupulously honest. The issue is therefore a matter of fact and degree, and of admission and toleration. First, in what circumstances is a person dishonest, with what motivation, and with what effect? In other words, at work, to what extent can a person be trusted? Secondly, how does the institution ensure that it admits as few dishonest people as possible, and how well does it look for, find and deal with such people?

83. It must also be remembered that the police, unlike almost every other occupation, deal with industrial quantities of dishonesty every day. There are few, if any, jobs where you can expect a significant proportion of the people with whom you deal day-to-day to lie or try to mislead you. And it must also be acknowledged that in order properly to gather intelligence on criminal behaviour and the activities of those planning or engaged in crime, it is sometimes necessary for the police to mislead those people, by operating undercover. Undercover operations require authorisation, supervision and control of the highest order, to ensure that they operate within the limits accepted and given by the community, and it is of course necessary and right that they do. It should also be remembered that police officers who operate undercover in serious organized crime gangs and in comparable conditions take perhaps by far the greatest risks with their personal safety—and the welfare and futures of their families—on behalf of the public; they are amongst the bravest police officers of all. Those who operate in such circumstances, within the constraints of their authorisations and of course the law, deserve very great thanks from the public they risk their lives to protect.

So HMIC poses some first-class questions but offers little by way of remedial suggestions. The following might be a starting point for discussion:
- Possibly my most far-reaching question is, with their regional offices already established, might HMIC in a new enlarged regulatory format be the body to take managerial control of PSDs throughout the country, including the Met's DPS? I'm not suggesting that HMIC become embroiled in the IPCC's police complaints procedure, no more than chief constables are involved now, but HMIC's managerial involvement should give HMIC a lead into may of the problems experienced by a disaffected public

and separate each PSD from their local police. That could be a
starting point to resolving the issue of local police investigating
local police. Furthermore improved PSDs might be the best thing
that has happened to IPCC since its inception.

- The majority of HMIC work seems to be triggered by more or
  less routine inspections of more or less comfortable situations
  yet, although there are thousands of disaffected members of the
  public with a range of similar complaints, none seemed to concern
  HMIC or trigger consideration. More intimate involvement with
  PSDs might change HMIC's perspective and trigger-points and
  consequently increase public confidence in policing generally.

- It is absurd for a local PSD police to investigate their local
  mates and consequently, I believe unintended but inevitable and
  unavoidable PSD bias is one root-cause of Britain's police integrity problems. Furthermore when suspected of a crime the police
  seem to get favourable attention from IPCC and/or the CPS and
  escape prosecution more frequently that Joe Public (see *Chapter
  19*) possibly because it is usually the local PSD that investigates.

- An IPCC recommendation for disciplinary action following a
  police error or crime can be ignored by the local police force.
  That needs to change. IPCC disciplinary recommendations
  must become mandatory. Furthermore police dishonesty needs
  to be countered by increased penalties. Some police dishonesty
  is accepted by the IPCC but this is not acceptable to the general
  public. Furthermore, where punishments *are* handed down, some
  are currently derisory. All allegations would be better investigated,
  charged and prosecuted by a single independent body.

CHAPTER 19

The Crown Prosecution Service

The CPS is one of the three parts of the criminal justice system that dovetail in the general fight against crime and justice for victims. The other inter-dependent limbs are the police (or other law enforcement agencies) and (once a prosecution is launched) the criminal courts. So far as the police are concerned, the IPCC (*Chapter 21*) is a fourth factor in respect of discipline and the provision of information leading to the prosecution of police officers.

I will discuss police prosecutions a little later but bearing in mind the main triumvirate are all working within one system to the same ends of justice, one might assume they were united not only with a common purpose but with common targets and indeed common lines of reporting. However all have differing lines of accountability, different bosses (hierarchies) and therefore, inevitably, differing objectives (see also *Appendix 1*).

The Director of Public Prosecutions heads and manages the CPS and he or she reports to the Attorney General, a Government minister accountable to Parliament for the work of the CPS. The CPS has some 8,000 employees responsible for prosecuting those people/crimes investigated and presented by the police. These people/crimes can and do include those relating to police employees that, as I've said, we'll look into later. Aside from CPS national headquarters based in London there are 13 geographical areas, casework divisions (e.g. terrorism, fraud, welfare and organized crime) and the 'direct' service (aka CPS Direct, below). Each is headed by a chief crown prosecutor.

In serious and/or complex cases the police are obliged to refer the case to the CPS for a charging decision but, as can be seen from the tables presented later in the chapter, the majority of simple/straightforward cases are charged by the police without pre-charge reference to CPS. The dividing line between cases that must be and cases not requiring referral is provided by CPS guidance which is also summarised later in the chapter. Whichever route to charging applies it is crown prosecutors who prepare and prosecute cases in court. They used to be targeted via a successful prosecution percentage but a FOI request revealed that individual prosecutors are no longer judged on the percentage of convictions they achieve.

Furthermore, as also used to be the case on occasions, the CPS informs me that it does not downgrade an investigated crime to be sure of getting some sort of conviction regardless of the police's opinion, frustration or wishes. The CPS does occasionally still downgrade a charge to something the Crown prosecutor considers more suitable but does not maintain data on the number or percentage of police charges changed by the CPS in advance of or during criminal proceedings.

The CPS is not responsible for the volume of work it generates for the police nor for agreeing with victims to downgrade to a lesser charge nor not to prosecute a suspect at all, even if better liaison and information schemes nowadays exist. But naturally it has other considerations beyond its conviction objectives. The tests applied when deciding whether to commence each individual prosecution, and for keeping it under review, are set out in the Code for Crown Prosecutors:[1]

There are some less obvious agendas too. Informally, the CPS assures me that the prison population and/or overcrowding are not considered, and nor is consideration given whether to choose a level of charge where the sentence is likely to be non-custodial. However there are a number of factors that are taken into account when deciding to prosecute and these are articulated in the Code for Crown Prosecutors (above). In every case where there is sufficient evidence to justify a prosecution, prosecutors are required then to consider whether a prosecution is in the public interest (see later in the chapter).. The degree of violence, if any, is one of the factors considered at the public interest test stage, but other factors are taken into account such as:

- the seriousness of the offence;
- the level of culpability of the suspect;
- the circumstances of and the harm caused to the victim;
- whether the suspect was under the age of 18 (a juvenile) at the time of the offence;
- the impact on the community;
- the proportionality of the CPS response; and
- whether sources of information require protection.

---

1.   See https://www.cps.gov.uk/publications/docs/code_2013_accessible_english.pdf

Experienced offenders may be aware of CPS systems, considerations and its reluctance to prosecute in certain situations, as are the police of course who are, understandably, correspondingly disappointed by some CPS decisions (but that are completely outside their control). So the police see shortcomings in the system that is supposed to translate their criminal investigatory work into successful prosecutions. However, to be fair to the CPS, there is much on record that should ensure minimal disappointment. The CPS Directors' Guidance on Charging (May 2013) sets out those offences which the police *must* refer to the CPS for early investigative advice or a decision to charge as well as a host of other useful details.[2]

CPS Direct (CPSD)[3] is responsible for all volume crime charging decisions that must be referred to the CPS 24 hours a day, seven days a week. Police officers contact the CPS using a dedicated phone number and provide case information to the CPSD prosecutor. Pilots have in seven police force areas tested cases dealt with digitally, and the police officer does not have to routinely telephone CPSD in order to obtain a charging decision.

In any case involving a death, rape or serious sexual offences, child abuse, large scale or long-term fraud, cases with substantial or complex video or audio key evidence and those expected to take a substantial amount of consultation time are referred by the police to CPS area-based prosecutors instead of CPSD. In such cases, early contact should take place between the officer and the CPS to agree whether the consultation will be provided in writing, by telephone or face-to-face and what material is to be submitted to the prosecutor. In some specialised or particularly serious cases the CPS assign a team of lawyer/prosecutors. The team selection takes account of the characteristics of each individual case and the skills and capabilities of the lawyer(s). When a case is received it is reviewed, assessed and allocated accordingly. Where the CPS has been notified that the accused does not intend to contest the charge(s) or where it assesses that charges are unlikely to be contested, then such cases maybe handled by various lawyers, not specifically one lawyer. However in cases where the CPS have been notified that the accused intends to contest some or all of the charges and where not guilty pleas are entered at court, the case will be allocated to an individual

---

2. See https://www.cps.gov.uk/publications/directors_guidance/dpp_guidance_5.html
3. See generally www.cps.gov.uk/direct/

lawyer who then has the responsibility for that case and, where possible, will handle all meetings and decision-making associated with it.

Over and above this general approach, the CPS has specialist teams who deal individually, or as a small group, with certain types of offending—for example all allegations concerning rape and serious sexual offending are deal with by units staffed with specialist prosecutors, as are matters involving the seizure and forfeiture of the proceeds of crime. Outside of these types of cases, every CPS area has a Complex Casework Unit that deals with any other matters that require specialist attention. At a national level, cases involving allegations of terrorism, organized crime, complex fraud and the like are dealt with individually by specialist lawyers in the CPS's central casework directorates.

Improvements in the police/CPS interface using digital technology are being introduced. The CPS believes that the introduction of digital working means that its work can be conducted without reference to geographical or process boundaries, for example, national charging arrangements for volume cases as introduced in 2013 and administered by CPSD. Equally, digitally enabled remote arrangement to allow prosecutors to work at short notice with the police, linked to police stations and courts. All of which is positive news and reflected in the huge workload the CPS handle as you can judge from the CPS caseload tables presented below.

Crown Prosecution Service: Caseload

Year	Convictions		Unsuccessful		Total
2009–2010	259017	79.40%	67034	20.60%	326051
2010–2011	261539	78.60%	71396	21.40%	332936
2011–2012	223504	79.00%	59466	21.00%	282970
2012–2013	185176	79.30%	48418	20.70%	233594

Table 1—CPS Charged

Year	Convictions		Unsuccessful		Total
2009–2010	587204	89.40%	69477	10.60%	656681
2010–2011	559792	89.40%	66107	10.60%	625899
2011–2012	547153	89.20%	66382	10.80%	613535
2012–2013	504577	88.10%	68287	11.90%	572864

Table 2 — Police Charged

Year	Proceeded to Prosecution		Total
2009–2010	305497	64.00%	477522
2010–2011	305494	65.20%	468656
2011–2012	249474	67.50%	369564
2012–2013	208644	67.50%	309315

Table 3 — Pre-Charge Decisions

Notes: *Tables 1* and *2* 'Convictions' comprise guilty pleas as well as convictions after trial and include proceedings in the defendant's absence. However, the CPS point out that with regard *Table 3* they count pre-charge decisions in terms of the number of *suspects* and prosecutions in terms of the number of *defendants*. The 'Unsuccessful Outcomes' listed in *Tables 1* and *2* include discontinued (i.e. 'dropped') prosecutions, administrative finalisations, discharged committals and, of course, cases where the accused is acquitted or the charge otherwise dismissed.

The CPS's volume of work and securing of convictions of civilians is impressive, even more so if you care to consider the data provided and available via CPS's Case Management System (CMS) and associated Management Information System (MIS). The data collected is assembled to aid its effective management and is not intended to be statistically accurate or comprehensive. Nevertheless there seems to remain a problem with bringing erring police employees to book. Because of the focus of this book, I want to particularly explore the prosecution of alleged dishonest police employees and ask whether ordinary citizens are on a level playing field when it comes to CPS fervour. FOI details provided by the CPS suggest that the police enjoy significant advantages.

Table 4: Crown Prosecution Service: Pre-Charge Decisions[4]

	2010–2011		2011–2012		2012–2013	
No Prosecution	535	73.7%	288	69.6%	131	58.2%
Total Pre-Charge Decisions	726		414		225	

Table 4.1 — Police Complaint Flagged

	2010–2011		2011–2012		2012–2013	
No Prosecution	119,609	25.6%	88,816	24.1%	73,785	23.9%
Total Pre-Charge Decisions	467,930		369,150		309,090	

Table 4.2 — Non Police Complaint Flagged

Notes: The Police Complaints Monitoring Flag is applied to all cases in respect of persons serving with the police.

CPS police complaints statistics are dependent upon lawyers and administrative staff identifying applicable cases and flagging the case on the Case Management System.

No Prosecution — Cases where the decision is not to prosecute for evidential or public interest reasons.

The official statistics relating to crime and policing are maintained by the Home Office and the official statistics relating to sentencing, criminal court proceedings, offenders brought to justice, the courts and the judiciary are maintained by the Ministry of Justice.

---

4.   CPS pre-charge decisions are counted in terms of the number of suspects.

As can be seen from *Table 4*, the likelihood of a police employee *not* being prosecuted as compared to a civilian is significantly higher. Over the three years that the CPS provided the figures, a civilian averaged around a 25 per cent chance of escaping prosecution while a police employee could look forward to 70 per cent avoidance. So it would seem the police enjoy post-crime fringe benefits, starting with reduced likelihood of prosecution through the combined efforts of the IPCC and CPS. Both departments are however coming under a great deal of pressure and criticism for the increasing number cases that they elect not to bring to court or that 'fail' in court for want of satisfactory evidence. Against this discouraging background one has to question why over these three years police officers seemed proportionally less likely to face prosecution than their civilian counterparts. Of course the CPS can only work with the information provided in the form of evidence supplied by *the police*, and in most cases by the *officer's local PSD*.

However the IPCC are the 'foundation' for police prosecutions. The IPCC process all complaints about the police and there seem to be many 'processing' opportunities for the IPCC to consider. During 2010/11 a total of 58,667 allegations and a total of 34,503 complaints were 'finalised' by the IPCC. The majority of complaints were about police officers as opposed to police staff, but in total 37,779 police employees were the subjects of a complaint. This needs to be considered against a police officer strength of about 130,000. Unfortunately the IPCC have, in my opinion, done neither their own reputation nor that of the police any favours by recording that some police dishonesty is acceptable and not worthy of their investigation (see *Chapter 21*). So who allowed the IPCC the right to be judge and jury on such an important matters, particularly at a time when public perception of police integrity is plummeting?

As per *Table 4* there is a disparity between the likelihood of prosecution of police employees and non-police civilians. To be fair the differential is closing, nevertheless the CPS provided no information as to the reasons for the civilian/police prosecution imbalance, but it is noteworthy that 'Pre-charge decisions' for both civilians/police are falling. Nevertheless it is appears on the face of things that you're better being a police officer.

Aside from it being your colleagues who investigate and provide the evidence, perhaps we should examine whether there are other reasons for the differences. The CPS needs not only adequate ('sufficient') evidence to be available but for prosecution also to be regarded by them as 'in the public interest' if they are to proceed (see above). The evidence *has* to be gathered and maybe my proposals to separate PSDs from their respective police forces will de-personalise the investigation and, hopefully, but probably optimistically, amplify the motivation to collect evidence (see *Chapter 20*).

Or perhaps the IPCC must be required in law to carry out managed or independent investigations when a police employee is involved in any and all questionable practices (*Chapter 21*).

As already mentioned, the CPS prosecutes only when this is deemed by them to be in the public interest, raising the question of whose judgement is it as to what is/is not in the that interest. Mindful of public disquiet perhaps, the CPS needs guidance, the facility for external consultations or legislation requiring, say, that they put the matter in the hands of a court whenever police officers are involved. I consider that it is in the public interest and should be obligatory for every offence by a police officer where even minimal evidence is available to be tried in a court of law: a 'zero-tolerance' approach as explored in *Chapter 22*. In the way cases are often automatically referred to the IPCC by police forces they should be referred by the CPS to the court. It may not increase the ultimate volume of prosecutions but may act as a deterrent for the police including in the context of 'naming and shaming'. An officer can continue to hold his or her head high if found not guilty and — as with more open disciplinary proceedings and in conjunction with some other recommendations put forward at the end of this book — justice will have been *seen to be done*.

Is there is a bias in the police's favour as the result of split responsibilities? Currently the IPCC are solely an investigative commission and the CPS responsible for charging police officers when appropriate. In fact the split in responsibilities is broader than it first appears because three departments are involved — the police who supply the evidence, the IPCC who investigate/propose and the CPS who prosecute. In other circumstances one could consider that overly complicated, an unnecessary split in responsibilities and, perhaps unworkable as current outcomes appear to confirm.

Whatever the present road-blocks, it is not right that a police officer is nearly three-times *less* likely to face prosecution than Joe Public. In fact these positions need to be reversed. So rather than looking around the edges at various departments for a number of individual solutions, perhaps a major rethink is necessary — such as appointing the National Crime Agency (NCA) to take up the total overall responsibility for investigating and prosecuting all police crime from start to finish. This closes any 'loopholes' brought about by split responsibilities where police integrity and public confidence is concerned and draws the failing IPCC out of this particularly sensitive issue as quickly as possible — which in itself will aid public confidence.

CHAPTER 20

Police Complaints and Professional Standards

Freedom of information responses to other enquirers revealed that 1,915 officers were guilty of misconduct, 382 dismissed or told to resign and a further 489 employees resigned or retired thus avoiding disciplinary processes during 2008/10. So we do have a problem that needs remedial thought.

As indicated in *Chapter 12*, there are reasons to sympathise with the pressures put upon the front line police officer from all sections of society, including their own senior officers and Government. The number of officers is decreasing, the direction they have been required to follow has been questionable and public dissatisfaction, echoed by the volume of complaints against them, is increasing. Neither the majority of the public it seems nor many officers themselves feel satisfied with performance levels of recent times. The Office for National Statistics publishes the *Crime Survey for England and Wales* (CSEW): see also *Chapter 18*. Two key points from the 2011/12 survey were:

[J]ust under two-thirds of adults (62 per cent) thought the police in their local area were doing a good or excellent job...

Over half of all adults (55 per cent) reported that they see the police or police community support officers (PCSOs) on foot patrol in their local area at least every month, based on 2011/12 interviews.

The report seems overly focused upon *seeing* a police officer or PCSO on foot patrol as the measure of satisfaction. It appears to have made no attempt to include a wider public perspective than sighting an officer and it would have been helpful to have consulted with and incorporated people who have had some form of contact with the police. I think perceptions might be rather different.

However, the CSEW 62 per cent satisfaction rating is hardly inspiring. Any commercial enterprise would go out of business with as low as a 60 per cent approval rating of their product or service, but we do need to remain mindful that the rank and file police staff were themselves probably dissatisfied with their (it would seem still largely target-driven) performance. As noted in *Appendix 2*, the media were generally unimpressed too and the IPCC (in *Chapter 21*) records an increasing number of complaints against the police. Furthermore and admittedly speculation, it is likely that more and more police work will be done in the office as specialists attempt to catch computer-orientated criminals practising scams, paedophilia, pornography, grooming, fraud, identity theft, hacking, blagging, piracy, harassment/stalking/bullying, the use of malware/viruses and, of course, straightforward theft from bank accounts. I have touched on several of these crimes in earlier chapters but the point I wish to emphasise here is that none of them are likely to be minimised by an officer on street patrol. The CSEW approach to assessing a satisfaction rating therefore needs more than subtle updating.

The Government has responded with police and crime commissioners (PCCs) (*Chapter 23*) intended to provide the public with a democratic say in how their police force operates but PCCs are not currently convincing the public as to their effectiveness. The Government also introduced changes to the basis of sanctioned detection targets designed to increase police discretion. These were outlined in *Chapter 12* and also remain unproven as to their value, but is it possible to detect a leap in public confidence as the result of either change? There have been several attempts to re-brand existing institutions but the public perception remains that they are powerless against a police force that rules, these days, neither by consent nor respect. As we have seen in *Part 1*, the police culture leads them to believe, with some justification, that some officers can act with impunity. The word 'apology' hardly exists in the police vocabulary.

Yet there is some progress. As can be seen in *Chapter 21*, the IPCC has increased the appeals it upholds to 44 per cent, which suggests that either it is becoming more understanding, or that applicants are getting better at lodging appeals … or even that police conduct is still deteriorating.

So what's to be done by someone faced by what he or she thinks are lies, poor performance, poor or non-responsiveness, rudeness, neglect, poor judgement, a lack of integrity, incompetence or straightforward harassment as were some of our contributors—and, if their experiences are indicative, many other citizens too? I strongly suggest that they complain—calmly, politely, succinctly, pointedly, but definitely *in writing* at or to their local police stations. They should retain a copy. Remember that for certain issues, say slow/non-attendance, neglect or corruption, the problem will likely not lie with the attending officers and complainants may even be doing them and their colleagues a favour by drawing the issue to their superiors' attention. However, the responsibility for lies, rudeness, bad judgement or dishonesty is most likely to remain with the individual attending officer, even if corruption can emanate from several layers of management. Remember that it will help any dispute if a recording of exchanges with the police exists—as can be seen from several of our contributors' cases.

Each police force has attached to it a department intended to ensure good professional standards are maintained within the force. For each complaint recorded by any police force the respective PSD is required to investigate but, as we've seen, if the police refuse to accept/record a complaint the complainant needs to write a second complaint to the IPCC copied to, I suggest, the PCC. The PSDs, like the police themselves, are generally held in poor esteem not only by the public but by the Parliamentary Home Affairs Committee too. The HAC records that while results vary from force-to-force, PSDs generally are attributed with an unacceptable 38 per cent error-rate.[1] The figure is provided by the IPCC when reviewing the subsequent appeals against the police and is likely to be the minimum error percentage because the IPCC is notorious for adopting the police/PSD position.

It is the contention of this book that in fact PSD errors and performance are *at the heart of the problems within the police complaints system*. The HAC has written to each chief constable asking for budgetary and staffing levels for their respective PSDs and the IPCC has been asked to insist upon written explanations from chief constables when appeals against any police force pass 25 per cent. This is welcome and long overdue but is just 'tickling around the edges'. We need legislation and changes that address the problems at the heart of the police/PSD/IPCC complaints system. I've mentioned my suggestion on a couple of occasions already in this book but, because of its importance, we will explore the issue again shortly.

1.   P.8 HC494, April 2013, 'Independent Police Complaints Commission'. See https://www.gov.
      uk/government/uploads/system/uploads/attachment_data/file/228950/8598.pdf

Firstly however, we need to recognise that, from unreported crime statistics and, worse still, reported but ignored crimes, too few people complain to and about the police. Consequently, I outline the system for complaints in the hope that more people do so when the police don't turn up, hide behind 'It's a civil matter', 'screen-out' cases, or simply say 'What crime?' Note too that the police see a reported crime as different to a recorded crime. We must complain more to the police and also insist that where appropriate the events in question are registered as a *recorded* crime. If there is doubt as to whether it has been 'recorded' it is essential to write to the police and also copy the letter to the IPCC, local PCC (more in *Chapter 23*), your MP and the Home Secretary until the current problems are dramatically reduced and/or the law is changed.

Ultimately, Parliament is the only way to get the current deficiencies addressed. However, as we learnt from the contributions in *Part 1* and indeed from the IPCC statistics, the police adopt various tactics to avoid recording some reported crimes and use workload management mechanisms to declare a complaint 'internal' or 'civil', i.e. an issue that does not require their involvement, time or merit investigation. To say the current system has shortcomings is an understatement. This is how it works in theory:

- The police force involved will probably prefer that you contact them direct and their respective websites include information about how to complain, but you can visit any police station. However, in itself, such a visit leaves no recorded trace of the complaint so I recommend a third alternative — downloading a form from the IPCC website. You can print and complete the form and post it to the relevant police force, but it is preferable you establish an external record by emailing a copy to the IPCC. This method does get your complaint indisputably 'on the record'.

- The IPCC says that, although it has no authority to enforce the statement, when you make a complaint, at least officially you can expect the police force to listen to you, act in a fair and balanced way and seek to put things right. If you complain direct to the IPCC about a police force or an officer within that force, your complaint will be routed to the PSD of that police force.

- If your complaint can be resolved by giving you some information or explaining what happened, then the police should do this. If it needs to be looked into, the police force should make a formal record of it and let you know they have done this. Recording a complaint means that it has formal status under the Police Reform Act 2002 and if the police do not record it you can and must appeal to the IPCC. The officer dealing with your complaint should contact you to make sure he or she has all the details of it and what you want to happen (e.g. an apology, rectification or an officer held to account). He or she will be able to tell you what is likely to happen and how they will deal with your complaint.

- 'Local resolution' outcomes deal with minor complaints (if there is such a thing) locally. The person dealing with the complaint will try to resolve it by meeting the person complained about, investigating the background, providing information or an explanation, or by apologising, and should let you know the outcome either in person or by phone and should confirm the outcome by writing to you. This process covers most complaints but where one is not suitable for local resolution a 'local investigation' will be employed. The force will discuss with you how the complaint will be investigated and a decision reached. The investigating officer should update you every 28 days.

- When the investigation is complete, you will be told the outcome and if any action is going to be taken as a result, what that action is and the outcome of that action. For example, an officer might have to attend a misconduct hearing and, as a result, receive a written warning. You should receive enough information at the end of the investigation to understand what has happened and what decisions have been reached. Sometimes this might happen by you being given a copy of the investigation report.

- If you are unhappy with the outcome you can appeal in some circumstances—this could be either to the police force or IPCC depending on how the complaint has been dealt with. The letter informing you of the outcome should include information about how to lodge an appeal and the (limited) time restraints involved.

Sadly my own experience fell far short of the above ideals. It revealed procedural errors, misinformation and bias at both the PSD and the IPCC that became the main triggers for this book.

Although mostly extracted from IPCC Annual Reports and presented below in tabular form the figures below endorse my contention that the PSDs are at the heart of the public's dissatisfaction with police complaints procedures. Why else would there be so many appeals to the IPCC after PSDs have investigated?

Percentage of year	'08–09	'09–10	'10–11	'11–12	'12–13
All appeal types upheld	29%	29%	30%	38%	44%*
Non recording appeals upheld	49%	54%	58%	61%	
Investigation appeals upheld	22%	21%	23%	31%	
Local resolution appeals upheld	34%	33%	33%	35%	

The Handling of Complaints Against the Police

*The above demonstrate a significant upward trend in appeals upheld against the police by the IPCC.

The 2012–13 data was unpublished at the time of writing but provided by an IPCC FOI reply dated 9th December 2013. The following information from the IPCC report for 2011–12 is interesting and marks a reduction in the criteria but does not explain the motivation for this easement.[2]

Reports—Previously, police forces were required to make a judgment as to whether there was evidence of misconduct at the end of an investigation into a public complaint. Where misconduct could be proven, the allegation would be substantiated. This has now shifted to a threshold of whether the service provided by the police 'did not reach the standard a reasonable person would expect' (IPCC,

---

2.   See https://www.ipcc.gov.uk/sites/default/files/Documents/research_stats/complaints_
     statistics_11-12.pdf

2010), as it is often the case that a complainant has received poor service even though the actions of officers involved do not amount to misconduct.

Perhaps because of this change in standard the following is becoming out-of-date but my dissatisfaction is rather widely shared judging by some of the post-appeal statistics issued in 2008/9 (last available to my knowledge) by IPCC's Directorate of Strategy and Communications which I précis:

> Of 1,629 questionnaires, 632 were returned and 27% of respondents felt that their appeal had been treated 'very fairly' or 'fairly' and 77% that it had been treated 'unfairly' or 'very unfairly'…slight variations were recorded when a respondent had previously complained about the police when 20% felt treated 'very fairly' or 'fairly' compared to 24% of those who had never made a previous complaint.

More encouragingly, 63% of those who had lodged an appeal against the non-recording of a police complaint said they felt treated 'very fairly' or 'fairly', and 55 per cent of these had decisions upheld. Twenty per cent of those appealing against a police local resolution said they were treated fairly; the same percentage who had their appeal upheld. A total of 19 per cent of respondents appealing about a police investigation indicated the appeal was dealt with fairly, again with the same percentage having their appeal upheld.

These are not a ringing endorsement of any part of the complaints process but as noted earlier the success rate for appeals may be improving, which may in turn improve these figures were IPCC to carry out another survey in the near future. However, bearing in mind the PSDs are there to filter and resolve the majority of problems, clearly they are failing but this is hardly surprising when one remembers the close association each police force has with its attached PSD. This arrangement may call for a PSD officer to investigate the work of his best mate, ex-teacher, early mentor, neighbour, wife's brother, a friend, someone he owes a favour to or a Masonic (or alternative secret society) colleague. Jack Straw when Home Secretary questioned the wisdom of having Masonic members in the criminal justice system but restrictions were dropped although police officers are still required to tell their superiors if they are Masonic members. Masonic or otherwise, the laudable stick-together/mutual-support/team culture within the police is unlikely to spawn criticism of fellow officers except in the most extreme cases. So in summary the current concept of local PSDs investigating local officers seems unlikely to result in objective assessments.

One wonders who devised a complaints system whereby a complaint about an officer within a particular force is investigated by the PSD of that same police force. While I imagine it unusual, in my own case the officer who carried out the initial investigation was subsequently tasked by the force's PSD to 'investigate' himself to the point that correspondence addressed to the PSD was either intercepted by or routed to that same officer. Finally, that very same officer wrote the PSD investigatory report. Consequently, I believe there was little likelihood of the outcome being objective although the IPCC thought that all perfectly satisfactory.

A change is required that will decrease the likelihood of recriminations, public appeals and follow-on complaints to the IPCC. I appreciate a 100 per cent successful PSD team may be an impossible aim but it would put a large part of the IPCC out of business and maybe save taxpayers expense. The question is 'What changes will bring about an improvement in PSD performance?' I believe the reporting structure is the fundamental flaw. Given that the IPCC has proved itself incapable it does not appear to be a serious option. One possibility that should be discussed could be to make each PSD team via its senior officer report not to 'its' chief constable but to another body. The NCA or the College of Policing might be options for debate but my suggestion would be HMIC. HMIC already has some local offices, an interest in ensuring policing is carried through professionally, and untainted by past performance thereby removing the contentious issue of local police investigating themselves. I think something along those lines is worthy of evaluation for the medium term at least.

But in the short term, pending major re-organization, should not PCCs be liaising with their neighbours to ensure that no PSD investigator investigates a local problem? A neighbouring police force should be required to step in and carry out each investigation. To my mind this issue is even more urgent than reforms to the IPCC.

CHAPTER 21

Complaints and Appeals via the IPCC

Starting in 2004, the Independent Police Complaints Commission was established as a result of the Police Reform Act 2002 which provided it with statutory powers and responsibilities in relation to the police complaints system. The 2002 Act guarantees the IPCC independence and, interestingly, places it under an obligation to raise public confidence in that system. It was in fact a re-branded from the 'Police Complaints Authority'.

The IPCC receives investigatory requests from two main sources. The police forces throughout England and Wales can and do 'refer' cases to it, sometimes voluntarily (where public concerns are voiced); but more often referrals are obligatory when an unusual death (after contact with the police or in custody or a shooting or a traffic incident) is involved or if any serious offence has been allegedly carried out by a police employee. Over 2,000 such cases are referred to the IPCC per annum. It deals with these in four ways:

- 'local' investigation by the PSD of the police force concerned;
- 'supervised' investigation' or 'oversight' by the local or a designated PSD;
- 'managed' investigation by a PSD under direction from the IPCC;
- 'independent' investigation by IPCC staff managed by an IPCC commissioner.

However, the Parliamentary Home Affairs Committee (HAC) believe that the second of these methods, 'supervision/oversight' by the original police force, is insufficiently rigorous and does nothing to increase public confidence in either the police or the complaints system. The detail can be seen in the HAC minute, paragraph 5, later in this chapter. I believe the HAC are right and that this option should be removed as part of the PSD/IPCC overhaul as is suggested later in this book.

In addition to referrals by and from the police, any aggrieved member of the general public who considers he or she has been unfairly treated by the police may complain to the IPCC via an appeal procedure provided he or she has been given leave to do so.

In 2009/10 such public complaints were running at nearly 34,000 a year and the system was changed requiring members of the public to address their complaints initially to their local force to enable that force to resolve as many complaints as possible. Those complaints that were sent direct to the IPCC were automatically referred back to the local force.[1] Thus the same PSD, maybe even the same officer, as handled the complaint initially is charged with reviewing it, so it is hard to envisage it being an objective review. Once the police force's PSD has investigated the complaint it may give leave to appeal its findings and decision to the IPCC. The IPCC is then supposed to study how the complaint was investigated but, perversely, not to investigate its validity. This restriction is the second major shortcoming in the appeal process; not the fault of the IPCC but of the legislation it is required to work within and requires updating.

As confidence in the police and IPCC appeals diminishes, the latter receives ever-increasing workloads as its accounts show:

- in 2009/10, *police forces referred* 2,646 cases (2008 + 12 per cent) to the IPCC. After initial assessment, 2,208 were sent back to them to be resolved locally or investigated. A total of 5,584 *public appeals* were received compared to 4,634 in 2008/9 (+ 21 per cent);
- in 2010/11 a further increase in the number of *public appeals* took place to 6,307 (+ 13 per cent) although the number of *police referrals* fell by 13 per cent to 2,401;
- during 2011/12 the IPCC received 2,165 *police referrals*, a ten per cent decrease on the previous year. However a further increase in the number of *public appeals* occurred albeit at a slower rate of growth, 6,476 an increase of three per cent on the previous year. However during this period, interestingly, the IPCC issued new findings about the public's view of police corruption and its impact on public confidence in policing;
- 2012/13 saw 2,309 *police referrals*; a 17 per cent increase compared to the same period in the previous year but for the first year since

---

1. But sending your complaint (or a copy of it) to the IPCC is still to my mind a good idea because it gets it on record and helps to prevent the police by-passing it: *Chapter 20.*

operations began no increase in the number of *public appeals* occurred. Between April 2012 and February 2013, 5,854 *public appeals* were received — a similar number to those received during the same period in 2011/12. However, while the number of non-recording and local resolution appeals has decreased, the demand for more complex appeals about how the police have investigated complaints has continued to increase.

On average the volume of police referrals stays more or less static at about 2,400 per annum but the incremental workload from a disillusioned public has gone from about 4,500 in 2008/9 to a going rate of about 6,000 pa in the three years 2010–2013. It would be encouraging to record that this was due to increasing public faith in the IPCC, but in fact confidence in the whole system looks to be decreasing as any internet search will demonstrate via the sites of respected bodies and/or the media sites. However, there are also those members of the public who do not appeal and just carry resentment. Inhibited initially by a lack of support/assistance they see no point in complaining about the police, believing that they act properly (and thus with impunity) is a foregone conclusion. Several contributors in *Part 1* were of this opinion. The allowed timescales can be an issue and the seriousness of mistreatment another factor in Joe Public deciding to cut his losses. Others are just not equipped to complain about the police never mind cope with the appellate processes. Then there is the fact that the IPCC decision is final unless you elect to try for a judicial review in the High Court but this is becoming more difficult as legal aid becomes harder to find. That would be easier to understand if the IPCC were not so supportive of the police's point of view and there was an opportunity to appeal IPCC decisions higher within the IPCC itself or to some other body.

The 'appeal upheld' percentages (i.e. when the IPCC judges the appeal against a PSD decision is justified) are interesting. In the three years 2009/10 through to 2011/12 the IPCC annual reports recorded a pretty consistent 29 per cent However, it can be noted that the 2012/13 annual report recorded that 'upheld' decisions increased to 41 per cent (but it made no comment about this considerable increment). An FOI question brought the following response dated 9th December 2013:

There is a discrepancy in the percentages you have quoted, the correct data is as
follows (for appeals upheld as to police conduct):

2009/10 — 29%
2010/11 — 32%
2011/12 — 38%
2012/13 — 44%

The above statistics demonstrate an ongoing upward trend for appeals
upheld. The IPCC has commented on this trend in the Annual Complaints
Statistics report for 2011/12 (the 2012/13 report has not yet been published).
The report also looks at the different appeal types and provides a breakdown
of the upheld rates for each type and by police force. The report is available
on the IPCC website.[2]

What, however, is equally interesting is that the IPCC annual report does
reveal that since November 2012 the determination/resolution of appeals
submitted to it has been shared with a local police force—presumably the
same force the complainant was unhappy about in the first place and the
force that the complainant appealed to IPCC about. So, since late 2012 it
would appear the IPCC is now returning that same complaint to that same
police force for a second bite at the cherry! If I understand the IPCC phraseology correctly, this route has determined 57 per cent of public appeals
from late-2012. However at the same time it would appear that there has
been a sudden increase in the volume of appeals upheld or, to use my own
word, 'endorsed'. This suggests that either the IPCC is becoming more
understanding, or that applicants are getting better with their appeals, or
that police conduct is degenerating.

I submitted an appeal to the IPCC mid-2013 (IPCC's 2013/14 year). It was
not upheld and the IPCC's conclusion came back largely written in terms
similar to the original PSD 'Investigative Report'. I asked the IPCC under
the FOI whether appeals are ever referred back to the 'originating' police
force. Its reply, dated 22nd October 2013 reads

---

2.   http://www.ipcc.gov.uk/reports/statistics/police-complaints

I can confirm that our appeal decisions are made independently and are not drafted, formulated or influenced by the police. It may be helpful if I explain more about the process for considering appeals. In situations where the IPCC is the relevant appeal body, our role is to see whether the police force has correctly considered a complaint in line with the Police Reform Act 2002 ...

This seems to run counter to the IPCC 2012/13 year report. In any event the whole process completely sapped my confidence in the PSD/IPCC/ justice system and initiated this book.

On starting my research I detected little public confidence in the police or the IPCC, although the IPCC reports (2009/10) that public confidence is 'high'. I suspect that the majority of independent investigations by IPCC staff managed by an IPCC commissioner, are thorough and effective but few and far between. At the other end of the scale local and supervised investigations (as described above) form the vast majority of the IPCC's workload and bring about the perception that it is jointly responsible with the police for the decline in public confidence in the complaints system; also that it is biased in favour of the police. Many blame the fact that a high percentage (I have seen 90 per cent erroneously mentioned) of IPCC staff are ex-police officers and therefore automatically suspected of bias regardless of the facts. I think the public lose sight of the fact that the IPCC is currently not there to investigate the validity of an initial complaint, which is a fundamental problem that festers in many cases and cries out to be corrected.

The IPCC is independent and required to ensure no commissioner has previously worked for the police service in any capacity, which is not to say that any member of IPCC staff is prohibited from previous police employment. I think public perception is that the IPCC is 'police-biased'. My own experience is of such bias and I've yet to read a contribution to this book that suggests otherwise. So given current perceptions, one wonders why the IPCC is not, as its name implies, more independent and thus objective. Perhaps the following staffing information explains a little:

March 2010

Job title	Total Staff	Ex-police	Ex-police Civilian	Total Ex-Police
Investigator	92	20	10	30 (33%)
Deputy Sen Investigator	31	13	5	18 (58%)
Senior Investigator	10	8	1	9 (90%)
Casework	122	1	8	9 (7%)
Total Investigative	255	42	24	66 (26%)
Other	210	12	25	37
Total staff 2010	465	54	49	103

March 2011

Job title	Total Staff	Ex-police	Ex-police Civilian	Total Ex-Police
Investigator	85	18	10	28 (33%)
Deputy Sen Investigator	27	10	4	14 (52%)
Senior Investigator	9	8	0	8 (89%)
Casework	123	1	7	8 (7%)
Total Investigative	244	37	21	58 (24%)
Other	181	9	23	32
Total staff 2011	425	46	45	91

March 2012

Job title	Total Staff	Ex-police	Ex-police Civilian	Total Ex-Police
Investigator	79	19	9	28 (35%)

Deputy Sen Investigator	20	8	1	9 (45%)
Senior Investigator	9	8	1	9 (100%)
Casework	116	1	6	7 (6%)
Total Investigative	224	36	17	53 (24%)
Other	147	6	19	25
Total 2012	371	42	36	78

March 2013

Job title	Total Staff	Ex-police	Ex-police Civilian	Total Ex-Police
Investigator	67	17	11	28 (42%)
Deputy Senior Investigator	20	9	1	10 (50%)
Senior Investigator	8	7	1	8 (100%)
Casework	137	4	8	12 (9%)
Total Investigative	232	37	21	58 (25%)
Other	177	7	20	27
Total Staff 2013	409	44	41	85

So there is a fairly constant 25 per cent ex-police background for IPCC investigatory staff that frankly, at first sight and given their tasks, does not seem unreasonable. The HAC consider (paragraph 19 below) that the percentage of ex-police employees should be reduced to 20 per cent however, even at 20 per cent, ex-police investigatory employees will influence the style and culture they and their colleagues bring to the work. In fact I suggest even if limited to 20 per cent, there is unlikely to be a major change in bias/ attitude at the IPCC. Influenced by our contributor's experiences, I believe the case officers are indeed biased towards the police to the point that I question the IPCC supervisory standards or whether there is any subsequent random checking carried out by supervisory staff on their case officers' work.

Hence my earlier recommendation whereby disgruntled would be appellants should be able to request a further review of their case. This partly removes the current case officer's status as judge and jury but also necessitates IPCC supervision reviewing re-appeals and thereby establishing which of their case officers is doing a fair, balanced, unbiased job. Further, and returning to the question of whether and to what degree reducing the percentage of ex-police officers employed by the IPCC will improve the objectivity of its findings, it seems likely that the HAC is correct in principle but I believe it has not gone far enough. I suggest in *Chapter 24* that this could usefully be reduced further.

However, I also believe that the cultural style and bias amongst the senior staff and mentors within the IPCC needs reconsideration. New recruits to the IPCC may not have a police background but can and will be taught to favour the police's point of view if their supervision remains biased. How and when IPCC senior staff can be judged unbiased is a major issue in itself and demonstrates the importance of getting the right chief executive in place and of providing some sort of re-appeal procedure when the complainant believes police bias has been shown. It was illuminating to note that the HAC, when hearing evidence from the chair of the IPCC in the federation officers' part of the Andrew Mitchell saga (*Chapter 9*), asked if the new investigating officer (IO) charged with bringing the IPCC investigation to a close was an ex-police officer. The HAC appeared pleased to hear that the IO appointed did not have a police background—which speaks volumes.

As can be seen above, the IPCC caseload has increased but from the staffing-level tables we can also see that the investigative staffs available to handle the increasing caseload actually decreased. This came about during the 2011/12 year when 45 staff at the IPCC were declared redundant. One presumes this was subsequently seen as an error because recruitment re-commenced in September 2012, about a year later. Consequently, it seems likely that a shortage of investigatory staff was the fundamental reason for the commission's increasing backlog and unacceptable investigative timescales. The HAC's constructive remedial comments can be seen, but some idea of the case backlog can be gained from the initial IPCC estimate for a resolution to my appeal (mid-2013). I was told 40 weeks.

To my mind there is also a question over the IPCC's priorities. It thinks it necessary to put resources into and publishing and distributing 'Learning the Lessons' to police forces three times a year. Furthermore it seems to squander money, later complaining of inadequate resources, on public surveys to try to establish what police corruption is acceptable. Better the IPCC focuses on more obvious and direct problems such as measures that improve its speed of response, effectiveness, transparency, accountability, public confidence and bringing erring police officers to justice. I am particularly uncomfortable with the time the IPCC devotes to investigating 'Public Views on Police Corruption' and incensed that it should be grading some police corruption as less serious. Less serious corruption occurs when others are not involved in the act/outcome or when low level false expense claims are submitted or officers falsify figures/targets. *All* police corruption is quite unacceptable. It could always lead to greater crimes at a later date. Yet the IPCC more or less says some examples are acceptable and, by implication, no investigation.[3]

I believe this demonstrates an inappropriate attitude by the flag-bearer for justice. It is the watchdog that is supposed to be striving to improve the police and public confidence in both the police and IPCC itself. Consequently, I seek an advocate of 'zero-tolerance' in the chair of the police watchdog, someone with a no-tolerance attitude to *any* police corruption. Bearing in mind the dubious information that the Home Office presents as its crime figures (*Chapter 17*), I am astonished that the IPCC is prepared to accept falsification of crime figures as acceptable corruption (Consider whistle blower PC James Patrick in *Chapter 17* and whether the IPCC is fit for purpose). The HAC's conclusions on the IPCC are paraphrased below:[4]

> 1. Police officers are warranted with powers that can strip people of their liberty, their money and even their lives and it is vital that the public have confidence that those powers are not abused. We conclude that the IPCC is not yet capable

---

3. The report issued in September 2012 can be read in full at http://www.ipcc.gov.uk/sites/default/files/Documents/research_stats/public_views_of_police_corruption_May_2012.pdf . You can however get a swift appreciation of their tolerance by fast forwarding to their chart on page 16 of that document.

4. The extracts contain Parliamentary information licensed under the Open Parliament Licence v1.0. See the full report at www.publications.parliament.uk/pa/cm201213/cmselect/cmhaff/494/49411.htm

of delivering the kind of powerful, objective scrutiny needed to inspire that confidence (Paragraph 4).

2. Compared with the might of the 43 police forces in England and Wales, the IPCC is woefully under-equipped and hamstrung in achieving its original objectives. It has neither the powers nor the resources needed to get to the truth when the integrity of the police is in doubt. Smaller even than the PSD of the Met Police, the IPCC is not even first among equals, yet meant to be the backstop of the system. It lacks the investigative resources necessary to get to the truth; police forces are too often left to investigate themselves; and the voice of the IPCC does not have binding authority. The commission must bring the police complaints system up to scratch and the Government must give it the powers needed to do so (Paragraph 5).

3. The public do not fully trust the IPCC and without faith in it the damaged public opinion of the police cannot be restored. Unfortunately, too often the work of the commission seems to exacerbate public mistrust not mend it. (Paragraph 15).

4. The independence and oversight offered by commissioners is at the heart of the role of the IPCC. It is wrong that their day-to-day work is frequently far removed from the cases being investigated. Commissioners should be given a more active role in overseeing major cases and take personal responsibility for ensuring a clear process and timetable is laid out for complaints and appeals. The independence and oversight offered by commissioners is at the heart of the role of the IPCC. (Paragraph 16)

5. More cases should be investigated independently by the commission, instead of referred back to the original force on a 'complaints roundabout'. 'Supervised investigations' do not offer rigorous oversight of a police investigation, nor do they necessarily give the public a convincing assurance that the investigation will be conducted objectively. This 'oversight-lite' is no better than a placebo (Paragraph 23).

6. The IPCC owes it to the families of those who die in cases involving the police to get to the truth of the matter—a botched job is an offence to all concerned.

When the IPCC does investigate it often comes too late and takes too long. The trail is left to go cold. IPCC investigators should be able to take immediate control of a potential crime scene during the crucial 'golden hours' and early days of an investigation into deaths and serious injury involving police officers (Paragraph 24).

7. It is deeply worrying that the commission feels its level of resourcing has dropped below a level at which it can properly discharge its statutory functions and meet public expectations, to the extent that a backlog of appeals is building up. We recognise it will not be easy to find significant additional resources. We recommend that the Home Office works with the commission to identify innovative ways in which the backlog might be cleared (e.g. temporary secondments). More robust procedures should be put in place at the permission stage of appeals to filter out more minor cases so the IPCC can focus on the most serious (Paragraph 32).

8. Important cases are under-investigated because of a lack of access to independent specialists. The Home Office should provide the IPCC with a specific budget for a serious cases response team. The resources within individual forces for investigating complaints dwarf the resources of the Commission. It is notable that the IPCC is smaller than the complaints department of the Metropolitan Police alone. In the most serious cases, therefore, there should be the IPCC's investigations into HM Revenue & Customs and the UK Border Agency (Paragraph 33).

9. Applying non-discriminatory practices is crucial as a disproportionate number of the cases that cause the most serious public concern involve the black and minority ethnic (BME) communities. All Commissioners, investigators and caseworkers should be trained in discrimination awareness and relevant law...(Paragraph 35)

10. Public confidence in the police has been shaken: Operation Yewtree, Operation Alice, the Hillsborough Inquiry, Operation Elveden and Operation Pallial all cast doubt on police integrity and competence. It is in these circumstances that the public ought to be able to turn to the IPCC to investigate and we believe that it ought to have a more prominent role in each of these operations (Paragraph 42).

11. Some kinds of complaint are simply not appropriate for Police Complaints Departments to investigate themselves. Cases involving serious corruption should

be automatically referred to the IPCC for independent investigation. The Government has committed itself to provide more resources for the IPCC to investigate the Hillsborough disaster. Once that investigation is complete, that funding should be maintained and dedicated to anti-corruption cases (Paragraph 43).

12. Allegations following the altercation between Rt Hon Andrew Mitchell MP and police officers raise fundamental questions about police honesty and integrity. The alleged unauthorised disclosure of information to the press on the night of 19 September 2012 and the alleged fabrication of an eye-witness account on Thursday 20 September 2012 are extremely serious; if officers could do this in a case involving the protection of the Prime Minister's own home, it raises the question how often might this be happening outside the gaze of the national media. As Mr Mitchell said, '[I]f this can happen to a senior government minister, then what chance would a youth in Brixton or Handsworth have?' (Paragraph 44).

13. We support the commissioner's 'relentless pursuit of the truth' and believe West Midlands Police Federation were wrong in calling for the resignation of a Cabinet minister. However, it was hasty of the commissioner to say he was 100 per cent behind his officers and to Rt Hon David Davis MP the investigation was closed when it had not been investigated with any rigour (Paragraph 45).

14. We note the commissioner's intention to ask another force to independently review the investigations underway in Operation Alice—whilst a welcome safeguard, it is no substitute for independent investigation by the IPCC. It should investigate this case independently and the Government should provide funds, if necessary, as with Hillsborough (Paragraph 46).

15. Mediation and restorative justice present rich avenues for improving the handling of police complaints. The commission should set out best practice protocols for their use in appropriate cases and the use of informal or local resolution systems should be independently monitored to ensure that it is not used inappropriately in relation to conduct that would justify criminal or disciplinary proceedings (Paragraph 49).

16. The root of the problem is that the front line of the police complaints system is not working. It is unacceptable that PSDs had made the wrong decision in 38 per cent of appeals. The number of appeals upheld varies wildly from force to force, as does the proportion of appeals upheld by the IPCC and PCCs must take decisive action where a force is shown to be failing. The commission's robust handling of appeals is welcome, but costly. Far more effort should be made to ensure correct decisions are made in the first instance. We have written to each chief constable to ask for the staff complement and budget of their PSDs (Paragraph 60).

17. Where a threshold of 25 per cent of appeals are upheld, the commission must demand a written explanation from chief constables and PCCs, which should be followed by a six month probation period. After that time, if the proportion of appeals upheld is not reduced below the threshold, a 'complaints competency investigation' must be held into decisions made at the local level. This should involve a joint report by the IPCC, HMIC and the local PCC, which would lead to proposals binding on chief constables. If applied now, these measures would affect all but four forces (Paragraph 61).

18. It is a basic failing in the system that there is no requirement for forces to respond to recommendations from the IPCC, still less implement them. We recommend that the commission be given a statutory power to require a force to respond to its findings. In the most serious cases, the commission should instigate a 'year on review' to ensure its recommendations have been properly carried out. Any failure to do so would result in an investigation by HMIC and the local PCC, as a professional conduct matter relating to the chief constable (Paragraph 69).

19. If the commission's primary statutory purpose is to increase public confidence, then it must act to rectify the impression that the police are investigating the police. The commission must improve its in-house investigative resources towards a target of 20 per cent of investigators who have moved directly from a career as a police officer, or fewer, so the number of former officers investigating the police is significantly reduced (Paragraph 78).

20. HMIC must play a more prominent role in investigations of the most serious cases. In cases involving serious police corruption, e.g., one of HM Inspectors

should review the IPCC's findings and be tasked with ensuring implementation of any IPCC recommendations. HMIC's responsibility for forces' effectiveness make it a natural candidate for involvement in the 'complaints competency investigation' and the inspectorate should ensure any findings for a particular force are taken up by other forces where necessary (Paragraph 79).

21. The issue of interviewing officers in cases involving death and serious injury is indicative of a culture of treating officers differently from members of the public. Where officers are not interviewed promptly under caution, this can lead to weaker evidence and loss of confidence in the process of investigating, e.g. s deaths in custody. The application of the threshold test should be reviewed, so that officers are routinely interviewed under caution in the most serious cases, exactly as a member of the public would be (Paragraph 85).

22. The Government should revise the definition of the threshold. One option would be that death and serious injury cases should be treated as 'conduct' matters with special requirements and officers interviewed under caution except if 'beyond reasonable doubt' that a misconduct or criminal offence has not been committed (Paragraph 86).

23. The adequacy of communications between the IPCC and the public can have serious implications. Some of the violence across London in the riots of 2011 may have been avoided if anger had not been intensified by inaccurate statements from the IPCC (Paragraph 93).

24. Accurate and timely information is also vital in retaining confidence in the complaints process. The commission should set out a timetable for an investigation for complainants and write to them to explain any deviation. If the commission orders a police complaints department to reinvestigate, it should also set a timetable for that and any deviation should be explained to both the complainant and the commission. There should be sanctions if not followed (Paragraph 94).

25. The commission should communicate positive outcomes through different channels, including social media. Prosecutions, misconduct findings and

recommendations must be more widely publicised in a way that openly demonstrates scrutiny of the police (Paragraph 95).

26. We note that although the IPCC is allowed to hear complaints about the Serious Organized Crime Agency (SOCA), the position regarding the new National Crime Agency (NCA) is less clear. We recommend that the NCA be subject to IPCC procedures as with police forces generally (Paragraph 102).

27. The landscape of policing is changing and the IPCC must change with it. Increasingly, companies like G4S, Capita, Mitie and Serco are involved in delivering services that would once have fallen solely to the police…yet the public cannot call on the IPCC to investigate their delivery of those services (Paragraph 109).

28. The commission's jurisdiction should be extended to cover private sector contractors in their delivery of policing services and appropriate funding should be available for it to undertake all the functions, which we consider it should have responsibility for (Paragraph 110).

29. The commission should be renamed to reflect its broader remit and functions, covering appeals and complaints for police, the UKBA, HMRC and the NCA. 'The Independent Policing Standards Authority' is one possibility (Paragraph 111).

One can only conclude that the supposedly independent police watchdog, intended to foster confidence in the police, is toothless, misguided, far too police-orientated and its findings can be and seemingly often are ignored by the police.[5]

Comment

In spite of their own assessment (Paragraphs 7 and 8 above) the HAC made a number of proposals including increasing the remit of the IPCC and changing its name to 'The Independent Policing Standards Authority'

---

5. See also *Chapter 17* where Dr Rodger Patrick provided figures to the HAC and listed methods by which police altered the Home Office recorded crime figures.

(Paragraph 29). It seems unlikely that the IPCC, currently unable to cope with its existing span of responsibility and workload, will cope with further tasks—at least before resolving the current raft of issues. Furthermore, another re-branding/renaming exercise will do nothing to revitalise public confidence in the system and will take the focus away from resolving the fundamentals of police, PSD and IPCC problems. I therefore disagree with these suggestions and counter-suggest that if any broadening of the IPCC remit is to be considered, let it be removing their current appeals constraints and, to improve the balance of their conclusions, by allowing challenges, at least until public confidence is restored.

CHAPTER 22

Policing Using a Zero-Tolerance Standard

Policing policies go through phases. The Home Secretary, usually influenced by political pressure, dogma and sometimes election promises, steers policing policy at national level. Politicians of all colours tend to promise hard-hitting measures against crime and few will forget Prime Minister Tony Blair's 1997 election slogan 'Tough on crime—tough on the causes of crime'. According to 'Community Policing in the 21st Century', a paper published 16 years later under the post-2009 Coalition Government,[1]

> The approach of the last decade has been for central government to intervene more and more in local policing in an attempt to make it more accountable. There has been an ever-increasing list of legislation with the specific aim of centralising policing. The Home Secretary has been given stronger and stronger powers to intervene; to set national objectives; publish data relating to performance; issue codes of practice and guidance; and direct police authorities. In 2001 this…continued through the creation of the Home Office Police Standards Unit.

Furthermore:

> The police have been tied up in bureaucracy following central guidance setting out how they should do their work rather than using their professional judgment to get on with their jobs serving their communities. Police have become form writers rather than crime fighters, taken away from the public by bureaucracy and overly prescriptive central guidance. Despite record numbers of police officers and staff, the police are spending less time on the street.

So currently we have 'community policing' that, according to the Coalition Government, will reconnect the police and the people.

---

1. Crown Copyright.

Increasing Government interference in recent years has changed the focus of
the police. They have become responsive to government targets and bureaucracy
rather than to people. They have become disconnected from the public they
serve. Crime is still too high; too many individuals and neighbourhoods suffer
anti-social behaviour; and only just over half the public have confidence that the
issues that matter locally are being dealt with.

It may be an unfortunate coincidence, but it seems that public confidence
in the police has plummeted since the Coalition Government came to power.
There is certainly much more, and still growing, public and media attention
on police integrity and one has to wonder whether alleged dishonesty has
always been there but is now in the spotlight. A couple of our older contributors to *Part 1* of this work confirm that police integrity issues were a fact of
life many years ago but the extent of it and the degree of exposure seems to
have increased exponentially. During the 2000s the pressure on the police
to get results increased, 'sanctioned detections' targets were brought in and
the underlying 'because we can' culture of questionable integrity seemed to
increase under the pressure to meet targets and earn bonuses.

In 2012, Paul Lewis, Vikram Dodd and Rob Evans wrote in *The Guardian*
a piece headlined 'Police recorded 8,500 corruption allegations in three
years'.[2] The IPCC report collated data for all forces in England and Wales
between 2008 and 2011. During that period, 8,542 allegations of corruption
were recorded by police forces. Of those, only 837 were referred to the IPCC
which only had the resources or powers to investigate 21 of the most serious
cases. Extracts include (summarised):

- Only 13 officers had been prosecuted and found guilty.
- The IPCC warned that although police corruption is not deemed
  to be 'widespread', it has a 'corrosive' impact on public trust.
- There was a specific reference to concerns about potentially
  corrupt relationships between police officers and the private sector.
- The IPCC investigates only a small fraction of corruption allegations, owing to its limited remit and resources, leaving individual
  forces to investigate their own officers in most cases.

---

2.   24th May 2012 at http://www.theguardian.com/politics/2012/may/24/
     police-watchdog-corruption-complaints

The Guardian reported that the IPCC's new chair, Dame Anne Owers would be seeking greater power and resources for tackling corruption, and would raise these concerns with Ministers directly. She was quoted as saying, 'This report illustrates the kind of behaviour that undermines public confidence in the police such as abuse of authority, perverting the course of justice and accepting generous hospitality.' Detailing hundreds of cases of alleged corruption and a steady increase in recent years, including of serious corruption, sometimes at senior level, the IPCC called for more teeth. The report also came in the same week Parliament heard allegations that officers within the Met's anti-corruption unit were paid bribes. The Met was investigating allegations that a firm of private investigators, composed of former Met officers, may have bribed serving officers. The next day, offices were raided, and a Scotland Yard detective and three former Met police officers arrested.

The police-forces/IPCC/CPS non-prosecution policy for anything other than the most serious police errors and the rather public live TV coverage of the HAC interviewing 'Plebgate' witnesses have all contributed to declining public confidence. In *Chapter 20* I drew attention to the poor performance of PSDs and noted that Messrs Lewis, Dodd and Evans tell us that only about nine per cent of the 8,542 allegations were referred to the IPCC. In other words 91 per cent of the initial allegations will have been investigated by PSDs which found no grounds for further consideration of colleagues' conduct.

An erring police officer has a further advantage because when the police commit a crime they seem to receive very favourable treatment as the figures in *Chapter 19* concerning prosecution demonstrate; leading to my view that one organization should take charge. It would seem that Deborah Glass, deputy chair of the IPCC, agrees with my one-organization thinking—at least she did when BBC News quoted her on 31st October 2011 in a *Panorama* report that was calling for stronger oversight as the police avoid scrutiny:

> There is no overall body that has responsibility for the police misconduct system other than the Home Office, I dare say…local police authorities play a role in the process and offer a measure of accountability but the lack of a single national overview does have an effect.

Not discussed by her nor the BBC was the question of whether on the occasions that the police *are* found guilty of an offence, whether actual sentences are appropriate. FOI information publicised that over the course of three years to 2011, 1,915 Metropolitan police officers were guilty of misconduct, which may not be a criminal offence in itself but nevertheless officers can and have been dismissed including following Plebgate and after Operation Alice. Of the 1,915 misconducts, only 20 per cent were dismissed, most resigned while 25 per cent of the total were allowed to retire before their disciplinary hearing. I addressed the resignation issue elsewhere but it bears repetition to ask if it is right that officers are allowed to resign or retire to avoid disciplinary hearings. The terms of each officer's retirement are rightly personal, but it is widely held that such retirements are on full pension. It is to be hoped that these officers who served the stipulated 20 years did not received a Good Conduct Medal!

Via FOI the Met also reported that 42 officers and staff were disciplined in two months early in 2013, 15 faced a misconduct hearings but were only punished by written warnings or reprimands. This seems typical of police forces across the country and to my mind is too lenient even for disciplinary issues. However, to mention another more serious example, Gloucestershire Constabulary revealed that five police officers resigned in 2013 over criminal offences but all resigned without dismissal and that five more officers left because of criminal activities in the two years 2010/12. In fact I believe you will find that as many as 1,000 police officers serving across the whole of the UK have criminal records.[3] How/why can this be allowed to happen?

You can enquire about your local police force via FOI but perhaps the most distressing of many is the Ian Tomlinson story. His death in April 2009 occurred in the context of the Met turning a blind-eye to the disciplinary record of the officer involved. The story of Mr Tomlinson's death is well-documented by newspapers and others so the detail behind the four years of purgatory the family were put through does not bear repeating here. Simon Harwood, the officer concerned, was acquitted of manslaughter but an apology was issued by the Met in August 2013 which included:

---

3. I rely here on my own estimation after seeing the research conducted by Paul Woods mentioned in *Chapter 16*.

> Issues concerning the failure to discipline Simon Harwood and his re-admission into the Metropolitan Police in 2004 have been a source of concern and upset for the family. It is clear that insufficient recording and checks meant that detailed information regarding the officer's misconduct history was not shared at key points. We got it wrong. The commissioner acknowledges that this case has highlighted significant failings in the vetting procedures of the Metropolitan Police Service and we have taken steps to put in place new procedures that will improve public confidence.

Sadly these 'We've learned something' responses do nothing to bring Mr. Tomlinson back and nothing to compensate for the over four year fight his family had to endure to bring about this admission and get some kind of justice. And it would be interesting to hear the Met detail what disciplinary/criminal-record lessons they have learnt and revised. Unbelievably when you consider matters, the Met, including during the officer's criminal trial (when he was found not guilty of the criminal charge of manslaughter) hid the officer's disciplinary history. However, the history was later revealed via five 'lever-arch' files. He had resigned from the Met police on the grounds of ill-health in 2001 just prior to a disciplinary hearing to investigate an off-duty road-rage confrontation he was involved with when he tried to arrest the other party and altered his notes to justify his actions. He then joined Surrey Police and transferred back to the Met in 2004 where, although it must be stressed most remained unproven, on nine occasions he was, true or not, supposed to have threatened and/or used force on suspects.

Discipline avoidance seems alive and well. What solutions are there? In *Chapter 21* I touched on zero-tolerance (ZT) of all police indiscipline, dishonesty, corruption or whatever euphemism is used. Those who call a spade a spade call it gross misconduct, perverting the course of justice, misconduct, bribery, lying, intimidation, conspiracy *et al* and argue that the police are that part of our society that upholds the law so *absolute* trust is an essential, non-negotiable requirement. In short the police must be 'whiter than white'. One reason for the growing public disquiet around police integrity is that officers seem to escape justice by excessive tolerance by their authorities and the IPCC or, if all else fails, by being allowed to resign/retire. The Government does seem intent on partly plugging the resignation loophole but much remains unaddressed and consequently I suggest we explore ZT because I believe this is standard that police discipline should be judged by.

Originally conceived as a neighbourhood policing strategy rather than a method of policing the police, ZT runs counter to community policing-style preferences. I accept that the Government can use whatever style of neighbourhood policing it believes works best. Nevertheless with current discipline and corruption suspicions, the police and all associated staff *should* be subject to a policy of ZT. No deviations whatsoever in their professionalism should be acceptable and a ZT standard should be applied to all ranks. The Government's consultation report 'Policing in the 21st Century, Reconnecting Police and the People'[4] fails to address the lack of confidence in the police, the apparent growth of impropriety (or at least the publicity of it) and the role that enhanced police discipline standards could bring about.

Interestingly, neighbourhood ZT policing enjoyed strong political and public support when it was the 'in' thing during the 1980s and 1990s but nevertheless was unpopular among some UK police forces. It was originally introduced in the New York Police Department as 'positive policing' and was seemingly at least partly behind the Blair Government's 'tough on crime' message of the late-1990s. The New York theory was that all crime, including minor misdemeanours, must be vigorously pursued and the policy is credited with dramatically reducing crime wherever it was adopted in the USA. This resulted in local residents feeling much more positive about their neighbourhoods and is said to have achieved a 39 per cent fall in New York crime figures. So one could be forgiven for thinking what's not to like about ZT policing. There were detractors and those who claimed the crime reductions were little to do with ZT policing but attributable to new computer systems that should be given the credit. There are also displacement theories, i.e. the idea that ZT simply causes offenders to offend somewhere else. But this is hardly open to your everyday policeman.

ZT was also successfully used in several areas of the UK, the most well known being Cleveland where a 20 per cent crime reduction took place in, famously, 18 months. Detective Superintendent Ray Mallon subsequently suffered damage to his policing reputation after he admitted receiving but

4.   See https://www.gov.uk/government/uploads/system/uploads/attachment_data/file/118241/policing-21st-full-pdf.pdf

ignoring reports that some of his officers were guilty of misconduct. This cast a shadow over the admiration and awareness of his crime reductions and social improvements brought about by ZT approaches. After leaving the police force, the local populace showed its appreciation by electing him mayor!

To paint a slightly broader picture of ZT policing of the streets in the 1980s, we also need to acknowledge that computer technology software was introduced about the same time and no doubt contributed to improved policing responses. 'Compstat' is the computerised crime-tracking system that ZT detractors feel had the greater influence on crime reduction. What is beyond doubt is that a combination of ZT polices aided by computer technology allowed police to deploy personnel and resources efficiently which, aided by the ZT message being delivered at every opportunity, brought about overall crime reductions of the order of 60 per cent.

I feel that ZT should be applied to police officers' discipline even if the neighbourhoods they police are more liberally supervised. Furthermore, the police, with their responsibility to provide a role model to society must receive meaningful, indeed hurtful, punishments when offending and the discipline must be administered without the opportunities of loopholes, transfers, full pensions and long-service retirement awards.

Comment

Currently and on the basis of what I can discern, police officers and police staff are more likely to avoid the disciplinary and/or criminal justice that civilians would be required to submit to by two preferential treatments. Some officers are allowed to continue to serve despite convictions while others are allowed to resign/retire and thereby avoid internal police disciplinary proceedings and/or criminal charges as a result of processes that remain behind closed doors. These loopholes require closing if respect and confidence is ever to be re-established.

CHAPTER 23

Police and Crime Commissioners (PCCs)

Police and crime commissioners (PCCs) replaced the earlier police authorities for each police force area in 2012 with a view to increasing the public's
democratic say in policing and policing priorities in 41 geographical areas
of England and Wales. PCCs are paid for their work in this full-time role.
London where the mayor carries out that function in relationship with the
Home Secretary is excluded. This is a plank of the Government's 'community policing' changes designed to reconnect the public with the police. The
first elections for PCCs were held in 2012 with incumbents taking up their
posts in November 2012. They will take place every four years.

While the former police authorities for each area may have been outmoded,
a new local body, the police and crime panel (PCP) has been introduced to
scrutinise the actions and decisions of PCCs and to ensure that information
is available to the public so that it may hold their local PCC to account.
Each panel comprises of a joint committee reflecting most of the authorities
in the area endowed with some legal powers to hold their PCC, but not the
police force, to account. Quite what the real differences, benefits and disadvantages of a PCP are compared to a police authority is difficult to assess
but the change has certainly brought about a raft of additional regulations
and statutory provisions.[1]

There are Government protocols outlining the respective roles of PCCs
and their chief constables and clear statements about both roles and responsibilities which they are expected to adhere to when working together.[2] Prior
to the changeover, police authorities consisted of appointed councillors
who were supposed to hold their area police force to account. There is little
evidence that they were effective but whether the succeeding PCP/PCC

---

1. See, e.g. http://www.ipcc.gov.uk/sites/default/files/Documents/complaints/complaints_
   guidance_for_police_and_crime_panels.PDF and http://www.legislation.gov.uk/
   uksi/2012/2271/made
2. https://www.gov.uk/government/uploads/system/uploads/attachment_data/file/117463/role-
   as-pcc.pdf

arrangements will eventually prove to be any more effective remains to be seen. PCCs collectively got off to a poor start when the electoral turnout for their appointments was one of the lowest on record. The Electoral Reform Society estimated that this followed some £75 million in pre-election costs:

> Ninety per cent of Britons have no idea who their elected police and crime com-
> missioner even is. November's bungled poll failed both candidates and voters.
> Government mismanagement has handed our elected commissioners a poisoned
> chalice, and it remains unclear how they can overcome it.

To an extent and to the best of my knowledge few apart from Home Secretary Theresa May have trumpeted improvements brought about by PCCs. Nevertheless, to present a balanced picture, she told the Policy Exchange on the first anniversary of the PCC appointments that (extracts):

> [O]nly seven per cent of people even knew that police authorities existed, but today
> around 70 per cent of people know about their police and crime commissioner.
> And even though police and crime commissioners have been in place for just
> one year, they are already receiving ten, 20, sometimes even 50 times the volume
> of correspondence received by police authorities.

> I believe there is more that can be done to improve the public's awareness and
> understanding of the performance of their local police force and their police and
> crime commissioner … I believe those signs do suggest that we will see a better
> turnout next time round.

> Many individual police and crime commissioners have played a visible role in
> incidents relevant to the communities they represent, like Matthew Ellis who
> responded to the revelations about Stafford Hospital and Mark Burns-Williamson
> who responded to allegations about the conduct of his chief constable, Norman
> Bettison[3] earlier in his career.

---

3. These extracts included under Open Government Licence v2.0. Sir Norman Bettison, already
    accused of covering up the causes of the Hillsborough football crowd disaster, was referred
    to the IPCC by West Yorkshire's PCC following claims that he was also thought to have
    influenced a witness for the Stephen Lawrence Inquiry. Bettison denies all such matters.

The second test I set for police and crime commissioners is to what extent are they driving reform, innovation and the delivery of more efficient policing? And here I think we're seeing some very encouraging signs…

Many police and crime commissioners are looking not just to reform and make savings by collaborating with other forces but with other emergency services. In Northamptonshire, Adam Simmonds has been bold enough to question why we have three separate emergency services. He is considering ways of integrating the police and fire service, and I know—with the support of his local county council—he's looking at setting up a combined headquarters, possibly inside a new county council centre. This is exactly the sort of innovation I want the Government not just to applaud—but take firm action across the whole country to help deliver…

The third test I set…is to what extent are they making full use of their powers to hold their forces to account? And here, I think, the picture is a little mixed. I know that many police and crime commissioners were horrified when they saw their counterparts rush to the defence of their local forces after the Independent Police Complaints Commission cast doubt on the internal disciplinary investigations into the treatment of Andrew Mitchell in Sutton Coldfield last year.

I've made my views clear on what the IPCC said about that case, and while I'm not going to stand here and condemn those commissioners, it will be down to them to explain to their local communities whether, in rushing to defend their local forces and condemn the IPCC, they showed good judgement.

On police budgets and precepts, I have already talked about the many innovations being driven by police and crime commissioners to make their forces more efficient…

Some police and crime commissioners are using other powers available to them to hold their force to account. Ann Barnes, the police and crime commissioner for Kent, called in the Inspectorate of Constabulary to look at the force's recording of crime and as a result uncovered practices that were frankly inappropriate. Action was quickly taken to put things right and as result the residents of Kent can have confidence in how the police record crime.

The ability of police and crime commissioners to hire and fire chief constables was perhaps the most controversial power we granted—especially to chief constables. And while I am not going to get into the rights and wrongs of every decision by a commissioner to hire or fire a chief constable, the truth is that this power is fundamental...I emphasise, without approving or criticising any individual decisions that have been made—it is a positive sign that the commissioners have been prepared to use this power.

So the Home Secretary thinks there are some encouraging signs but there have also been one or two rumblings. Kent's PCC made some unwanted headlines firstly by appointing a 16-year-old youth crime commissioner who resigned slightly ignominiously before commencing her work. The same PCC allowed a TV programme to be made about her work. It seems that people found this less than impressive and it brought about calls for her resignation which she declined. This brought to light the fact that no-one, not least the relevant PCP, can remove a PCC if they decline to resign until the public has had that opportunity at the next PCC elections. One has resigned[4] and four PCCs have necessitated IPCC investigations, presumably after complaints. The IPCC took no further action in North Wales or in Hampshire. One, retrospective to when the PCC was a deputy chief constable, while a further report was passed to the CPS. The investigation was in fact concluded in March 2013 when the IPCC report concluded 'therefore it is not considered that there is a case to answer in respect of honesty and integrity.'[5]

Such stories are disappointing but nevertheless the theory of publicly-driven policy guidance to the police actually sounds good to me. However, I found unsettling the Home Secretary's account of the mixed PCC reactions to the disciplinary/integrity questions brought into the public spotlight by the televised HAC meeting over the conduct of three Police Federation

---

4. The PCC for South Yorkshire did in 2014 'for the sake of victims' after allegations of historical links to a local social services department when his then staff oversaw child welfare at a time of extensive child abuse. In essence his position had become untenable.

5. See https://www.ipcc.gov.uk/sites/default/files/Documents/investigation_commissioner_reports/Bettison_Final_Report_incl_Foreword_FINAL_for_publication.pdf

representatives. The Home Secretary commented that the respective PCCs rushed to the defence of their chief constables after internal disciplinary investigations into the conduct of the federation representatives. The three senior police officers, after studying the IPCC report, concluded that those representatives had no case to answer. To be fair, the PCCs will not have had the benefit of the subsequent HAC witnesses and evidence when they made their decisions. But they were clearly aware and had the opportunity to consider that the IPCC had held an inquiry into the conduct of the federation representatives which had cast doubt on their conduct and integrity. Furthermore, earlier events in the same Plebgate saga (*Chapter 9*) had brought the Met police to submit evidence about five different police officers to the CPS. Consequently, on the information that was available, the PCCs should have exercised some caution and the chief constables seem to have established their 'superiority' from these events. In the context of their respective long-term working relationships, which I'll hypothesise on shortly, that does not auger well for the future of PCCs.

I would have thought there was never a better time, case or cause for the PCCs of West Mercia, West Midlands and Warwickshire to make their mark by supporting the IPCC. Maybe from divided loyalties, they stood behind their officers. In outline, to save the reader leafing back to *Chapter 9*, three federation representatives made questionable public statements after a meeting with Andrew Mitchell MP in October 2012 and thus before the PCCs were appointed. However, during an IPCC supervised joint investigation through spring/summer 2013, when the PCCs were in post, the deputy or assistant (as appropriate) chief constables of West Mercia, West Midlands and Warwickshire police forces looked into the conduct of the federation representatives, all serving police officers, and found there to be no case for the federation representatives to answer. The IPCC drafted a report suggesting misconduct but the senior rank officers effectively altered the report's conclusion. In October 2013, the IPCC released a statement that strongly disagreed with the revised conclusion offered by these senior officers, instead suggesting there was a case for gross misconduct hearings.

In effect, the PCC/chief constable relationship involves a meeting of equals. Any one-on-one relationship requires mutual respect and necessitates an effective working relationship. The theory is that each PCC holds his or her chief constable to account for policing in the respective force area but without a direct line of authority. This arrangement seems not dissimilar to a consultant/company doctor's relationship with the client's chief executive. If it works, it works and can work very well. If it falters, there are problems. Theoretically, PCCs have hiring and firing authority over their chief constable but the firing part isn't so easy as it once was in other contexts and furthermore that authority doesn't automatically ensure a harmonious, co-operative, productive working relationship. A newcomer, particularly without extensive experience of policing and with a minimal public mandate, will likely find some chief constables hard to handle. Anyone with a lifetime of policing, seniority, bullet dodging and (most likely) support from the ranks will understandably find the new arrangement hard to stomach if push comes to shove. Hiring and firing authority is also quite different to the inevitable differences in views, priorities and methods that a one-on-one arrangement brings about on a daily basis. I have no doubt many PCCs are getting along famously and working productively with 'their' chief constable. I also have no doubt some are not. Re-election time might be quite interesting too.

So the Home Secretary's view may have been a little rose-tinted and would appear not to be shared by the majority of voters, as Alan Travis and Patrick Wintour, writing in *The Guardian* on 14 November 2013 reported under the heading 'Public confidence in Police and Crime Commissioners drains away':[6]

> The limited public support for PCCs has drained away further in their first year of office, according to a survey that shows only 10% of people polled agreed that the commissioners gave them more say in how their local area was policed. The public opinion poll, by YouGov, comes on the anniversary of the PCCs' introduction and as Home Office proposals are announced that would allow members of the public to have their 'everyday complaints' about the police dealt with by the commissioners. A summer 2012 poll showed 27% expected PCCs would give them a greater say. In the new poll, only 9% of those polled thought PCCs had contributed to a fall in crime in their area.

Furthermore, in her speech to the College of Policing on the 24 October

---

6.   http://www.theguardian.com/uk-news/2013/nov/14/
     public-support-waning-police-crime-commissioners

2013, the Home Secretary also told us that, referring to the extra resources planned for IPCC, she knew that some forces and PCC were resisting the transfer of resources necessary for the IPCC to take on this bigger role which hardly enhances the image of the new PCCs driving forward improvement through a cooperative liaison with their chief constables. However, with the IPCC already failing, one has to question whether the PCCs are not in fact right to be resisting this particular move. So, were I able to put the clock back a couple of years, I would also question why the Home Secretary chose to have a one-on-one top police structure in each of the 41 policing areas outside London. I may agree with the concept of the top police executive for each area being subjected to election and re-election every four years but why add another tier, an extra public body and extra cost to the policing structure? Why not pass legislation that requires the chief constable's post itself to be electable?

Furthermore my personal contact with the Sussex PCC, co-incidentally one of those singled out by the Home Secretary for praise, suggests that at least some commissioners see their responsibility as rather narrower than the above Government policy states. The pith of the reply I received from Sussex PCC in April 2013, when complaining about Sussex PSD was

> Please note that it is the police and commissioners statutory duty to investigate complaints against the chief constable of (respective county) police (where he has been personally involved). The chief constable is responsible for investigating complaints against police staff and officers and on operational and policy matters.

On that basis, it seems unlikely these appointments will have much effect on the flywheel of police inertia, culture and, to my mind the all-important improvement, integrity.

Finally we can note that the Home Secretary is not in favour of 'the traditional Association of Chief Police Officers solution of continually merging forces' although one would have thought an inventive mind could have devised ways of reviewing both the geographical and types of responsibilities without 'taking accountability further and further away from local communities'. At present the police forces of England and Wales are too numerous and I believe each is required to cover too many issues. Better they cover less ground but do so effectively—so in fact the Government's advisers should focus on consolidating the police's primary role of preventing and solving crime.

Consequently, road safety patrols, traffic policing and speed cameras are a major bone of contention with the public who feel they do little to cut accidents and are there to raise revenue. Of course the police will strongly deny that assertion but the image of the criminal-investigating police would be improved if all traffic policing responsibilities were amalgamated into a specialised nationwide traffic division separated from crime-prevention and criminal detecting. This will help the criminal police both by narrowing their focus and improving their image. Few things are more upsetting than seeing a police car sitting, usually in a carefully obscured spot, waiting for a motorist to creep by a few miles above the speed limit when he or she has just had his or her house burgled, called the police and nothing happened as described in earlier chapters. A dedicated 'highway patrol' would help separate their often less than kindly demeanour from impinging on the criminal police's image.

At the other end of the policing scale and possibly at a later date, serious crime investigation such as murder could automatically become the responsibility not of local police forces but a national murder investigation team. That would seem to bring the specialist experience to bear earlier in an investigation and clearly the National Crime Agency (NCA) might be the ideal recipient of these responsibilities.

Subsequently the reduced-size geographically orientated but now crime-focused police forces and their numerous PCCs could then be amalgamated as the geography/population of regions dictate into perhaps half the present number of forces, with consequential economies of scale and hopefully greater effectiveness. Changes that bring about simplification and provide accountability have great merit. The election of PCCs and having them report to an unelected PCP seems to be increasing complications and cost.

PART 3

Summing-up

CHAPTER 24

So What's to be Done (and by Whom)?

This book's contributors, the national press, television programmes, lobby groups, victim support groups, MPs, the Parliamentary Home Affairs Select Committee, the Parliamentary Privileges and Public Administration Select Committees — not to mention those within the general public who have experienced involvement with the criminal justice system — will likely know there are problems with at least parts of the system. Little seems to change for the better and many people want answers.

Lord Maginnis of Drumglass, addressing the House of Lords, said, 'Basic justice is distorted by the system, but I can see nothing to address this major issue in the Government's plans.' So it seems the Government already knows of the problems but, to use my earlier phrase, has just 'tickled round the edges' to effect minor improvements. However, many people not only want answers but solutions that get to the root of problems. This final chapter weighs-up some of the possible options, certain of which may be controversial, in an effort to create discussion, debate, promises, manifestos, policies, but ultimately remedial action.

One thing seems clear: changes are needed to improve the justice system generally, but way the role of the police is discharged in particular. And the changes are so fundamental and, because the system is so entrenched in its ways, only the Government can bring these about, raising the question of which party or parties is or are proficient, strong and committed enough to take the necessary action. They would be breaking the mould, which is usually painful and always resisted, so it remains to be seen if *any* politicians will rise to the challenge. It probably largely depends upon how much public pressure is applied to MPs in their constituencies. What seems clear is that neither the police nor the IPCC in particular are willing, capable or interested in bringing about these changes of their own accord.

So what needs to be done? First let's spend a moment on the 'how' question. In the wake of a spate of press complaints, the Government set up an enquiry under Lord Justice Leveson to assess the culture, practices and ethics of the press. While I have the greatest admiration for Leveson and his enquiry's work, there were at least six months of hearings and, understandably, many more months' delay while an extensive report was prepared. When it was finally available, the recommendations were disputed and implementation fudged to the point where, at least at the time of writing, I cannot recall whether anything fundamental was achieved by that entire endeavour? So a special committee of MPs perhaps or maybe an augmented Home Affairs Committee, since they have already met to consider the IPCC and other aspects of policing, might help find solutions which could gain Parliamentary support.

There could be one chink of light. As 2014 turned to 2015, the Home Office published an invitation for public contributions to a review of policing integrity and discipline. A summary of this book was submitted within the allotted timeframe and will hopefully be taken into account.[1]

As explained in the book, even some MPs have experienced a 'because we can'-style approach to policing in which the complaints system acts as a barrier rather than an encouragement to resolution of disputes with citizens. This surely confirms that it is in the interests of the whole country to seek change: an unfettered police force but with essential deterrents to 'freestyle'-policing. I would summarise my conclusions as follows. They are not presented in any particular order:

(a) The police should not investigate themselves

There can be little doubt that this entrenched practice, unchallenged for decades, now appears to be inappropriate. It not only fosters cover-ups and potentially corruption but causes resentment and detracts from public confidence in the police. To remove all doubt I'm referring to the fact that currently each police force investigates all complaints lodged against that same force using its own Professional Standards Department (PSD or DPS in the case of the Met), so that local PSDs investigate their own local colleagues'

---

1. https://www.gov.uk/government/consultations/
   improving-police-integrity-reforming-the-police-complaints-and-disciplinary-systems

alleged bad conduct. Each PSD reports to the same chief constable as the rest of that force. What could be more perverse?

The volume of complaints lodged by the public against police conduct remains high as do post-PSD appeals to the IPCC, perhaps endorsing the contention that PSDs are at the heart of the public's dissatisfaction with the complaints system. Whilst it is good news that the IPCC is upholding more appeals after having softened the criteria as to whether the police reached 'the standard a reasonable person would expect' nevertheless this is a 'sticking-plaster' repair avoiding the roots of the problem.

Many professions have an in-built reluctance (understandable perhaps) to find a colleague's efforts wanting. The police in particular, whose job involves close teamwork often under difficult and sometimes dangerous conditions need dependability, loyalty and to watch one another's backs in the field is likely to mean closing-ranks when criticism is levied. Furthermore, it becomes much more difficult to objectively investigate officers and staff who you've worked with for some time and who could be friends, mentors, neighbours or simply known to you. Any chief constable will see little benefit in his or her PSD finding his or her police officers or teams wanting. Consequently, the system of local police investigating local colleagues needs to change.

I believe that PSDs should be divorced from chief constables altogether and made responsible to another body. That could, e.g. be the National Crime Agency or National Police College upgraded to a regulatory body, but placing this under Her Majesty's Inspectorate of Constabulary (HMIC) might be the better solution. With their regional offices already established, and with HMIC's more objective style, it should have the capability to separate local police from investigating local police. This would improve investigations and consequently contribute to reducing the number of police complaints lodged at the IPCC. Simultaneously, HMIC would learn of the problems experienced by a disaffected public.

(b) Improve discipline and introduce meaningful sanctions

All the accounts I heard whilst compiling data for my book reveal police shortcomings: several tell of falsification, fabrication and corruption. To add insult to injury, the sanctions meted-out by the various police forces can often be derisory and make the police and the IPCC, which may have made a quite reasonable recommendation, appear weak. There are instances of quite serious misconduct resulting in words of advice and others where even after gross misconduct proceedings officers have soon been promoted or despite a written warning being added to their file. More sensitive and proportionate use of powers to promote/demote erring officers would be welcome..

Police errors seem to attract little by way of deterrent and perhaps, consequently, we have a problem with integrity, a fact confirmed by many of the experiences I have heard of. This despite extensive lists compiled on my behalf of those public servants, mainly police officers, convicted in the last few years in spite of the current inefficiencies and reluctance to prosecute. Many it seems still escape this net.

We frequently hear of chief constables over-riding and/or simply ignoring discipline recommendations for their officers. In one case three chief constables 'altered' an IPCC conclusion but there are other examples of no, or derisory, disciplinary action. Since they have shown themselves as unable to recognise the wider issues that such authority brings, discipline should be ceded to a single independent authority, perhaps under the auspices of the NCA or NCP, and whose key focus is the investigation, disciplining, or advising on prosecution of police and other employees within police services.

The Government needs to consider and perhaps legislate in such a way that police malpractice is unacceptable at any level and so that zero-tolerance (below) is applied to police (as well as prison, prosecution and court personnel) found erring from the highest standards of integrity. Furthermore, although there may be howls of protest from some quarters, strong deterrents need to exist and be implemented. All those who do their jobs in an honest, fair and balanced manner have nothing to fear, but discipline equating to civilian standards needs to be applied, not only for lapses in honesty, conduct, behaviour, or integrity but perhaps with an additional penalty for the officer's breach of public trust. This does not seem to be the case at present.

The Home Secretary has announced that officers 'retiring' to avoid disciplinary hearings will be added to the 'struck-off' list if a hearing in their absence finds them guilty. This is a positive move but is it really sufficient? Obviously there is a difference between some purely disciplinary matters and an actual criminal conviction in the courts but I'd point out that if a civilian commits a crime whether or not it is in the course of his or her work, prosecution and justice does not stop if they retire, resign or normally when they suffer ill-health. Should not those civilian principles now become applicable to all guardians of law and order so that officers are unable to avoid discipline or justice by whatever route, device or tactical manoeuvre?

I would also suggest what can be best described as a 'complaints accrual check' whereby any officer who amasses, say, three complaints (whether individually upheld or not) should be interviewed by a local assessment panel to confirm his or her suitability for police work, whether re-training is needed or different assignments should be allotted to him or her. If that officer then accrues a further three complaints (six in all, including in relation to minor motoring matters such as speeding) he or she should be assessed by a panel external to his or her own force, say from the NCA or National Policing College.

Further, should we not debate whether officers who resign/retire/are dismissed following 'difficulties' should continue to qualify for sick-leave/pay in lieu of notice and the travesties of benefit justice we read about in the media? Pensions for erring officers could be limited up to the time when that officer's service was blemish-free.

Surely all police officers who establish a criminal record should be dismissed unless it is a relatively minor, say a marginal offence such as a speeding conviction, when it should be recorded as a third-party complaint and included in the officer's disciplinary record/total.

Above I advocated that the NCA, or a similar such body, could handle all aspects of the investigation and (in conjunction with the Crown Prosecution Service) prosecution of erring police employees, taking the local police force out of the loop entirely. Some senior officers may prefer that solution and it will be for the Government to declare its predilection. It could resolve one of the more difficult obstacles: making sure evidence is gathered free from obstruction, delay or other hampering.

Currently, all disciplinary hearings within the police are held in private. Thus, rarely does an aggrieved party hear what takes place and, to the best of my research, never is a non-police employee allowed input or participation. Only since quite recently in civilian criminal proceedings is the victim allowed not only to act as a witness but to address the court to explain the grief the perpetrator brought into his or her life. In the light of a crisis of legitimacy should we not be questioning whether police 'in camera' practices are in the best interest of justice? Progressing a little further into the level of seriousness of allegations against officers, might there be some virtue in allowing civilians, to sit on the enquiry/disciplinary board and for victims to be heard in person. Last but not least, should there be a special police prosecutor appointed?

(c) Reduce, re-assign and refocus the IPCC

As a police 'watchdog' the IPCC is not succeeding. In my view it sets poor standards for something as important as police integrity and many believe it needs to be relieved of all police-related prosecution duties.

Extending the coverage and workload (suggested by the Parliamentary Home Affairs Committee) of the IPCC to provide an appeal route for private sector contractors might be a good idea in concept but with the IPCC in its present form, with its current reputation and disappointing performance, the suggestion seems quite impractical unless and until major changes are first discussed and agreed by Parliament

I would make a number of related comments:

- The HAC recorded its wish that the percentage of ex-police employed by the IPCC be reduced to 20 per cent. Does this go far enough and would not a much lesser figure (possibly as low as ten per cent) be even better in the interests of greater objectivity?
- How does changing the IPCC's name, say to 'Independent Policing Standards Authority', help to improve its performance, effectiveness and public image rather than look simply like as a re-branding exercise?
- How might IPCC management address and improve the cultural style/bias of its staff?
- Should not any broadening of the IPCC remit be focused on easing its current appeals constraints so as to allow it to examine the reasons for and/or the underlying validity of an initial complaint? This is a major shortcoming in the appeal process particularly as long as the police are investigating themselves, but

it is not the fault of the IPCC rather of the legislation it works within. As confidence in the police decreases and IPCC appeals increase, this significant detail needs addressing in legislation.

- What benefits might ensue for the IPCC were the PSD function managed more independently as already suggested?
- Should not the IPCC pass any public appeals where any level of corruption is suspected to, say, the NCA, which could be empowered to carry through the whole investigation and (in conjunction with the CPS) prosecution?
- With better focus would the IPCC have more capacity to directly manage more of the investigations presented to it by police forces rather than simply have an overview with a delegated investigation back to the police force?
- Would the IPCC be more effective and present a better public image were it to focus solely on core activities such as improving its speed of response, effectiveness, transparency and accountability, i.e. are time and resources on market research, seeking public opinion, circulating newsletters and other 'non-core' activities counter-productive?
- Some IPCC investigation and report work is commendable, but significantly undermined by the fact that the IPCC has no powers to ensure implementation. Might the IPCC be able to make a case for mandatory report implementation powers?
- Does not the IPCC need an empowered top level executive ('fire-brand', 'figurehead'?) in control, someone who understands that all police corruption is unacceptable and with the force of character to ensure that the police 'watchdog' makes a sufficient mark?
- Questions hang over the IPCC's own integrity as when it apparently adjusted the supporting evidence sent to it as part of one appeal noted in *Chapter 6*. Furthermore, is not its reputation sufficiently poor that by declaring its decision final this generates public disquiet. With less workload from elsewhere would not its reputation/effectiveness be more likely to recover if there was an opportunity to question its judgement (short of judicial review)?

There seems to be widespread agreement that the IPCC is not currently fit for purpose but opinion is divided when it comes to the solution. The two main positions are: replace it with a new effective, empowered independent 'watchdog'; or enlarge and strengthen the present organization. I take a third 'give it a chance' position. Delegate some of its current tasks, eliminate non-core activities and distractions, feed it with less work via improved and independent PSD processes and give it improved management and direction and thereby a chance to improve performance. If its role is to continue, the IPCC should perhaps be given authority to enforce its recommendations or be told by chief constables why not, and, say, five years to effect major improvements.

(d) Establish a duty of candour, of care and protect whistle-blowers

Legislation is required to impose a 'duty of candour' as part of the terms and conditions applicable to every member of our police forces, including members of a PSD, the IPCC (or their replacements) and the NCA, and to give practical help, possibly anonymity, to protect whistle-blowers.

Not entirely without some justification, the police see themselves under attack from many sides: public-enquires, politicians, the public, the legal profession, senior officers and, of late, police and crime commissioners (PCCs). Like other human beings police officers will fear change and consequently consolidate their tight-knit groups with a culture that involves using those powers they do enjoy and keeping outsiders from 'their world'. Consequently, 'whistle-blowing' will seriously harm any officer's future career in the police and the damage may extend far beyond getting the sack. Were all police straightforwardly honest in all respects an official 'duty of candour' would be unnecessary, because the obligation would be assumed, as it used to be, to be part of a police officer's role.

However in parallel with the obligation of candour for each officer, the Government needs to provide adequate, practical protective legislation to ensure the safety of officers doing their duty. It is in the best interest of all involved that officers disclose matters of inaccuracy, dishonesty or injustice and are then given real assistance to avoid the subsequent fall-out in a similar way to provision in relation to the National Health Service as this book was going to press. PCCs could be ideally placed to play an important intermediary role here although one civilian I heard from contacted his PCC three times and got no help, interest or support with police integrity issues.[2]

PC James Patrick (*Chapter 12*) is to be commended for his exemplary integrity and courage in drawing attention to under-reporting of crime but had to resign from the Met in June 2014 (as no doubt other whistle-blowers have felt the need to do over the years).

In the context of adding a duty of candour to police officers' terms and conditions, since none of us can serve two masters, there probably should now also be a provision prohibiting membership of secret societies at all levels within the police force. Home Secretary Jack Straw tried some years ago to bar Freemasons but was rebuffed. However given the present crisis of legitimacy, this aspect of police employment surely needs reconsideration. How can police think that they should be able to operate on such a basis?

When considering a duty of candour should the Government also be reassessing the current emphasis on the police's and associated standards of care? How can it be right for senior staff in particular employed in the police, CPS, IPCC and/or HMIC, empowered with checks and balances, to shy away from such duties and to allow what seem, repeatedly, like cover–ups (which could be said to be worse than the initial errors complained of) and/or to allow their staff to put obstacles in the way of the public.

One complainant who contacted me continued for eight to nine years to get his complaint heard. It's not that the senior officers did not know about his situation (more than enough letters were written) but one cannot help but conclude that they thought they had to. In seeking to preserve the reputation of their organization they appeared to abandon its integrity. If reputation is shown to have been placed before integrity should senior or other responsible staff, including those within the IPCC, not themselves face the prospect of investigation?

---

2. Personally I would dispense with PCCs altogether as a failed experiment.

(e) Stop manipulation of crime statistics and other records

The integrity of the police information provided to the Home Office has become a source of public mistrust and consequently detracts from confidence in the Home Office statistics. Might they not they be discontinued and the resources diverted to supplementing/increasing the *Crime Survey for England and Wales* victimisation surveys?

If the police/Home Office crime statistical information continues the police must become obligated to record every crime reported to them. Such devices as 'screening-out', splitting 'reported crime' from 'recorded crime', classifying matters as a 'civil', 'street/area' groupings and other manipulation must be avoided and records opened-up to an HMIC review. I recognise that removing police discretion puts them in a difficult position if/when some local residents are habitually at the police station attention seeking. However, on the other side of the coin, the public must be encouraged to report each genuine crime, which might become more likely if citizens know the police will record their report and not fob them off. All these matters touch on police discipline and its systems of enforcement,

Some crimes are in decline, but others like internet crimes are increasing. We need to be prepared, even to call for, consequential changes in policing. Perhaps fewer constables patrolling the beat but with additional officers available for swifter responses while there ought to be more IT specialists sitting away from public view but catching criminals who are using computers for fraud, child pornography, hate crime, etc. That will necessitate overhauling the already archaic 'public satisfaction' based on seeing a patrolling officer.

(f) Enforce the Home Office 'ban' on target-setting

The concept of 'sanctioned detection' targets, although well-intended has, with the advantage of hindsight, proved to be ill-conceived and consequently national targets have since been prudently abolished by the Home Office. Nevertheless some chief constables are reintroducing targets independently of the Home Office and national policy and the Met in particular would appear to be implementing them aggressively! Since targets force the focus onto core activities and the discontinuance of anything outside of those set borders, they seem detrimental to the whole community. It might clarify the way forward if we understood who was setting policy because, while chief constables must have a high degree of independence and autonomy, that should not extend to unfettered freedom like ignoring the wishes of the Home Office and the IPCC (the latter on police disciplinary issues).

In the previous section I mentioned 'screening-out' and other work-minimisation ploys that leave the complainant convinced the police are disinterested and/or not particularly helpful. Giving the police the benefit of the doubt, let's assume this policy was a by-product of target-setting but whatever the 'reason' the police should be awakening to the fact that it only further disengages them from those they strive to police by consent.

(g) Make sure victims of the police or its complaints system are compensated

Sadly, various of those I heard from confirm that getting police mistakes, corruption, bias or injustice rectified is time-consuming, extraordinarily stressful and for most complainants prohibitively expensive. Rarely is an apology available, never mind adequate sanctions so the police continue to be careless, even lawless on occasions, because 'they can be' and rarely face collective or individual consequences. Although the Government is understandably trying to reduce the extent and cost of publicly-funded legal aid, for the foreseeable future there seems to be a case for extending such support to those alleging that they have been wronged in this way and who are seeking rectification or damages. This sounds extravagant, but could be a route to getting the police to be more attentive to the legality of their methods.

(h) Record every police/citizen contact by audio or video

I have come across several examples of the incalculable value of recording conversations with the police or police staff to avoid later disputes. Several of those I heard from would have been unable to prove police lies and hold them to account were it not for having the foresight to make records. The police have started to use video in face-to-face meetings but retain the power to switch the recording off at their discretion. In any event a police record of the encounter can be doctored to suit their purpose and currently there is not even the facility to provide the apprehended person with an instant copy (which would be easy and not expensive). Consequently, in spite of this development, citizens currently fare better if they rely on their own recordings.

The Government should actively encourage covert or other recording of interactions the police or their employees and make clear that this is perfectly permissible, not some kind of obstruction of the police. Though unlikely, police officers should welcome confirmation that their face-to-face behaviour, attitude and accuracy has been exemplary and while recording such interactions will not stop all false allegations, it should at least keep face-to-face contacts factual.

(i) Increase support for domestic violence/abuse and for a (renewed) Victims' Charter

Few report rape or other sexual abuse, and here I'm including not only of male/female but gay/lesbian rape, sex within arranged marriages and the like, probably because the current level of support provided seems inadequate. Many cases of rape are going unrecorded but no-one knows how many and what percentage. That is not satisfactory given the seriousness of the crime and the lasting damage it does but, although attention is gathering pace, the authorities appear not to be doing enough to get a measure of the true volume of violence, abuse and rape, nor are they combating it.

On the face of it HMIC's Rape Monitoring Group is a start — but everything appears to be from a police viewpoint and there is no evidence as to the constructive work or policies that fact-gathering exercises have brought about. Without consequential action the whole exercise is nothing more than time-consuming. Might it be practical for rape victims to write anonymously to their PCC at least to reveal the scale of this horrendous crime? Thereafter local and indeed national remedial polices might start to emerge.

(j) Make the most of HMIC

Of the bodies I researched, at around 130 strong, Her Majesty's Inspectorate of Constabulary may be the smallest but that department comes over as the most impressive and trustworthy. Therefore should not HMIC be elevated to the status of a regulatory authority with powers of direction and intervention but, at the same time, required to take more account of disaffected members of the public. Currently, none seem to interface with HMIC.

However we are left asking why, with all their work and skill, we have so many outstanding questions about police performance, mistakes and integrity? There must be more that needs to be done so, perhaps with regulatory powers, HMIC might bring about greater improvements?

(k) Adopt a zero-tolerance approach to prosecution

In spite of the present difficulties of evidence-gathering (police investigating the police), split departmental responsibilities and 'public interest' decisions by the Crown Prosecution Service (CPS) it naturally does prosecute some police officers and I have charted many instances where charges or prosecutions have been levelled (hundreds of cases involving police officers and other public servants in fact). Even so the likelihood of the CPS prosecuting a police employee compared to a civilian counterpart is, according to my research, significantly lower, which brings into question the current tripartite police/IPCC/CPS prosecution arrangements.

It seems that it is the current system rather than the intent that's mostly to at fault. Thus 'road-blocks' need to be removed, probably starting with a presumption that prosecution of allegations against police officers are in the public interest unless there is sound reason to the contrary. Where there is doubt about police integrity it is in the public interest that each issue be tested in a criminal court, openly and by judicial processes rather than behind closed doors, if public confidence is to be restored.

Further this should be linked to a zero-tolerance approach so far as investigators, prosecutors and sentencing courts are concerned.

Conclusion

Hopefully, most police officers do a commendable and essential job but some colleagues taint that work. This and the nature of many working methods raise questions about police integrity as a whole. Whenever a force's reputation is contaminated this affects public confidence without which policing by consent becomes impossible. Despite huge advances in policing in modern times, the police complaints and disciplinary systems lags behind.

Despite passing reference to police integrity in public discussions, the remedies suggested tend to be vague. For example, there has been mention of establishing a code of ethics but no revision of the police officer's oath known as 'attestation'—and currently I believe only new constables are required to attest, another detail that needs reconsideration. Ultimately and for the majority of police officers the extent of complaints against the police is more likely to be governed by the duty of care exercised by officers in contact with citizens than by sanctions of whatever kind. But until that stage is reached major reform of the present system along the lines set out above seems essential.

Criminal Justice System Organizational Structure Pre-Court

The organizational structure for the policing and crime reduction side of the justice system is complex. Thus the details in this book are better appreciated if the respective organizations are placed in context. The Home Office Accounting Officer's system diagram on page 4 of its Accountability System Statement[1] shows some of the lines of responsibility and opportunities for scrutiny. The following summary, also kindly provided by the Home Office, will assist in understanding some relationships explored within these pages (paraphrased).

- Directly elected **Police and Crime Commissioners** (PCCs) are accountable to their electorate for ensuring the policing needs of local communities are met effectively;
- **Police and Crime Panels** provide a statutory oversight and scrutiny function modelled upon scrutiny committees in local authorities;
- **Chief constables** are responsible for the operational delivery of the local police force and direct and control officers and staff in the force;
- Independent **regulatory and inspection bodies** such as Her Majesty's Inspectorate of Constabulary, the National Audit Office and external auditors, and **the public** who, through robust transparency arrangements, can assess the performance of their local force and hold their PCC to account; and
- The statement sets out the legislation and guidance that underpins the system and signposts changes that are expected to be made ... It also describes the sources of information, published locally as well as by independent sources, which allow judgements

---

1. https://www.gov.uk/government/uploads/system/uploads/attachment_data/file/181705/ Accountability_System_Statement_13_04_03_v3.pdf

to be made about the efficiency and effectiveness of policing and crime reduction.'

However, the above is not all embracing. Noticeable by their absence are the IPCC and the Attorney-General's office/CPS and consequently I have taken the liberty of also providing a simplified structure of my own which I hope will assist in exploring the strengths, weakness, responsibilities and functions of the various bodies and individuals that make up the pre-court policing organization.

The IPCC is the 'watchdog' overseeing the police complaints system in England and Wales. It is described in more detail in *Chapter 21*. It sets standards by which the police should handle complaints, carries out some important investigations itself and reviews appeals about police conduct put forward by the public. However it is independent, and not responsible to or for what the police, Government or Parliament may do and this is reflected in the following (much simplified) chart.

The CPS is the independent department responsible for prosecuting criminal cases investigated by the police and other public law enforcement agencies as outlined in *Chapter 19*. It comes under the Office of the Attorney-general rather than the Home Office or Ministry of Justice. The CPS will consider cases for prosecution from these investigating authorities, such as the police and the IPCC.

The Ministry of Justice is among other things responsible for the courts, prisons, probation and legal aid and consequently not directly relevant to the effectiveness or integrity of police forces. However, interestingly, it is responsible for improving the transparency of the justice system as detailed at https://www.gov.uk/government/policies/creating-a-transparent-justice-system

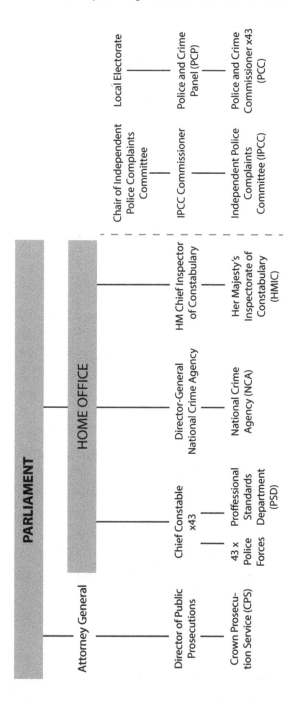

Table: Law and Order — Outline Organizational Structure

Some Further Examples of Cause for Concern: No Smoke Without Fire

Henry Porter told *Observer* readers on 20th October 2013 that his researcher had assembled 330 newspaper reports containing complaints about police conduct and corruption over the course of just a few days. Here are a rather smaller number that I assembled during my research but which are sufficient to confirm that there is no smoke without fire.

The Independent, 8th February 2014. Police officers arrested on suspicion of sending each other 'extreme pornographic images' (Three officers, whose duties included guarding Downing Street, have been arrested on suspicion of 'being involved in the possession and distribution of obscene images' using mobile phones).

> http://www.independent.co.uk/news/uk/crime/police-officers-arrested-on-suspicion-of-sending-each-other-extreme-pornographic-images-9116209.html

The Independent, 7th February 2014. Plebgate row: PC Keith Wallis admits misconduct over lies about Andrew Mitchell.

> http://www.independent.co.uk/news/uk/crime/plebgate-row-pc-keith-wallis-admits-misconduct-over-lies-about-andrew-mitchell-9051291.html

BBC News, 19th November 2012. IPCC advised to take soft tone with police (IPCC's Deborah Glass sent an email advising a soft approach be taken with police suspects).

> http://www.bbc.co.uk/news/uk-20366968

The Daily Telegraph, 10th January 2014. Police officer Keith Wallis admits lying over Plebgate (Pc Keith Wallis, 53, of West Drayton, West London, admitted misconduct in public office between September 19 and December

16 2012, by saying that he had witnessed the incident and arranging for his nephew to support the claim).

http://www.telegraph.co.uk/news/uknews/law-and-order/10563108/

Police-officer-Keith-Wallis-admits-lying-over-Plebgate.html

BBC News Wales, 25 January 2012. Twelve of 32 police in Wales kept jobs after breaking law (Figures obtained by BBC Wales through a freedom of information request to the four forces in Wales show at least 32 serving police and community support officers have committed crimes since January 2007).

http://www.bbc.co.uk/news/uk-wales-16508670

Mail online, 9th May 2011. Sacked in secret: The hushed-up hearings of police who are found guilty of crimes and misconduct (In the past three years, a total of 477 officers were sacked, 52 demoted and hundreds more fined or reprimanded—all in private hearings. Many of the accused were suspended on full pay for long periods or had their duties restricted).

http://www.dailymail.co.uk/news/article-1385009/Hundreds-UK-

police-sacked-secret-misconduct-committing-crime.html

The Guardian, 3rd November 2013. Esther Rantzen claims she had first-hand experience of police lies (The BBC presenter claimed she and her late husband Desmond Wilcox were the subject of police lies after he was stopped by a traffic officer while speeding: see *Chapter 7*).

http://www.theguardian.com/tv-and-radio/2013/nov/03/esther-rantzen-claims-police-lies

BBC News, 12th November 2012. IPCC advised to take soft tone with police (Under oath at the subsequent inquest in December 2010, the officers admitted to removing potentially key evidence from their written statements to the IPCC claiming they were told to do so by a police federation lawyer).

http://www.bbc.co.uk/news/uk-20366968

The Independent, 24th October 2012. Sixty-one per cent of police complaint appeals upheld (Almost two-thirds of appeals to the police watchdog over ignored complaints were upheld last year, i.e. 2011).

http://www.independent.co.uk/news/uk/crime/61-of-police-
complaint-appeals-upheld-8224447.html

BBC New Magazine, 9th March 2012. Would you want to be a Freemason (Martin Short found that 'corruption in the police was enhanced and shielded by the Masonic lodges.')

http://www.bbc.co.uk/news/magazine-17272611

The Institute for the Study of Civil Society (Civitas). Never has the police service had so much money, so many officers or such access to technology. Yet never has public dissatisfaction with the police been so widespread. Complaints against the police have increased.

http://www.civitas.org.uk/press/publicpolicesummary.php

The Telegraph, 5th August 2011. David Cameron's US 'supercop' blocked by Theresa May (while in New York he pioneered the 'zero tolerance' approach to policing where no offence was considered too small to be dealt with).

http://www.telegraph.co.uk/news/uknews/law-and-order/8685423/
David-Camerons-US-supercop-blocked-by-Theresa-May.html

Daily Mail, 3rd March 2013. MP subjected to six month £100,000 police racism probe for telling man he is 'unkempt'.[1]

http://www.dailymail.co.uk/news/article-2287219/Tim-Loughton-MP-subjected-
6-month-100-000-police-racism-probe-telling-man-unkempt.html

The Guardian, 23rd October 2012. I know just the man to put the police's house in order: Andrew Mitchell ('Bear in mind seven of the nation's 43 chief constables were sacked, suspended or forced from their jobs for misconduct in just 18 months up to the end of last year').

http://www.theguardian.com/commentisfree/2013/oct/23/
andrew-mitchell-britain-police-problem

---

1. See alo *Chapter 10*.

The Independent, 6th May 2012. Police 'in denial' over rise in racism complaints.

> http://www.independent.co.uk/news/uk/crime/police-in-
> denial-over-rise-in-racism-complaints-7717639.html

The Guardian, 12th April 2012. Justice is impossible if we cannot trust police forces to tell the truth.

> http://www.theguardian.com/commentisfree/2011/apr/12/police-truth-blair-peach-tomlinson

Mail Online, 15th August 2012. Two Met Police officers 'smashed their way into aircraft engineer's home with a battering ram and kidnapped him'.

> http://www.dailymail.co.uk/news/article-2188837/Two-Met-Police-officers-
> smashed-way-aircraft-engineers-home-battering-ram-kidnapped-him.html

The Independent, 18th October 2013. Private citizen wins right to prosecute Met police worker.

> http://www.independent.co.uk/news/uk/crime/private-citizen-wins-
> right-to-prosecute-met-police-worker-8890313.html

The Guardian, 10th May 2013. Former judge to examine role of police corruption in murder investigation.

> http://www.theguardian.com/uk/2013/may/10/judge-police-corruption-murder-investigation

IPCC ignored complaints reported against IPCC commissioner Gary Garland during 2007.

> https://www.whatdotheyknow.com/request/complaints_reported_against_ipcc_2

Lord Maginnis of Drumglass in House of Lords.

> http://www.theyworkforyou.com/lords/?id=2012-05-15a.258.7&s=hofschroer#g332.0

Freedom of Information Request. (Does the IPCC's Chair or Deputy Chair possess the Lawful Authority to Conduct Criminal Investigations in Accordance with Police and Criminal Evidence Act 1984?).

> https://www.whatdotheyknow.com/request/does_the_ipccs_chair_or_deputy_c

The Guardian, July 2013. *Crime Statistics for England and Wales.*

http://www.theguardian.com/news/datablog/2011/jul/14/crime-statistics-england-wales

The Independent, 16th July 2013. Collapse of Britain's biggest police corruption trial: 'No misconduct involved' in Cardiff Three fit-up case (Police fit-up and self-investigation overlooked).

http://www.independent.co.uk/news/uk/crime/collapse-of-britains-biggest-police-corruption-trial-no-misconduct-involved-in-cardiff-three-fitup-case-8711679.html

Mail Online, 3rd January 2012. How can the public respect police who have no respect for the law? (serious crimes and officers still serving).

http://www.dailymail.co.uk/debate/article-2081700/How-public-respect-police-officers-respect-law.html

Office for National Statistics. *Crime Survey for England and Wales* (Year ending June 2013).

http://www.ons.gov.uk/ons/dcp171778_331209.pdf

The Telegraph, 4th September 2013. Police do not investigate six out ten Reported Crimes.

http://www.telegraph.co.uk/news/uknews/crime/10285564/Police-do-not-investigate-six-out-of-10-reported-crimes-admits-chief-constable.html

The Telegraph, 21st November 2009. Police Fail to investigate one third of crimes ('Screening-out').

http://www.telegraph.co.uk/news/uknews/law-and-order/6623745/Police-fail-to-investigate-one-third-of-crimes.html

IPCC May 2012. Corruption in the Police Service in England and Wales (Second report based on the IPCC's experience from 2008 to 2011).

http://www.ipcc.gov.uk/sites/default/files/Documents/research_stats/Corruption_in_the_Police_Service_in_England_Wales_Report_2_May_2012.pdf

The Guardian, 24th February 1999. Macpherson report summary (Seventy proposals to take on our 'institutionally racist' police).

http://www.theguardian.com/uk/1999/feb/24/lawrence.ukcrime12

Minutes of Home Affairs Select Committee dated 23rd Oct 2013.

http://www.publications.parliament.uk/pa/cm201314/cmselect/cmhaff/756-i/756.pdf

The Observer, 20th Oct 2013. Police Corruption Rife.

http://www.theguardian.com/commentisfree/2013/oct/20/
police-corruption-demands-royal-commission

'Police and Crime Commissioners, one year on: warts and all' (Home Secretary speech, November 2013).

https://www.gov.uk/government/speeches/
police-and-crime-commissioners-one-year-on-warts-and-all

The Guardian, 19 December 2012. Police conduct undermining service (Report finds 'inappropriate behaviour' by officers on social media and high-profile corruption cases damages integrity).

http://www.theguardian.com/uk/2012/dec/19/
police-conduct-undermining-reputation-watchdog

List of police officers charged with offences in 2010. (A full list of more than 1300 public employees is available by registering at the site).

http://www.fmotl.com/forum/viewtopic.php?f=17&t=6251

'Never Never Never talk to the police' (An American video with some good advice).

http://www.rottentothecore.co.uk/viewtopic.php?f=13&t=23

Panorama 31st October 2013. Call for Stronger Oversight as Police Avoid Scrutiny.

http://www.bbc.co.uk/panorama/hi/front_page/newsid_9624000/9624787.stm

The Guardian, 24th May 2011. Fiona Pilkington case: Police face misconduct proceedings.

http://www.theguardian.com/uk/2011/may/24/
fiona-pilkington-police-misconduct-proceedings

The Herald, 27th July 2013. Files reveal Devon and Cornwall police misconduct cases.

http://www.plymouthherald.co.uk/Files-reveal-Devon-Cornwall-
police-misconduct/story-19578511-detail/story.html

h Mail Online, 7th July 2013. A vicious crime boss, his corrupt police cronies and a scandal that could have been buried forever. (It is being all but swamped by one claim of misconduct or cover-up after another, which add up to a devastating and fundamental indictment of the force).

http://www.dailymail.co.uk/debate/article-2357977/A-vicious-crime-
boss-corrupt-police-cronies-scandal-buried-ever.html

The Telegraph, 7th October 2013. National Crime Agency: Does Britain need an FBI?

http://www.telegraph.co.uk/news/uknews/law-and-order/10361009/
The-National-Crime-Agency-Does-Britain-need-an-FBI.html

The Guardian, 14th May 2013. Whistle-blower's claims ignored ('It was clear from the off that I would be ostracised, victimised and ultimately sacked').

http://www.theguardian.com/business/2013/may/14/whistleblowers-claims-ignored

Daily Express, 27th November 2013. 'I was stitched up by police'; and 'What chance would a kid in Brixton have (After the announcement that PC Keith Wallis is to be charged with misconduct in a public office, Mr Mitchell described his ordeal after being 'fitted up' by police. But see *Chapter 9*).

http://www.express.co.uk/news/
uk/445355/I-was-stitched-up-by-police-over-Plebgate-say-Andrew-Mitchell

The Guardian, 26th July 2013. Sir Norman Bettison faces investigation over Stephen Lawrence evidence (Allegedly from the evidence provided in support of the referral the intelligence gathering requested appears to have been both inappropriate and intrusive).

http://www.theguardian.com/uk-news/2013/jul/26/
norman-bettison-investigation-stephen-lawrence

The Guardian, 5th July 2013. Norman Bettison 'had smear file' on anti-racist campaigner (The PCC for West Yorkshire and the force itself say documents raise serious concerns that a witness due to appear before Macpherson's hearing in Bradford was allegedly targeted).

http://www.theguardian.com/uk-news/2013/jul/05/
norman-bettison-mohammed-amran-allegations

The Guardian, 3rd July 2013. Norman Bettison referred to IPCC over Stephen Lawrence inquiry (This allegation may suggest an attempt to intervene in the course of a public inquiry and influence the manner in which the testimony of a witness, who was due to present evidence before it, was received).

http://www.theguardian.com/uk-news/2013/jul/03/norman-bettison-ipcc-stephen-lawrence

The Guardian 28th March 2013. Hillsborough police officer faces fresh criticism from watchdog.

http://www.theguardian.com/uk/2013/mar/28/hillsborough-disaster-officer-norman-bettison

The Guardian, 14th April 2013. Hillsborough victims' families demand swift justice for people behind cover-up.

http://www.theguardian.com/football/2013/apr/14/hillsborough-victims-families-justice

The Guardian, 23rd October 2012. Hillsborough: police chief 'boasted' of role in smearing fans.

http://www.theguardian.com/football/2012/oct/23/hillsborough-police-chief-bettison-eagle

Index